Colonel Edward E. Cross,
New Hampshire Fighting Fifth

ALSO BY ROBERT GRANDCHAMP
AND FROM MCFARLAND

*"Rhody Redlegs": A History of the Providence Marine Corps
of Artillery and the 103d Field Artillery, Rhode Island*
(by Robert Grandchamp, Jane Lancaster and Cynthia Ferguson, 2012)

*The Boys of Adams' Battery G: The Civil War Through
the Eyes of a Union Light Artillery Unit* (2009)

*The Seventh Rhode Island Infantry
in the Civil War* (2008)

Colonel Edward E. Cross, New Hampshire Fighting Fifth

A Civil War Biography

ROBERT GRANDCHAMP

Foreword by Mike Pride

McFarland & Company, Inc., Publishers
Jefferson, North Carolina, and London

LIBRARY OF CONGRESS CATALOGUING-IN-PUBLICATION DATA

Grandchamp, Robert.
    Colonel Edward E. Cross, New Hampshire Fighting Fifth : a Civil War biography / Robert Grandchamp ; foreword by Mike Pride.
    p.   cm.
    Includes bibliographical references and index.

    ISBN 978-0-7864-7191-1
    softcover : acid free paper ∞

    1. Cross, Edward Ephraim, 1832–1863.
2. United States. Army. New Hampshire Infantry Regiment, 5th (1861–1865). 3. New Hampshire— History—Civil War, 1861–1865—Biography.
4. United States—History—Civil War, 1861–1865— Biography. 5. United States—History— Civil War, 1861–1865—Campaigns. 6. Soldiers— Vermont—Biography. I. Title.
E520.55th.G73 2013
973.7'442092—dc23
[B]   2012042812

BRITISH LIBRARY CATALOGUING DATA ARE AVAILABLE

© 2013 Robert Grandchamp. All rights reserved

No part of this book may be reproduced or transmitted in any form or by any means, electronic or mechanical, including photocopying or recording, or by any information storage and retrieval system, without permission in writing from the publisher.

Front cover: Colonel Edward E. Cross (Library of Congress)

Manufactured in the United States of America

McFarland & Company, Inc., Publishers
  Box 611, Jefferson, North Carolina 28640
    www.mcfarlandpub.com

For Brigadier General Richard J. Valente
an officer, a gentleman, and a friend

Table of Contents

Acknowledgments ix
Foreword by Mike Pride 1
Preface 5

ONE: An Eagle Is Born 9
TWO: Restless Wanderer 23
THREE: American Party Reporter 35
FOUR: Tubac 48
FIVE: Mexico 66
SIX: "At once entered upon my duty" 72
SEVEN: Baptism 87
EIGHT: The Fighting Fifth 100
NINE: Marye's Heights 116
TEN: A Star 127
ELEVEN: Hooker's Campaign 137
TWELVE: The Wheatfield 148
THIRTEEN: "The boys will miss me" 162

Appendix: "The Young Volunteers" 181
Chapter Notes 193
Bibliography 207
Index 215

Acknowledgments

This book began in the state of Cross' birth, early years, and burial and it is in the Granite State that the deepest thanks are owed. Mike Pride, who I first met one hot July day in the Wheatfield, contributed records, advice, and research leads. Mike's concerted effort to assist in the details made this project a reality. He kindly read drafts and shared his knowledge of the regiment, in addition to writing the foreword to this volume. In Concord, the staff of the New Hampshire Historical Society pulled volumes and boxes from the magnificent repository that is the Tuck Library, allowing Edward Cross and the men who served under him to come back to life once again. At the New Hampshire Division of Archives and Records Management, the official records of the Fifth New Hampshire were put at this author's disposal to study Cross' relationship with the governor and state officials, allowing new material to be gathered into his contentious relationship with those in power. The New Hampshire State Library, New Hampshire State House, and New Hampshire Army National Guard also provided material.

While the bulk of the research occurred in Concord, several wonderful visits took place in the small town of Lancaster, New Hampshire, where Cross remains the local hero. Betty E. Newell of the Lancaster Historical Society kindly opened the doors of the Wilder House Museum on a cold December day, allowing ready access to the wonderful collection of Cross-related material. The author is grateful to the Lancaster Historical Society for allowing the publication of images from their collection. Additional thanks are also extended in Lancaster to the staffs of the Coos County Courthouse and Coos County Sheriff's Department, the Lancaster Town Hall, Lancaster Library, the members of North Star Lodge 8 Free and Accepted Masons, the *Coos County Democrat*, and every citizen who took the time to answer questions and provide directions.

In Durham, home of the University of New Hampshire, the archivists in the Milne Special Collections provided ready access to Cross' personal papers, sent home after Gettysburg, and the recently acquired letters of Sergeant George Gove, which gave a critical enlisted man's voice to Cross' character. It has been this author's privilege to be associated with the men of the Fifth New Hampshire Volunteers, a Civil War living history association that strives to re-create the life and times of the men under Cross' command. Chris Benedetto, Jim Blake, Bill Shea, Paul Parvis, Nick Pouliot, George Hall, Marc Vallee, Tyler Bergeron, and others offered research advice, kindly read early draft chapters, and provided good comradeship in the writing of this book. Across the Granite State, librarians, town clerks, and others kindly searched their repositories for information, especially at the Rauner Special Collections Library at Dartmouth College.

Terry Thomann of the Civil War Life Museum in Fredericksburg, Virginia, is owed a special thanks. Terry kindly opened his doors and freely shared his own decade worth of research into Cross' life, allowing access to much needed material that could not have been found elsewhere. In addition, Dave Morin kindly pointed out Fifth New Hampshire images at the USAMHI.

Outside of New Hampshire, where Cross spent most of his adult life, is where many resources are located. At Norwich University the archives staff kindly provided assistance, as did the American Antiquarian Society in Worcester, Massachusetts. The Cincinnati Historical Society conducted over the phone research and added tremendously to the project during a hectic visit. In Arizona, the Tubac Historical Society and the Arizona Historical Society saved this author a trip to the Southwest and were able to fill in many voids about Cross' time and service in the territory, kindly mailing copies East, much as Cross did in 1859. In Washington, DC, the Library of Congress and National Archives again contained the bulk of the official records consulted and cited. No Civil War study is possible without the assistance of the historians of the United States Army Military History Institute at Carlisle Barracks, Pennsylvania.

At Fredericksburg/Spotsylvania National Military Park, Don Pfanz allowed ready access to the wonderful park library at Chatham and filled in details about Cross' Apache fights with Richard Ewell. At Antietam National Battlefield, John Hoptak and Ted Alexander went the extra distance, as did Bob Krick at Richmond National Battlefield and John King and John Rudy at Harpers Ferry National Historical Park. At Gettysburg, John Heiser, the park historian, provided a great service in copying voluminous material to support this project.

I would be remiss if I did not mention my grandmother, Joyce Knight Townsend, for instilling in me at an early age a deep love of the Granite Hills of New Hampshire. When this author was sixteen and began to develop a lifelong interest in the Civil War, she drove me to a small town in the mountains, Lancaster, where my interest and fascination in this remarkable man took root. She followed me on several more research expeditions to New Hampshire and was always interested in the latest material gathered on "Ed Cross."

To those not mentioned, thank you for assisting in this study of the life of Colonel Edward E. Cross.

Foreword by Mike Pride

Edward E. Cross stood out in a crowd. There was a lot of vertical to him, not much horizontal. He was tall and lean, eagle-eyed, fidgety, more graceful on horseback than on his own two feet. Prematurely bald on top, he grew a tawny beard nearly as long as his face. Growing up in Lancaster north of New Hampshire's White Mountains, he imbibed Shakespeare, went to work for the local newspaper, and took a keen interest in all things military. He developed a dualistic worldview: Life was full of humbug (one of his favorite words) and yet life demanded discipline and order. He came of age in a young country. He revered its past, especially the Revolutionary legacy of his grandfather, Richard Everett, while embracing Manifest Destiny, the dominant nationalistic idea of his time. He considered white Protestants to be superior people and thought their values should rule the country. No friend of slavery but no friend of black people or abolitionists either, he also looked down on Mexicans and Irish Catholics. He thought American Indians should either be confined to reservations or wiped out to make room for national expansion. A powerful writer and blunt speaker, he loved to bluster, skewer, and romanticize, but a substantial core lay beneath his posturing and political cant.

Cross was a self-made man in the American mold. Though born and raised in a far corner of the United States, he took to the road before he was twenty. Curiosity and wanderlust pointed him westward, but even as he established himself as a journalist in Cincinnati he found ways to travel to neighboring states, to the South, and to Washington and the other political centers in the East. Eventually he took the first printing press to the Arizona Territory. In an age of horses and trains, Cross saw far more of the continent during his short life than most Americans do today in a much more mobile society. He was no idle tourist. Without a safety net he had to make his own way wherever he went, in Cincinnati, in Washington, in the Arizona Territory, in Mexico. By the time the Civil War came, he had made and remade himself several times. He had been a crack political reporter, travel writer, editor, trail hand, silver mine supervisor, and Indian fighter. Experience and study had also made him a keen military analyst.

For Cross, the war was the opportunity of a lifetime. He was just twenty-nine years old when he came home to command the Fifth New Hampshire Volunteers, but everything he had done in life had prepared him for the task. He was a leader — all-seeing, demanding, knowledgeable, fearless, and confident. He understood what it took to make a regiment work. He was quick to root out shirkers, malingerers, drunks, and men who thought they deserved commissions or promotions on the basis of their fathers' prominence and political connections. Because he had conquered difficult challenges as a young man, he eagerly chose men of nineteen or twenty for positions of authority and trained them to lead. His regiment had the advantage of months in the field before it faced its first battle, and Cross used this time to train the men. When the Fifth New Hampshire had to fight, it was ready. Preparation did not protect Cross' men from harm, but it gave them their best chance on the battlefield. As he knew, the ability to act as a unit made the whole more powerful than the sum of its parts. The colonel's response to being in a tight spot was to attack. After the Fifth's many battles under Cross had reduced its number from a thousand men to a hundred, its corps commander referred to these survivors as "refined gold." It was no exaggeration.

Edward E. Cross had ink in his blood. Had he not been killed in battle, he would no doubt have written his memoirs, burnished his own legend, and weighed in on many a postwar controversy. Instead he has waited in the grave for a biographer for a century and a half. In Robert Grandchamp he has found one, and I think he would be pleased. Like the men the colonel liked to promote, Robert is young and determined. Cross left behind a wealth of words, but because he was a wanderer who died young, his writings scattered to the winds. Robert has traveled far and wide to dig them out of archives and extract them from the microfilm reels of long-forgotten newspapers. Along the way he has found many new caches of letters written by soldiers who knew Cross personally and fought under him. He has read voraciously about the war and Cross' role in it. He has traced Cross' roots to a far greater extent than any researcher before him. He has investigated Cross' prewar life and walked in his footsteps on battlefields and in his hometown of Lancaster.

Mark Travis and I brought out *My Brave Boys: To War with Colonel Cross and the Fighting Fifth* in 2001. Robert read our book. As he began to consider Cross as a subject for a full biography, he contacted me and we began an e-mail correspondence. Our first actual meeting came in 2010 at the Civil War Institute in Gettysburg. He was a participant in the institute and I served as a lecturer and tour guide. He signed up for my tour of the Fifth New

Hampshire's battlefield positions and movements on July 2, 1863. As we walked on that great battlefield, I had the uneasy feeling that, although I was doing all the talking, Robert knew more than I did. When the tour group reached the "Cross' Brigade" marker on the edge of the Wheatfield, a fellow I had met at the institute whispered an idea in my ear. Rather than just stand there waiting for everyone to read the marker, he said I should ask someone to read it aloud. I called on Robert. Without hesitation he barked out the information on the plaque in a brisk martial voice. If I had lulled any of my listeners to sleep on their feet, Robert certainly woke them up. Colonel Cross would have loved it.

When Mark Travis and I started researching our book nearly twenty years ago, someone said to us, "You won't find much on Cross and the Fifth." It was the best challenge a historian could have had, and we promptly set out to prove its poser wrong. As I followed Robert's research, I had new cause to chuckle about the assertion that there wasn't much out there about Cross. *Colonel Edward E. Cross, New Hampshire Fighting Fifth* should lay that idea to rest once and for all. It is a rich biography of a great soldier.

Mike Pride is the author of several books, including the acclaimed "My Brave Boys": To War with Colonel Cross and the Fighting Fifth (coauthored with Mark Travis) and Abraham Lincoln in New Hampshire. The retired editor of the Concord Monitor, *he lives in Concord, New Hampshire.*

"What a magnificent fighter Cross was."
—Major General Winfield Scott Hancock, 1866

Preface

You have never disgraced New Hampshire; I hope you will not this time. If any man runs, I want the file closers to shoot him, if they do not, I shall myself. That is all I have to say. — COL. E.E. CROSS, September 17, 1862

With blood streaking down his face from a head wound on a shot-torn field in western Maryland on the seventeenth of September in 1862, a man stood above all others. One shoulder strap shot away, this man, a lanky six-foot, two-inch tall New Englander with a flowing chestnut-colored beard and thinning hairline, led his men into action. Maneuvering his regiment with precision that few troops could accomplish even on the relative calm of the drill field, he led these New Hampshire farmers, laborers, and professionals with exacting care, executing rapid movements under a raking storm of musketry and artillery fire to meet the Confederate threat. With one-third of his regiment down, and the enemy only yards away, this officer knew that only direct inspiration would allow them to hold their perilous position. A red handkerchief wrapped around his bloody head, he gave the order to "put on the war paint and give 'em the war whoop." Instantly responding to the command, the soldiers smeared black powder onto their sweating faces and began to yell like a band of Apache warriors at the approaching North Carolinians. This act of defiance in the face of death led these men to stand their ground as they succeeded in blocking a Rebel force bent on flanking the entire Union line. On this battlefield of Antietam, the regiment gained immortality as the Fighting Fifth.

Many considered the man responsible for creating this unit to be the best regimental commander in the Army of the Potomac. For some he seemed to stand ten feet tall in combat, "the epitome of fire and brimstone." He was a man who led by example and did not take his soldiers any place where he would not be willing to lead first. For others he was a drunken tyrant, a man with a short temper who pushed too hard, whose Democratic politics were a threat to the administration in power. In either light, no one could deny that in action he was at his best. This man was Colonel Edward Ephraim Cross of the Fifth New Hampshire Volunteers.

In the pantheon of heroes who served the Union cause, Edward Cross is a man who, although relatively forgotten, seems to be a constant presence. In Concord, New Hampshire, his portrait continues to glare down at visitors as they enter the state house, while in his hometown of Lancaster he remains the local hero. In Arizona, Cross was the man who published the first newspaper. On battlefields in Pennsylvania, Maryland, and Virginia, park rangers and guides exalt his actions in battle, a fiery man who did not hesitate to threaten to shoot his own men in the back if they ran away. There is much more, however, to this remarkable man.

In his thirty-one years on earth, Edward Cross lived an incredible life. Born in a small town in far northern New Hampshire, he died in command of a brigade at Gettysburg. Educated in the local district school, Cross became a printer in his teens. At the same time, he developed a lifelong passion for politics and the military, something that proved a dangerous combination in years to come. A traveler of the West in his twenties, he became the editor of a major newspaper and a respected political correspondent. Seemingly abandoning a comfortable life in Ohio, Cross traveled to Arizona, where he almost lost his life in a duel over his inability to silence his pen. His next step brought him immortal fame as colonel of the Fifth New Hampshire. As an officer, Cross served only eighteen months in the Civil War, but that year and a half represented some of the bloodiest and most important battles fought by the Army of the Potomac: Fair Oaks, Antietam, Fredericksburg, Chancellorsville, and Gettysburg. Cross' participation in these events have led to an interesting interpretation of his life.

Because he died in the war as a colonel from a small state, Cross was forgotten in most postwar histories. Just a few contemporaries from the Granite State wrote about him. Some of his comrades portrayed him in a terribly inaccurate manner, as a man with no faults who was the beau ideal of a soldier, an officer who could do no wrong. In this light, Cross is someone whose only exploits worth recording occurred in the battles in which he participated. Still others ignore certain salient facts in his life that contributed to what he was, such as his upbringing and prewar adventures that forged him as a combat commander. Then there are those who portray Cross in a manner that is not befitting of a savage: He was someone who hated everyone but himself, who would shoot anyone who did not see eye to eye with him. This Cross was a man who threatened those in power in Washington through his fiery rhetoric. Some of his detractors even went so far as to portray him as a southern sympathizer, "a damned Copperhead," after his death. The truth of the matter is that the real Cross lies somewhere in between these two portrayals.

Over the last century and a half many people have tried to tell the story of Cross' life, but until now it has been all but impossible to bring out the full story, as the primary sources — the lifeblood of history — have existed but have not been exploited. With recently discovered manuscripts, newspaper articles written by and about Cross and a nationwide search for historical material it is now possible to write a detailed biography of Colonel Cross. The veil of time has lifted to reveal details previously unknown about his life, both before and during the war.

As a regimental and later brigade commander, Colonel Cross was brave to the point of recklessness in combat. He treated his men well, as long as they in turn obeyed his orders explicitly and without question. Cross led by example in a time when leadership was a very rare commodity at all levels; in many instances, his presence was enough to motivate his men forward or scare those into complying with his demands. The regiment that he molded, the Fifth New Hampshire Volunteers, was known in its time as a group of men who could be depended on to do their duty in the face of overwhelming odds, but this came at a terrible cost. His regiment suffered more men killed in action than any other infantry regiment in the Union army, among them Cross himself. After his death, the Fifth continued to soldier on, but it was never the same. If ever a man was the heart and soul of a regiment, it was Cross and his Fighting Fifth.

Cross had many faults that contributed to his character. These issues however, have added to the mystique of his life over the years. He possessed a sharp temper, was quick to jump to conclusions, and exerted favoritism to a high degree. Like many of his time, Cross loathed blacks, abolitionists, and immigrants. In addition, like the other male members of his family, he had a lifelong affliction with the bottle that contributed to his actions off the battlefield. For Colonel Cross, however, it was his inability to conform that made him an enemy of many. He was unable to put his own beliefs and politics aside, even as it cost him what he wanted most: a general's star. Word of his temper, combined with scathing articles and letters circulated to the highest levels in Washington and Concord, brought him enemies who otherwise would have supported him for his battlefield exploits. Cross believed firmly in the rights that his grandfather had helped to establish in the Revolution and did not see any reason why as a soldier he himself should lose his First Amendment privileges.

If ever a man was a paradox of two opposites, it was Edward Cross. He was a firm supporter of the cause of preserving the Union as it existed, with a clear distinction between slave state and free. Cross felt the administration was destroying the country rather than reuniting it, especially as scores of his men died on the battlefield and in camp for a cause that in time seemed hopeless. While many other officers resigned in the face of such odds, Cross remained with his New Hampshire men, in essence supporting the very politicians he hated so much. In combat, his actions, especially at Fair Oaks and Antietam, were the stuff of legend. Here he maneuvered his men as if they were a battering ram striking the Confederacy. Although a superb commander of men, he persistently drove his soldiers to never back down from a fight, costing many of his men, and ultimately himself, their lives.

This biography of Colonel Edward Ephraim Cross will present a full picture of this controversial man, his achievements, his failures, and his many faults. Because of the large amount of material written by Cross in his formative years, and surviving Civil War papers, the narrative unfolds as he saw the world. In addition, the letters and diaries of those who knew Cross and saw both the good and the bad in him are utilized to round out the subject and present a comprehensive view of his life. This book is designed to fill a critical gap in the vast literature of the northern Civil War experience, about a man whom Major General Winfield Scott Hancock, one of the Union's ablest combat generals, once called "a magnificent fighter."

CHAPTER ONE

An Eagle Is Born

Posterity owes to the Almighty a debt of gratitude for sending down to us the brave Col. Cross. — C.B. JORDAN, 1895

The white settlers named the place Coos, after the Abenaki who once lived there. Like their predecessors, the settlers were "dwellers of the pine tree place," a vast land of boreal forests, majestic moose, and sparkling lakes. Hardy individualists, devoted to family and set firmly in their beliefs, these people carved a hard life out of the granite hills of far northern New Hampshire. To the north was Quebec, still home to the natives many fought to expel from this rugged landscape. To the south were the majestic White Mountains, peaks soon to bear the names of great statesmen such as Washington, Jefferson, and Adams. On the eve of the Revolution, pioneers left their homes and settled in the land north of the "notches," the final frontier of New England. With a short growing season, farmers planted wheat and potatoes that took best to the rich soil near the Connecticut River, while others took advantage of the vast forests, once reserved solely for the use of the Royal Navy. Among those who made the decision to settle here was a young man named Richard Everett. From his line came a writer, explorer, adventurer, and soldier named Edward Ephraim Cross, whose roots were set deep in the earth of Coos County, New Hampshire.[1]

Richard Clair Everett was born in 1764 in Attleboro, Massachusetts, a descendent of one of the thousands of Puritans who journeyed to the new colony in the 1630s. Orphaned at age ten, he went to live with an aunt in Providence, Rhode Island, but in 1779 he ran away from home to enlist as a private in the Second Massachusetts Regiment of the Continental Line. Garrisoning the line of fortifications near West Point, New York, the Second Massachusetts did not see combat during this time, but the young soldier was present at the execution of Major John Andre, and like many suffered the severe privation that was common to the Continental soldier. Everett served three separate enlistments totaling six months and fourteen days of active service. The young man served his country in her time of need, and with the war all but over he faced a terrible dilemma. He was eighteen, his parents were dead, and he did not have any place to call home. In camp one day, Everett heard of a place called Lancaster, New Hampshire, a town first settled in 1764 with "cheap and fertile land."[2]

At this time, the town consisted of one hundred residents, who lived off the land, selling timber, pitch, and potash to the seafaring towns of Portland and Portsmouth. The recent conclusion of the Revolutionary War had carried away most of the able-bodied men in Lancaster, leaving behind few of the early founders. These settlements in the north needed an increase in population to remain stable. The increase came from a large influx of immigrants from Massachusetts and those who took up their land grant offers from the United States following their service in the Revolution. According to one resident of Lancaster, "From that class all these northern towns can count scores of the most important families that have helped to make them what they are today. Of that class Lancaster received many men of the most sterling worth and integrity." New people brought new industry, business, and professionals. Soon the small town was flourishing with life.[3]

A veteran of the Revolution and a prominent attorney, Richard Everett was the grandfather of Colonel Cross and an inspiration during his writing career (courtesy Lancaster Historical Society).

Returning to Providence in late 1782 to gather his few personal belongings, Everett knew some neighbors were also planning a move to Lancaster and decided to accompany them. After a toilsome journey of twelve days, the party scaled the White Mountains and arrived at their new home. As Everett was without his own family, Jonas Wilder, one of the founders of Lancaster, adopted him into his family. Wilder employed his new charge to help build roads on the frontier and to bring potash to the market at Portland, Maine. Everett decided early on that he wanted to do more in life than manual labor, and he began saving his money for greater pursuits. The young veteran fell for Wilder's eldest daughter, Persis, and knew that he needed to have a career that provided for his future wife. In 1786, Everett proposed to her and the next day left for Dartmouth College in Hanover. Graduating in 1790, he finally received the inheritance from his family's estate in Rhode Island and bought land in Lancaster. There were no lawyers in northern New Hampshire at this time, and Everett, faced with few options other than going to Concord or Portsmouth, decided to read law in an office in Albany, New York. Spending another three years away from his home and fiancée, Everett returned in 1793 as a member of the New Hampshire Bar; he was the first attorney in town.[4]

Finally marrying, the new couple built a large home on Main Street in Lancaster, and Everett opened a practice in the now thriving community, whose population increased yearly and where the services of a lawyer was needed to draft deeds, wills, writs, and other legal documents for those unable to understand the law themselves. Besides his law practice, Everett took to the interests of his town, serving as a selectman and, for five years, as a representative to the general court in Concord. Among the many ideas he brought to the capital was the need for vast internal improvements in the areas away from southern New Hampshire: roads were desperately needed to link the remote settlements with the outside world. Furthermore, he took a deep interest in maintaining bridges and expanding public education and libraries throughout rural New Hampshire. In Lancaster, he operated a gristmill and hired hands to collect the valuable pitch pine to sell in Portsmouth. This brought the growing family, which eventually included five daughters, a vast income, which he invested into huge tracts of real estate. By 1803, Richard Everett had established himself as one of the leaders of northern New Hampshire. As he was respected by the neighbors he served, Everett sought to abolish a longstanding tradition.[5]

Established in 1771, Grafton County comprised the northwestern part of New Hampshire. With the increased settlement of the area north of the White Mountains, and its very poor roads, the residents, including Richard Everett, found it increasingly difficult to travel to Haverhill, the county seat, to conduct their business. The general court conceded that the large tract north of the notches to the Canadian border should constitute its own county, beginning in 1805. With the new county came new county officials such as militia officers, sheriff, attorneys, clerks, and registrars. For Everett however, there was a plum prize involved. In the fall of 1804, Governor John T. Gilman appointed him as the first justice of the court of common pleas of Coos County, while Lancaster, through his influence, became the shire town.

In addition to this high honor, he became the first commander of the Coos County militia. As in civil affairs, Everett was well respected as a jurist, leading New Hampshire chief justice Jeremiah Smith to write, "I cannot help thinking people bred on mountains, or used to them, have more genius and more understanding than the low country." Another observer wrote that the new judge was "upright, fair, and learned." In 1813, Everett received an appointment as an associate justice of the New Hampshire Supreme Court.

Travelling the circuit to various locations in the state, Everett was constantly on the move, spending little time in Lancaster. Returning from a trip to Dover in the winter of 1815, erysipelas set in, and on March 22, 1815, Justice Richard Clair Everett died at his home in Lancaster. He was fifty-one. In writing about his life in later years, another prominent Coos County attorney said of the legacy he left to Lancaster, "Posterity owes to the Almighty and to him a debt of gratitude for sending down to us the brave Col. Cross."[6]

When Justice Everett died, he left a "low house with piazza in front, its roof perforated by a huge chimney; in rear the wood-shed and out buildings," to his wife, Persis, and their five daughters to live in. One by one, the daughters married and moved away, but Abigail, born in 1805, remained behind at the "Everett place." Another man who sought his fortune in Lancaster was Ephraim Cross, someone with "the rudiments of a common education" but "hopeful, buoyant, and progressive." Born in 1795 to a Revolutionary War veteran in the farming community of Windham, Connecticut, Cross came to Lancaster at an early age and apprenticed as a hatter. Despite this training, he constantly searched for the next enterprise to which to devote himself. In 1817, Cross married his first wife, Lucy P. Messer, of nearby Colebrook, but it ended in 1825 with her death. The union produced three children, but only one, Nelson, survived to adulthood. Cross again married in 1826, to Susan M. Wilder, who died several months later in 1827. Following the deaths of two wives and with a small child, Ephraim Cross turned his attention to the resident of the large house in the commercial district of Lancaster and married Abigail Everett in 1830, moving into her home. The house gained the title of the "Cross Place."[7]

The union with Abigail Everett produced five children: Edward Ephraim, born April 22, 1832; Richard Everett, born in 1835; Persis, born in 1840; Frank, born in 1843; and Helen, born in 1850. Each one of the Cross children left their mark on the world, but none greater than the first-born son.[8]

Ephraim Cross lived a very varied existence, much as his father-in-law had done. His hat-making business was the only one in Coos County and produced fine beaver fur hats that "did not wear out." In 1827, Ephraim opened the Coos Hotel, a massive structure raised to support the new tourism industry to the White Mountains, which the hatter-turned-hotel-owner operated until 1837, when he sold it to another party. An observer wrote, "Cross would attempt anything, and was never daunted by failure." A master woodsman, he was constantly out hunting for the abundant deer, bear, and moose that inhabited the north woods. In 1832, Cross and five other incorporators chartered the first bank in Coos County. Raising a capital of 50,000 dollars, the six men began a somewhat profitable business in what was once a purely barter economy. Ephraim Cross did not contribute to the raising of the funds. Instead he entered a note, stating that he would raise the money within a given amount of time; it was never paid. Cross took a major role in the bank and became an expert in detecting counterfeit money. Heavily involved in the civil affairs of his town, Cross was a Mason in the North Star Lodge, serving as Worshipful Master. He also served as a trustee with the Lancaster Academy, a private school in town that sought to provide those enrolled with more than the common education available at the time in the "district school." While he served in these business and civil capacities Cross also harbored a darker side. He suffered a lifelong affliction from alcohol use.[9]

Although heavily active in business, Ephraim Cross was more in his element in politics and the military aspects of Lancaster. He thrived in both and passed his interest in them down to his sons. In addition, he was a Jacksonian Democrat to the core. Lancaster was typical of the places where the party thrived: "they were hilly, poor, and small; they had few industries, and few Congregational churches; they were growing rapidly, but they were not yet on the main lines of communications." In an isolated community of 1,000 people, those who took the initiative to serve in public office often had to serve in more than one capacity. Cross served as a fire warden in his district in Lancaster, ensuring that all able-bodied persons had a bucket available in the event of a fire in the business district. At various times from 1840 to 1854 Cross was a deputy sheriff in Coos County. Throughout this time as well, Cross was a revenue collector, selectman and, as the town moderator, served during the annual town meeting in March, when many important financial decisions were voted on.[10]

At sixteen, like all other males in the town, Cross joined the Lancaster Company of the Forty-Second Militia Regiment; he soon found himself the regimental adjutant. Eventually, like Richard Everett before him, Cross became the regimental commander, in 1831, and became known to all as Colonel Cross. The militia was organized into forty-two regiments and subdivided into brigades and divisions; every town mustered a company, while several towns formed a regiment. The New Hampshire militia was a complex organization. Every able-bodied male aged sixteen to forty-five was required to arm himself with a musket and the proper equipments. Each year, the men, in the tradition of New England democracy, voted in their company officers, while the company officers in turn voted for those of the battalion; the brigade and division staff officers were appointed by the state. Each spring and fall the company mustered in Lancaster for drill. Here the men went through their paces, learning to load and fire their muskets. Afterwards, the soldiers traveled to the nearest tavern and drank to excess to celebrate the victory; the company officers usually paid the cost. Each September, Lancaster played host to a general muster of the Forty-Second Regiment, comprising men from the towns of Lancaster, Northumberland, Dalton, Whitefield, Stark, Jefferson, Carroll, Nash, and Sawyer's Location. Although ten companies paraded each fall, barely 150 men mustered on the drill field.

The regimental muster was the equivalent of a military exercise, political debate, and county fair all in one. The companies arrived early in the morning with "the shrill of fifes and rattling drums" and the discharging of muskets to wake the town up. Farmers and peddlers also arrived to sell their wares, while the entire village showed up to watch the spectacle. Yankee farmers and mechanics faced no real threat in their community and answered the call only to respect the law and not pay a fine. It was often a comical affair as they tried to keep the line dressed; uniforms were unknown, and many wore their everyday working outfits. Maneuvers as simple as a wheel often ended in a tangled mass of men and muskets. All the while, the hard cider flowed freely, while on occasion a poorly managed musket was prone to go off and kill its owner. The day typically ended in a "sham battle" as half the battalion fired on the other half with blanks, trying to demonstrate the tactics learned before the whole town. The War of 1812 effectively ended the once feared threat from Canada, while the Abenaki were broken as a tribe after the French and Indian War. Ephraim Cross was one of the few men in town who took his militia duties seriously, and he passed this sense of honor and duty on to his sons.[11]

From 1844 to 1846, Cross served as a state senator in Concord, representing the district comprising southern Coos County. Unlike the hundreds of members of the New Hampshire house, the senate was a small, elite body of only twelve members. Based on his years of experience serving in the militia, Colonel Cross served on the Committee of Military Affairs. Unlike his years of dedicated service to civil affairs in Lancaster, Cross was a mediocre senator and did not sponsor any legislation or accomplish much during his term. In 1845, however, he was the subject of a special vote in both chambers and received over ninety-seven dollars of back pay for his service as commander of the Forty-Second Regiment. The motion failed to reach the floor twice, then passed on the third motion and the colonel received his pay.

In 1846, Cross decided not to run again and returned to Lancaster. He spent the next few years in charge of a survey crew for the state, trying to determine the size of the remaining unclaimed land in Coos County, and at the same time finally determining the international border between Canada and the United States. While many inhabitants lived along the banks of the

Connecticut River, the interior of the county remained sparsely populated. Cross' results were well received by the State of New Hampshire when he found it owned nearly 90,000 acres of unclaimed land in the north, which the state quickly sold off to generate income. He continued to play a role, albeit lessening each year, in town affairs. Instead, his children took over the legacy and began to enter active public life.[12]

Henry O. Kent, a close Cross family friend, wrote of Ephraim Cross: "I do not think that he has been appreciated in this community on which he really left so marked an impression and which has received so much honor through the fame of his children." All were involved heavily in great events and contributed to their community, state, and country. Of the six however, it is the story of Edward Ephraim Cross that proved to be the most compelling.[13]

Many of the details of Edward Cross' life before he turned fifteen are unclear. He attended District School Number 1 in Lancaster, as well as the local Lancaster Academy, "an institution in those days of a very high degree of excellence," until he reached the equivalent of eighth grade. He learned the rudiments of reading, writing, and math, but also took a deep interest in history. From an early age, he displayed "an unusual literary talent" common to every member of the family and spent long hours reading and practicing writing composition. He enjoyed sports, such as the testing of one's strength by attempting to throw a stone over the steeple of the courthouse and an early form of baseball. His childhood hero was Revolutionary War general John Stark, and he enjoyed stories passed down from the aging Revolutionary War veterans in town who had served in the great battles of Bennington and Saratoga. Cross enjoyed the outdoors life of northern New Hampshire, being especially fond of fishing trips along the Androscoggin and Connecticut rivers each summer, and constructing earthworks in the woods, harkening back to the days of Abenaki raids along the frontier. His father's property contained a number of acres, and Edward, along with Richard, was responsible for tending to the family cows. Besides his lifelong friend Henry Kent, Cross enjoyed the companionship of his "big brindle dog" Rouse. Even in his youth, he was above average in stature and went by the nickname of "Long Ned" in the village. He was very devoted to his mother, Abigail, supporting her throughout his life. The stories that she told of her father's service, albeit brief, in the American Revolution gave Cross a firm footing in the study of military history and served as an inspiration when he became a writer.[14]

From the earliest age, Cross, inspired by his father and grandfather, devoted himself to military service, enlisting at age twelve in the Lancaster Company and rising through the ranks to become a lieutenant at sixteen. From this young age, he learned to believe firmly in the ideals of the American

EVERETT HOMESTEAD BUILT 1794 COL. CROSS PLACE 1844

Nelson Cross sketched the family homestead where the four Cross brothers grew up. On the front porch, added later, is where Edward Cross' funeral took place (courtesy Lancaster Historical Society).

Republic and the role of the citizen-soldier in defending it. He read tactics and mastered the manual of arms. The land of northern New England where he lived was the scene of scores of bloody fights in the French and Indian War, the Revolution, and the War of 1812. Even in his later years, Cross recalled a summer visit that he and Kent took to Fort Ticonderoga in New York. Cross wrote, "Do you remember Fort Ticonderoga? The warlike stores and formidable weapons there collected? Ah! theirs [sic] where you and I got our taste for the '*milingtary*' which with me will always be a part of my existence." In 1847, with the coming of the Mexican War, New Hampshire provided two companies to join the Ninth United States Infantry. Company H of the regiment was recruited in neighboring Grafton County, while several men from Lancaster volunteered to go south in a war that was terribly unpopular throughout New England. Although Cross did not go to Mexico, he paid careful attention to the stories the veterans told of Contreras and Chapultepec when they came home, which played an important role in his life for years to come.[15]

The Lancaster Company of the Forty-Second Regiment at this time also sponsored an artillery company, composed of a single brass three-pounder cannon "without limber or caissons, manipulated by drag ropes." The gun, known as a "grasshopper," came from the capture at Saratoga in 1777. Cross' unit was the Forty-Second Regiment Artillery Company, of which he became lieutenant in 1846, with Henry Kent serving as gunner or first corporal. They fired the piece during Independence Day celebrations and during annual training days. The company housed the cannon in a "little red gun shed" and the gun "was always the most attractive feature at the trainings." It was with the cannon that Cross learned the necessity of military discipline, for even the smallest misstep in loading and firing the piece could result in the death or dismemberment of every member of the gun detachment. Obedience to orders was paramount; the cannoneers had to work together to ensure a safe discharge. Cross took this experience of discipline, courage, and resolve and used it throughout his life.[16]

Edward Cross entered the ranks of the New Hampshire militia at a critical time. The once powerful organization that his grandfather and father had known was quickly breaking down. Without a serious military threat, training day was turning into more of a spectacle. Fewer men turned out each year, less to train than to drink. An increasing temperance movement attempted to end the traditional musters, as they turned into a drunken festival with firearms. Cross, as did his father, continued to do his duty, turning out each year. By the late 1840s, the militia laws that had been in place since the early part of the century were being repealed and modified yearly, as the regimental musters were dropped, and the companies mustered only once a year in September so the officers could ensure that the men of age in town were enrolled. By 1849, the adjutant general of the state was forced to write this: "By these alterations and amendments, the militia of the State became a mere skeleton upon paper, and soon possessed very little of vitality." In 1854, the once powerful enrolled militia disbanded due to a general lack of interest. At fifteen Cross made a critical decision about his future. While he greatly enjoyed the pageantry of the militia, he decided not to pursue the army as a career and enter West Point. Instead, he used his talents with pen and ink and entered another profession.[17]

Journalism came early to Coos County. In 1838 Henry Kent's father, Richard P. Kent, who ran a prosperous dry goods business in Lancaster, along with several others purchased a press and began publishing the *White Mountains Aegis*. Whig in its politics, the *Aegis* failed and ceased operations in 1842. While the *Aegis* did not turn a profit, another paper begun in the same year in Lancaster did make one. Successfully published for nearly fifteen years, the *Coos County Democrat* became the party organ of northern New Hampshire, as well as a respected journal, covering the news in Coos County. According to one of the employees, the *Coos County Democrat* was "a power in the community — a power because instead of *emasculating* it, it educated, strengthened and vivified public opinion. It was not a chronicle of gossip. It was the medium through which the news of the world was weekly presented, discussed, and analyzed to a critical and independent community." The editor of the *Democrat* was James Madison Rix, described by one of the printers as "a nervous, rigorous writer, and an acute politician." He served in both chambers of the New Hampshire general court, and in 1854 he became the president of the New Hampshire senate. It was under his watch that Edward Cross learned the skill of politics and writing.[18]

Rix established the *Democrat* in a vacant space above Richard Kent's dry goods store on Main Street and promptly began publishing the journal. His creation was soon "in every remote homestead in Coos, in the best room, there would be found a 'light stand' covered with a white cloth, and on the cloth the family Bible and on the Bible a folded copy of Rix's *Coos Democrat*." With little employment in Lancaster, outside of the farming or professional trades, Rix was fond of taking many of the teenage boys in Lancaster under his charge and instructing them in the printers trade. Many believed that the hard, demanding work of properly formatting the type to produce the paper, combined with the talent and skill of writing, prepared a young man well for any position he wanted in life. Years later, Edward Cross wrote of the profession, "A printer is well versed in human nature — there is no place like a printing office to sharpen a man's ideals, and give him a knowledge of the *real* motives, intents, and actions of humanity. Thus a printer grows wise, as it were, has an inexhaustible store of miscellaneous information, and no one can say that they would not do their part towards moving on the world." An observer wrote of Rix's apprentices: "From his office went out into the wider world many men who became prominent."[19]

The publisher of the *Coos County Democrat*, James Madison Rix, taught Edward Cross two important lessons in life, journalism and politics (courtesy Lancaster Historical Society).

Cross began working for Rix in 1847. In later years, Cross described his new employer as "a strange, misanthropic man — the coarse weeds of *miserdom* had checked down nearly all the cordial and happy impulses of his heart, and a relentless system of hatred towards all those who did not agree with him in politics, was the second great fault of his nature." From the start, Rix taught two things to his new apprentices — the art of writing and publishing a successful newspaper and the ideology of the New Hampshire Democratic Party. This consisted largely of "scorning Negroes and attacking abolitionists." The small black population in New Hampshire lived mostly in Portsmouth, while few, if any, runaway slaves were smuggled through Coos County on their way north to Canada and freedom. Because of the isolation of Lancaster, prejudice was widespread. Under Rix, Edward Cross learned how to hate and marginalize groups and to use the power of the press to his advantage. Rix's belief system produced men like Cross who carried hatred of most things and were blunt and to the point, never afraid to speak their minds. The United States Constitution promised freedom of speech and freedom of the press, two things Cross fundamentally believed in. He did not, however, believe in the limits that an individual sometimes has to restrain himself by when using the right.[20]

At various times during the 1840s Rix had several young apprentices in the office who took their experience at the *Democrat* and used it as a stepping-stone to greater things. These apprentices included the three Cross brothers, Edward, Nelson, and Richard, Henry O. Kent, and Henry Denison, who married Cross' sister Helen and became an ambassador to Japan. For Cross, it was an enjoyable time, and he would later write, "Some of my happiest days were passed in the old room over the store of R.P. Kent." Of all the apprentices who spent time at the *Democrat,* perhaps none gained more fame or became more of a pain to both James Rix and Edward Cross than a young man from Maine named Charles Farrar Browne.[21]

Two years younger than Cross, Browne took up writing at an early age. His mother supported her son's career plans and in 1847 sent him via stagecoach to Lancaster to become an apprentice with the *Coos County Democrat.* The driver of the stagecoach told Browne as he dropped him off in town that "Mr. Rix was very pious and that his best passport to success lay in knowing his catechism." Browne was very surprised, as he had never studied religious matters in his life. Arriving in Lancaster late one night, Browne immediately walked into the offices of the *Democrat,* where Edward Cross, now the paper's foreman, and his brother Richard were busily working. The Cross brothers were in on the joke about Rix and religion and made Browne read a passage of the Bible, the two brothers questioning him intensely. When the young man from Maine failed, Edward Cross promptly announced he was doomed to an existence in hell. The following day, expecting the same results, Browne returned to the office, only to find Edward and Richard passed out "sleeping the sleep of the inebriated under the back stairs." Together with the town tinsmith, they had drilled a small hole in the floor in the office leading into Richard Kent's store below. A small tube passed through the hole, leading to the rum barrels below; they could drink as long as the rum was there. Besides a love of the military, Ephraim Cross had also passed to his sons his affliction with alcohol, something Edward and Richard battled throughout their lives and that caused many problems for both.

Cross befriended Browne, in the beginning at least. Both men enjoyed practical jokes such as painting a white temperance pole in town with red stripes to look like a barber's pole, and throwing the contents of chamber pots onto pedestrians walking down Main Street. The two teenagers enjoyed the mischief that they could get away with in a small town without many other opportunities for amusement. While Cross enjoyed such practices on occasion, he knew when to work. Charles Browne did not.[22]

Browne was "a wayward brother in the minor duties, a pronounced lover of the good things of this life, and the constant author of scrapes and bad jokes." He lived with Rix's family and, as Henry Kent wrote, "was the plague of his life." The other printers at the paper knew Browne as "Fungus." One day Rix sent Browne out to the barn to milk the family cow. He had never milked a cow before, and when the cow did not produce, he took the milking stool and smashed it into the cow's hip, breaking its hip. For the editor of the *Democrat,* this was the beginning of the end of his association with Browne. Rix had appointed Edward Cross as the foreman of the *Democrat,* responsible for insuring that the apprentices, such as his brother Dick and Browne, were doing their duties properly formatting the paper to be printed. When he attempted to instruct Browne in the "mysteries and miseries" of typesetting, the young man from Maine simply did not listen to Cross and continued to misbehave, even on the job. Cross wrote, "How I used to train him, how he *would* act he seemed to be the decoration of damned foolery." Unable to be trusted in the office, Rix sent Browne out into Coos County to sell papers and collect money and other goods in exchange for subscriptions. Even at this he failed: "He would rather talk to the people and tell stories, rather than ask them for money." With little revenue coming in, Rix eventually had to send his daughter Eliza along with Browne to insure the collection of funds. James Rix began to think of a way he could discharge his wayward employee.[23]

While Cross and Browne were friends for a time and even played the same practical jokes with each other, soon the foreman grew tired of the apprentice's mischief. In the summer of 1848, after only a year with the *Democrat,* Browne went a bit too far, by playing a joke on Edward Cross. Browne stole Cross' uniform on the day before a militia drill. That morning the lieutenant went to get dressed and could not find his uniform, so Cross promptly borrowed a red sash and a sword and went to the drill field to instruct his men how to operate their cannon. A few hours later, the town drunk, who when intoxicated believed he was Napoleon himself, was located in a shed wearing Cross' uniform, which "once so bright and gay, was now besmeared with mud." The young lieutenant knew exactly who had done the deed and he immediately proceeded to the *Democrat* office to get satisfaction with Browne. Cross barged into the office, and Browne "never experienced such anxiety in his life."

The confrontation soon turned physical, and the two young men were crashing around the office. The small cases containing the individual letters used to assemble the paper fell to the floor, scattering

Charles Farrar Browne, better known as "Artemas Ward," apprenticed at the *Democrat*, where he became a thorn in everyone's side (author's collection).

the contents and creating a nightmare to reorganize them. Even worse for the office staff, the plates containing the almost-assembled *Democrat* for the week were ruined. A four-page weekly such as that published in Lancaster required nearly sixty hours of work each week just to assemble the type to print the paper. The two had destroyed this hard work as well, and the office was out of order for a week as the staff worked vigorously to put each piece of type back in the proper place. Henry Kent walked in and saw his friend "in deadly grapple with his opponent, writhing, and reeling among the debris." As Kent was about to enter the fray to support his friend, Browne reached for a small hammer to strike Cross. At the same instant, Rix himself walked in—and fired Browne on the spot. Running out of the building, Browne still had the hammer in his hand and threw it back into the office, through an open window. The metallic object struck Cross in the stomach and caused considerable pain for several days. Browne returned to Maine, telling his mother that he needed more education to succeed in the field, much to her dismay, as she never learned what actually had transpired in Lancaster. Charles Browne gained, rather than lost, from his short time in Lancaster. He found editing work in Portland, Maine; New Bedford, Massachusetts; and Toledo, Ohio. In 1857, Browne went to Cleveland, where he became a columnist for the *Plain Dealer,* writing comedy under the penname "Artemus Ward." While others found humor in his work, Edward Cross did not.[24]

With Browne gone from Lancaster, Cross continued to work at the *Coos County Democrat* for the next year and at the same time occasionally travelling to Canada to work with his father in the shipbuilding firms on Lake Memphremagog. Finally, in late 1849, Cross decided to leave the paper and enter the journalism profession. The three years spent at the *Democrat* prepared him well for his chosen occupation; according to Kent he "served his time justly and legally." In leaving Lancaster behind, Cross was embarking on a new career that took him far from the mountains he held so dear. He traveled far, witnessed remarkable things, and made history, but Lancaster, New Hampshire was always home.[25]

CHAPTER TWO

Restless Wanderer

> *You don't know anything about what it is to be 2000 miles away and wonder and wonder what is going on at home.* — E.E. CROSS, JUNE 1, 1850

In late 1849, Cross and several of his boyhood friends gathered on the bridge across the Connecticut River leading into Vermont. Here he shook their hands and with a "grin" on his face left Lancaster to make his mark on the world. He had a good education, had developed a strong sense of duty serving in the militia, and had learned the newspaper trade at the hands of a masterful and "misanthropic" politician. Leaving his youth behind, Cross traveled north to Quebec. The Coos Bank that his father was involved in had, in the economic upheavals of the 1840s, lost much of its capital and the support of the local community. By 1849, creditors moved in and the bank closed, while the incorporators had to pay the debt. Ephraim Cross owed heavily on his part, writing a note for payment many years earlier. Cross was "discouraged by its failure and ran away to Canada where he remained nearly five years." The elder Cross promptly went to work in Magog, Quebec, assisting in the construction of the first steamship on Lake Memphremagog. Edward Cross spent the winter of 1849–1850 assisting his father in building the ships, but at the same time he began to develop a lifelong passion for discovery and experiencing new things.[1]

Having grown up in a small, isolated community where the inhabitants were all white, Anglo-Saxon Protestants, Cross developed and harbored a lifelong passionate dislike for anyone who did not fit his ideology of what an American should be. The Canadians lived in "antique houses," which when they burned Cross thought to be a blessing as this allowed the Quebecois to rebuild in a modern style. The Quebecois were just the first ethnic group that Cross observed and learned to admonish. After just a few months in Canada, he again became restless and began to plan his next move, this time south to New York City.[2]

In the spring of 1850, Cross arrived in New York City. He was eighteen years old, out of work, and looking for adventure. By May, he found it in a secret organization run by Narcisco Lopez, a Venezuelan who planned to liberate Cuba from Spain and establish an "Antilles of the Republic." Using the United States as his recruiting ground, Lopez wanted to land 2,500 men on Cuba and take over the government. The filibuster had the support of many southerners, including then Senator Jefferson Davis of Mississippi, who believed the island could then come into the Union as a slave state. In his brief time with the organization, Cross added to his knowledge of military affairs, studying with Mexican War veterans. President Zachary Taylor heard of the planned expedition and ordered one of the vessels Lopez planned to sail, already loaded with arms and provisions, impounded in New York Harbor. The financiers of the operation were to pay one thousand dollars to land 1,500 men, which included Cross, on the Cuban coast. The second vessel was seized as well, thus ending Cross' first opportunity for adventure and military glory. The young man from New Hampshire was fortunate at the seizure, as the following year Lopez landed in Cuba and was captured by Spanish authorities. Lopez and most of his men died. The incident was among many narrow escapes with death Cross had in his life.[3]

While Cross was beginning his life abroad, Henry Kent remained behind in Lancaster. He continued to work at the *Democrat* and took over Cross' role as commander of the Forty-Second Regiment Artillery Company, although the company was already suffering from "a lack of discipline" without Cross to lead it. In addition, the company books disappeared, leaving the new lieutenant unable to determine who was on the rolls. During the next thirteen years, Cross and Kent kept up a sporadic correspondence that allowed each man to know what the other was doing and the affairs of each other's communities. While Cross traveled and wrote, Henry Kent remained behind in New England, becoming involved in politics and the newspaper business. In the beginning of his correspondence with Kent, Cross wanted to know all of the details of life in Lancaster, writing in 1850, "What new buildings are going up—who is flirting with the girls—where's Julie Bellows—in fact damn it Kent write me all about things. You don't know anything about what it is to be 2000 miles away and wonder and wonder what is going on at home." As time went on, however, he cared less about the details of life in Lancaster than he did sharing with Kent his own adventures and ideas. His mother, Abigail, wrote as well, but it was Henry Kent who always was Cross' closest and most confidential correspondent. The letters allowed Cross to remain connected with Lancaster, but as his time away from the town lengthened, he came to see the west as his home.[4]

With the Cuban expedition dashing Cross' hopes of remaining in New York, he again turned his attention to another destination and followed in the footsteps of his half brother Nelson, now a lawyer and well respected probate judge, to the bustling commercial center of Cincinnati, Ohio. The difference from Lancaster was remarkable. By this time, Lancaster contained nearly 1,500 residents, while Cincinnati bristled with 250,000, with more immigrants, especially those from Germany and Ireland, arriving every day. In addition, the city contained many sights that Cross would never have experienced in Coos County. Eight museums and two theatres provided entertainment and relief, and Cross attended performances of Shakespeare and "a French ballet troupe." While he generally found life in the city pleasant to begin with, the hot June weather quickly bore in on him as he who was used to the cool summers of northern New England: "The weather is awful warm to me though the *natives* assure me that this is nothing — at any rate I call it something to stand at eighty-five to ninety in the shade day after day." Cross passed the summer days of 1850 drinking sherry cobbler, "to which compound I have the strongest regard," exploring the city, and looking for work. He quickly found it in the office of the *Cincinnati Times*.[5]

Established in 1824, the *Times* was published daily. Also printed was a collected edition each week called the *Dollar Times*—as a one-year subscription cost a dollar—and the paper had subscribers all over the country, including some in Coos County. According to the paper's subtitle, the journal was "A Paper for the Million, Independent in all things, Neutral in nothing." In early April 1851, Cross wrote, "I work hard and am doing well—that is if $40 to $45 per month is good wages." The funds were more than he could ever have made in Lancaster. He did send money home to his mother on occasion to support her, as his father continued to live in Canada, saving up to pay his debts.[6]

Cross' new job, much as it had been at the *Democrat*, was setting and laying of the type to produce the paper; he had to work his way up the ladder to become a reporter and finally an editor. Unlike the single hand press in Lancaster, manned by a few teenage apprentices, the *Times* was a major national paper, employing nearly sixty men and with a dozen new steam powered presses. While Cross worked hard at the paper he also had many opportunities to travel throughout the local area, including visiting Kentucky and Indiana for the first time. In New Hampshire, the growing season was short and unpredictable. In the Midwest, the farmers began harvesting their early crops in April. He continued to enjoy the various opportunities that Cincinnati offered, including catching glimpses of Mexican War hero General Winfield Scott and "Gen. Tom Thumb."

In April of 1851, Cross observed his first municipal election in the large city, which again was dramatically different from the peaceful practices of New England democracy seen in Lancaster. In one day, "there were two men shot, 1 man severely stabbed, and several knocked insensible in sight of our office. Why the proceeding of the day would cause a New Englander to shudder. However, it was pronounced by the newspapers as a 'quiet day.'" Not yet of legal age to vote, he remained intensely interested in the political process.[7]

Although Cross decided not to enter West Point or join the Regulars after leaving New Hampshire, the military spirit continued to burn in him. Even from Ohio, he continued to inquire of Kent how the artillery company was doing, including giving hints for how to train the men, although by now the Forty-Second Regiment was almost extinct. Although he was making good money at the *Times* and was enjoying life in Ohio, he was beginning to formulate plans to return to New England. Cross wanted to go to Vermont and study at Norwich University, the nation's first private military college. In his correspondence with Kent, he wrote, "If I work steady till Oct next I shall have about $300 which will I think pay my expenses at the school a year. Perhaps some of you boys may also conclude to go and we will have some of our old times again." As with working as a printer, even if the graduate did not enter the military profession, the tough standards of education at Norwich, especially the writing and engineering classes, were thought to prepare a man to meet all of life's challenges. As time went on however, Cross realized that his future, at least for the time being, was in journalism, not the military. His friend however, was on his way to the college.[8]

As the holidays approached in 1851, Cross longed to be home in Lancaster with his family and friends. Ohio presented itself as a place that he was coming to terms with, even as he yearned for home. Cross wrote, "It is very uncertain when I shall see home, and my old friends again. Sometimes, when I sit down alone, and am thinking of our school days, our thousand boyish scraps—and even some of more recent date, I am half inclined to pack up and pay a short visit to you all. But it is not time yet. I don't like to see boys running home so soon — it looks as though they found themselves inescapable of taking care of themselves. I think I have done very well so far. You know I am not yet 20! Only think of it a boy yet!" He was willing to pay to have his eight-year-old brother, Frank, come and join him in the city, but his father sent the youngest Cross brother to St. Johnsbury, Vermont, to further his education. Unwilling to purchase or obtain his own housing, Cross rented a room with an acquaintance from Vermont. He also planned to enjoy the holidays with several of his co-workers, who like himself had left New England searching for opportunity in the West.[9]

By this time, Cross had developed the physical and mental characteristics that marked him for the remainder of his life. He was six feet, two inches tall and woefully lean, with piercing dark grey eyes that "could flash well, and withal," a high forehead, and a prominent nose. An observer wrote that "he was a handsome man." Cross was a nervous individual at times. He had a habit of constantly pacing up and down, stroking his long "chestnut colored" beard, constantly rotating his head, as if searching for something. He was more comfortable in the saddle, and perhaps because of his height, walked awkwardly at times, with his hands clasped tightly behind his back. Despite this, he had a commanding presence when he entered a room, or faced a situation, that made people respect him. He was a methodical individual who thought deeply and planned events down to minor details; even when things went contrary to what he planned, he was able to think on his feet and execute his plan.[10]

Routine played an important role in Cross' life in Cincinnati. By having a set routine, he was able to cope with the separation from New Hampshire. Whenever he received a letter from Lancaster, he repaired to the St. Charles Hotel, where he ordered an eggnog and a cigar, and read the letter several times. Like the other males in his family, and many in the antebellum era, Cross enjoyed drinking and often drank to excess, leading to a violent temper whenever confronted by those who did not obey his commands or who disagreed with him. He constantly wrote mock toasts home to Kent and listed what he was drinking, including sherry cobbler, whiskey punches, and Cross' personal favorite, eggnog, an old New England favorite. "Egg Nogg is *divine*. Angels could with propriety sip it, and no saint that I ever heard of would object to a foaming tumbler." He advised his friend not to start drinking, as it was bad for the liver, but at the same time he wrote how it did not seem to affect him. One night, however, when Cross was in a bar engaging in his favored pastime, he mocked "the cabbage heads of the Dutch." A fellow printer, a German immigrant, took offense, and a fight ensued. Cross took a "letter cut in one hand" but managed to break a stool over the German's head before making good his escape.

In 1852, when the *Coos Democrat* cut back on publication, Cross was severely disappointed, as "with its fall goes down a great source of clarity and divers misdemeanors." Kent had been a constant supplier of the paper to Cross, and it continued to inform him of the affairs at home. The printer from Ohio also sent copies of the *Times* home to Lancaster, notifying family and friends of the events he was experiencing in the West. This exchange benefited both parties and allowed a decrease in the slow passage of information through frequent newspaper exchanges.[11]

While working as a printer consumed much of Cross' time, he devoted himself to civil affairs as well. He became adjutant of a local militia company, responsible for maintaining the "orderly + roll books." It was a time-consuming task, taking almost two days before one muster to complete for the unit of sixty men. In addition to this, he served in a city fire company, taking part in musters and reviews on special occasions throughout Ohio and occasionally into Indiana. In the rough and tumble world of the *Times* office, Cross kept a "brain knocker" available at all times in the event of trouble. The local culture was starting to grow on him as he became involved in the city he now called home. He joined a local subscription library, which contained 15,000 volumes in addition to major magazine and newspaper subscriptions. The Mercantile Library provided Cross, with a place to repair during the long winter nights to read and study history and Shakespeare. A local gymnasium also saw the tall New Englander added to their rolls. Here he took boxing lessons and mastered the art of sword fighting. Several things about the city that did not impress Cross, however, included the oppressive heat in the summer, cholera, cockroaches, and the catfish in the river, which, although inexpensive and good to eat, he considered "damned mean things they are."[12]

Cross daily saw free blacks and abolitionists working in Cincinnati, and a party was rising up that went along with his political and ideological beliefs. The American Party, or as it is better known, the Know-Nothing Party, due to its members' stance to remain silent, was almost tailor-made for Cross. The philosophy of the party, which began as an underground movement in the 1840's were now just coming to force as a political party, included severely limiting the influx of immigration to the United States, putting restrictions on what those already in the country could do, and allowing only English as the national language. They thought Catholic priests would lead their congregations in a revolution to stage a coup and take over the country. The two groups most feared by the Know-Nothings were the Irish and the Germans, the Irish for their willingness to take any job offered after fleeing the potato famines and the Germans for the bloody revolution of 1848. It was unknown if the fiery rhetoric and the leaders that fled to the United States might start a fight in their new country. The party began as a small, insignificant movement but was soon capturing offices at all levels. The American Party's power lay in white, Anglo-Saxon Protestants; a group to which Edward Cross belonged and believed was the rightful heir to the government that his grandfather fought to establish. The Democratic Party soon lost all meaning for Cross, as he took those ideals and combined it with those of the American Party. Although he never stood for office, Cross became a major voice in Cincinnati politics through his work for the *Times*.[13]

In the presidential election of 1852 Cross, still twenty, could not vote. He did, however, take a deep interest in the events in New Hampshire, as former Mexican War general and Senator Franklin Pierce, a Concord native and ardent Democrat, carried the presidency. Pierce won in a landslide contest against another Mexican War general and chief of the Regular Army, Major General Winfield Scott, who ran as a Whig. Cross respected Scott as a soldier, but he could not support him as the nation's leader. He wrote to Kent, still working at his father's dry goods store and the *Democrat* (but soon to leave for Norwich): "Far be it from me to detract anything from his fame, or to seek to tarnish the laurels which 40 years of service have placed on his brow, but he is a *General*, he is fitted for one, and nothing else and it appears to be the opinion of 29 states out of 32 that he must remain a General or nothing." Although Pierce was a Democrat, Cross believed even before the election that he would be a one-term president. "To the devil with him," he wrote. Pierce believed firmly in the Constitution; as others in New Hampshire began agitating heavily against slavery, the president remained firm in his beliefs to support the governing principals of the nation through any means necessary to prevent civil war. This turned many in New Hampshire against him, as they believed he was a southern sympathizer. While he did not support Pierce when he was president, Cross in his later years came to rely on the former president as a confidant in his darkest time.[14]

With the election of 1852 over, Cross settled into his usual routine of setting print, but in early December he went out to celebrate an unspecified occasion with several friends. After a meal of punch, tripe, and pig's feet, Cross and his companions began walking home and singing "in not very melodious but very exhilarated tones." The party soon attracted the attention of the Cincinnati police. In a letter home, he wrote of the confrontation:

> Now having arrived in the peaceful precinct of the 14th ward — the guardian of the night overtook us and demonstrated in a fatherly manner against the continuance of the said music. Now it happened that one *Thos Lynch*, a man of *small* stature (not so tall as I) but of a very valorous disposition retorted, and did applied to the Hibernian Watchman sundry epithets and hard names. The said Hibernian hereupon set forth to Thomas Lynch the terrors of the watch-house. Thos replied in terms of unmeasured scorn — complaining all policeman were thieves, beggers, and other person of bad repute — and further, saying he would see him (the Hibernian) in the place where "sulpherous flames" (I use the language of a highly respectable host to his son; viz: Hamlet's father) are supposed to exist, before he would be arrested. Now policeman No. 2 is a mighty man and without more ado he clothed Thomas Lynch by the collar and began to take his body away. Great commotion at once arose, it being without precedent to see the smallest man in a party of six "*nabbed*" in such a summary style. A rush was made and policeman No. 2 was obliged to release the said Lynch, and to make use of his club to protect himself from bodily injury. I say use his club and the first use made with that named device, was to tap in no ungentle style the head of one, Cross, who was engaged in the praiseworthy act of shouldering the before mentioned Lynch, preparatory to a rapid retreat. The said "*tap*," being delivered in a skillful and appropriate manner had the effect of causing the said Cross then and there to

drop, and falling partly on the body of Thos Lynch, totally disabling that small individual. However, one Molledone Seiegel, with a brick, immediately attacked policeman No. 2 and assisted the rest of the party by the time the said Cross had rejoined his feet, disarm the functionary of his club. Then giving him several severe raps with the same and the subscriber having vigorously applied his boot to the fallen individual — the body of Thos Lynch was secured, and a rapid and orderly retreat made to a certain place known as the "Excelsior," where excellent spirits were sold at all hours. Then the said Lynch, in consideration of his rescue, produced a piece of paper of the value of three dollars, and insisted on its being "broke," and accordingly divers invigorating beverages were calmly handled and drank — and then, in a respectable manner the party broke up. The papers next morning said, "Policeman Patrick Malone was attacked last eve and badly beaten, after having knocked down one of his assailants." A report to which I cheerfully subscribe.

Cross was quick to add in his story home that this was not typical of his behavior, and he did not take pleasure in attacking police officers. He had done so only to help his friends. He did, however, have some satisfaction in knowing it was an Irish officer.[15]

During the same time he battled the police and studied at the library, Cross began to write professionally. Reading Shakespeare and Homer's classics, he developed a love of poetry and began to sell his poems to the *Times* as a means to earn extra money. In the tradition of the era, he took the pen name of his maternal grandfather, Richard Everett, and soon his reputation as an author was established. Almost as quickly as he started writing poetry, Cross tired of it and began to write "prose" or fictional stories, often devoting his after-hours time to it.

In one night, he produced a six-page piece titled "The Rescue: A Tale of Lake Winnipesogee." The story set the standard for the Richard Everett tales. Although a work of fiction, it did contain many elements of fact, mostly culled from Cross' visits

As a young man, Henry O. Kent pursued a military education at Norwich University that led to a successful career as a surveyor, journalist, politician, and soldier (courtesy Lancaster Historical Society).

throughout the Granite State growing up. In writing his first story, Cross introduced his readers to the setting of the story on Lake Winnipesaukee, a massive lake in the central part of the state. Many of his readers never saw New Hampshire, and this gave them their first introduction to this beautiful place just as the tourism industry was starting to develop. "The name of this sheet of water, in the figurative and mysterious language of the Indians, signified smile of the Great Spirit. From the summit of Red Hill, an elevation of about two thousand feet, a fine view may be obtained. At the base lies the lake, twenty miles in length, and from two to twelve miles in breadth; three hundred and sixty-five islands dot its blue surface, here and there one of many acres, inhabited and highly cultivated, while the majority are but a few rods in circumference, covered with trees, grass, and a few wild flowers."

The rest of the story, although fictional, illustrates Cross' ability to conduct research and write. Focusing on the destruction of a white settlement by a band of Abenaki warriors during the French and Indian War, the heroin of the story is Louisa, a fair and virtuous teenage girl whose family is killed by the attacking tribe. Losing both her parents, she becomes a captive at a nearby camp, where the natives decide to burn her alive in retribution for the lives of two warriors killed in the raid. Cross always seemed to put an element of his own life into his stories, writing, "Among the band was a young chief named Metalleck; distinguished for his bravery as a warrior and his great success as a hunter, he was a favorite with his tribe." Metalleck realized that Louisa was the daughter of the man who had saved his life on a previous occasion. Determined to save her, Metalleck destroyed the other Abenaki canoes and, seizing Louisa the moment she was about to be torched, safely delivered her back to the white settlement, then took refuge in what became Coos County. The stories, much as Cross' poetry, had been, was widely reprinted, especially in the Midwest and South. The writings attracted the attention of the editors of the paper, and Cross was in for a major promotion.[16]

The editors of the *Cincinnati Times* appointed Cross as a reporter, and soon he began spending much of his time traveling, following story leads into Indiana, a landscape that although Cross found interesting through its large assortment of crops, but was dull and flat in comparison to New Hampshire, a place he continued to long for. The *Times* was now the American Party's primary instrument of power in Cincinnati. Cross was thoroughly involved with the cause that supported his beliefs in the United States. He wrote, "Our paper is a strong Anti-Popery one." In addition, sometimes he let his fears of the immigrants get the best of him, thinking that Catholic priests were going to lead a bloody uprising and "all the Catholic Churches keep arms in them, and there is 60,000 Catholics in our city."

More important, was the event on April 22, 1853, Cross' twenty-first birthday. He wrote, "I am a *man*— that is, I cease to be an *infant* in the French sense, being 21 years old. Were you here, we would celebrate — as it is no particular demonstration will be made." Even as Cross took up the important task of writing, he never lost the sense of adventure that always drove him. One night, in almost a sense of mental delusion while working on a series of his journeys and work, he wrote, "Henry I am anxious to see a war. I hope we shall have trouble with England. I want to see Canada annexed and the whole continent Americanized. I would volunteer at once in case of a rupture."[17]

Kent, now deep into his studies at Norwich, continued to be bothered by Cross, who wanted him to come out to Ohio and take a job with the paper. Cross, already away from home for nearly three years, was beginning to plan a summer visit to Lancaster. In the meantime, Kent started to write himself, on one occasion taking an entire semester to produce a paper on military history. Cross' response to Kent was typical of his editorial style, blunt and to the point, even to his best friend:

> I have examined it carefully, and will tell you frankly what I think of it. I am aware that you are cautious to acquit yourself well, that you want to have something *good,* something that will bear criticism. I feel almost the same interest in the matter as you do- therefore you *must* do better than this. I am convinced you *can*, if you try. For fear the pencil marks on the "copy" may not prove plain. I will state.
> 1st. I do not like the subject:
> 2nd I do not like the style:
> 3rd I do not like so many adjectives:
> 4th Nor so many far-fetched and novel-like expressions
> You had not ought to go out of the U.S. for a subject; and a historical fact dressed in flowery language is not the thing. You take the strings of old, common place expressions, *interlaced* with adjectives, which mean nothing. It is more like a school girls' composition than the product of a military student. You have too many *far fetched* words—too much circumlocution. Why, my dear fellow all that you have written could be condensed into half a page. It starts off in the same style as "Regulars," and while reading it, I seemed to see Frank H. as he used to appear on the "boards" of the Academy. Take some such subject as our means of National Defense, Our Militia, Character of John Stark, and his services; or some thing where you can evidence some *new idea*, or arrange things in a new light. Use few commas; have your sentences short. Be *terse*, not verbose. Use few *flowers* of speech. Arrange your subject. Turn it over in your mind. Dissect it. Think of it above all take time. Better spend an hour on six lines than not have them good. Now dont fly into a passion. Dont swear. Dont think hard at what I have written; for as the Lord giveth you'll say alright some day. My friend Leavitt — a college graduate concludes with me. If you do not use that essay modify it, simplify it. But my advise is— Try again.[18]

It was pure Cross, a direct blow, always willing to speak his mind, unmindful of the consequences. His comments also illustrate his keen eye for being methodical and leaving no stone unturned to ensure that something was accurate.

At the same time Cross tried to sway his friend into changing his writing style, he also continued to play a major role in the Cincinnati American Party, organizing and writing propaganda pieces as it began to take control of the politics in the city. Now of age, he was paranoid at the immigrants he encountered on a daily basis, seeing a threat in anyone who was not a white, native-born American. In April of 1853, Cross thought for sure there was

A previously unpublished early photograph of Edward E. Cross, taken in Cincinnati (Gettysburg National Military Park).

going to be "a bloody row" when a group of Protestants had a revival, and the Catholics determined to block it from occurring. His fears were often unwarranted, as many of the immigrants simply wanted a better life in the United States. However, the fear motivated Cross and gave him a purpose and a place to devote his talents. When Cross believed the mayor was a Jesuit, Cross and several others approached him to resign. The fear that the Catholics might gain office led him to write, "Never so help me the Eternal God will I vast a vote for a foreigner or a Roman Catholic."

Although the party held sway in Cincinnati, it was having trouble gaining momentum at the national level, over the issue of slavery. Northern abolitionists opposed to immigration were unwilling to budge on their stance against slavery; likewise Southerners, especially with the publication of *Uncle Tom's Cabin*, began to feel the scorn of the more powerful northern party. Cross was on the fence. He hated blacks and loathed southerners, yet his loathing also extended to immigrants, northern abolitionists, and Catholics, this fact led him to begin to wonder what direction the party might take. As early as the summer of 1853, Cross knew one thing for certain — that the United States as he knew it could not last forever. He wrote, "We cannot tell what a day may bring forth. One great event is evidentially approaching, namely, the destruction of this Union. Neither you or I will wear grey hairs before the deed is commenced unless Providence interposes." The sense of duty imparted to him at an early age continued to burn. Cross believed firmly, even his mid-twenties, that the Union had to endure, even if it meant civil war.[19]

As Cross contemplated the future, he spent the late summer of 1853 back home in Lancaster for the first time in three years. Rekindling his boyhood acquaintances, Cross found a changed town, with more people and businesses. The artillery company disbanded, and most of his friends were married or had moved away from the small town to other pursuits. His father was still in hiding in Canada, while the bank placed a lien on his mother's house for the debts that his father still owed on the failed Coos Bank. Together with Henry Kent and other friends, he took a multiday fishing trip on the Connecticut River, a tradition that he attempted to repeat nearly every summer until his death. In addition to enjoying his time at home, he also sold subscriptions to the *Times*. It was over all too soon, and Cross again was on his way to the West. He was not there for long, as the editors of the paper assigned him to cover events in the House of Representatives in Washington, D.C.[20]

CHAPTER THREE

American Party Reporter

> *An Abolitionist is a lunatic and nothing else. I am opposed to the extension of slavery, but consider its immediate abolition a chimera, an impossibility, an insane idea.* — E.E. CROSS, APRIL 3, 1855

Although politically active since his early teens, first in the militia, and then in the Cincinnati American Party, Edward Cross first entered the realm of American politics when the *Cincinnati Times* sent him to report on the proceedings in the House of Representatives during the winter term of 1853–1854. With Franklin Pierce in the White House and a Democratic Congress, the nation continued with the debate over slavery. The Compromise of 1850 staved off the threat of civil war for the time being, but the debate and continual hawking by southerners for state's rights as the Kansas-Nebraska Act was enacted in 1854. It was into this firestorm that Reporter Cross went.

Cross made an instant impression with the delegation from Ohio, who promised a paying clerkship in a House committee, but he did not "calculate very strongly upon it." While he did not receive the appointment, Cross went ahead with the business of the day. He occupied nearly every hour attending sessions, visiting members, studying at the Library of Congress, and seeing the sights, including Mount Vernon. He attended a drill of the Amoskeag Veterans, a militia company from Manchester, and wrote, "They are a splendid body of men." In essence, the Veterans and the Governor's Horse Guard were the only militia companies still active in the Granite State. Cross continued to attend the theatre and went on one occasion with a friend from home who "hates the Know-Nothings, and adores the administration." Despite their vast differences in politics, the two men got along.[1]

While he observed the sights and his meetings with members of Congress, Cross turned his attention to the presidential election of 1856, nearly two years away. The American Party was a rising power, but the issue of slavery was slowly beginning to divide this party as well. Northern abolitionists were in the process of forming their own party, the Republicans, while southern Democrats continued to hammer for an increasing expansion of slavery. For president, Cross wanted Millard Fillmore to return to office, as a compromise between northerners and southerners. He did, however, issue an almost prophetic message: "Kent, the Union is safe if Northern men will only let it alone."[2]

The session ending in the spring of 1854, Cross returned to Lancaster for the summer. As before, he accompanied his friends on a fishing expedition, reveling in recounting his adventures in the West. In August he again visited Canada, this time to write an article for the paper. His brother Richard enlisted in the Regular Army and was then on his way to being stationed in Texas with the First Cavalry. Cross made his way to Montreal and Quebec, and, as he did throughout his travels, wrote back to the *Times* about his adventures.

Always a student of military history, in Quebec Cross visited the Plains of Abraham, where General Wolfe captured the city in 1759, and the Gates, where in 1775 a force of New Hampshire men failed in their assault to capture the citadel during the opening days of the Revolution. Cross wrote, "Montreal is yet old fashioned. The streets are narrow, the houses are antique, and the manners of the people speak of the ancient regime." As an ardent American Party supporter, Cross took particular note of the Catholics of the two cities. In Montreal, he believed the Cathedral of Notre Dame, capable of accommodating 15,000 worshipers, was impressive on the outside, but "inside the work and decorations are very poor and cheap." After some priests showed him a box of relics, thought to provide a cure for ills, Cross gave his characteristic reply of its being a "humbug."

Of Quebecois nuns, he wrote, "Each face was a wan, hopeless, sorrowful picture, as though all life, happiness, and youth had been crushed from their hearts." When he tried to enter the convent, the nuns turned him away. Cross took no stock in the Catholic belief that a particular house he heard about was haunted, but he enjoyed watching the building of a bridge across the St. Lawrence River. Many of the Protestants that he encountered knew of the Know-Nothing movement and hoped the movement would expand into Canada to expel the Catholics who continued to hold onto local power, from Quebec. Of particular note was Cross' interest for British Regulars, then providing the garrison of Montreal. Having been in the militia most of his adult life, Cross knew what he was observing. The Yankee was not impressed at the Scottish troops he saw, writing, "The men were very small, old, and had a dispirited look." After spending time ridiculing and observing the Quebecois, Cross returned to the United States and his beloved New Hampshire.[3]

Although relatively remote, by the 1830s and 1840s, the White Mountains of New Hampshire became accessible to the masses by railroads that brought visitors to Concord and then by the turnpikes, which brought them north to the mountains. Cross visited 6,288 foot Mount Washington in late August, shortly before returning to work. Much as he did in his article from Montreal, he provided readers around the country with a glimpse of this place. He wrote, "The aborigines held these mountains in great veneration believing that evil spirits, tempests, thunders, and lightning dwelt there." Ever observant of his surroundings, Cross noted that there was a twenty-five degree difference in temperature between the summit and the valley floor; there was snow and ice as he ascended into Tuckerman's Ravine, a steep walled valley on his way to the summit. The ascent took nearly all day and ended with a stay on the summit overnight. His companions included wealthy men from Boston and women who "looked very much like Irish wash women, only worse." The sights from the top amazed Cross, even though he had once lived amid the rugged beauty of the mountains. At the base of the mountain, Cross wrote, "I spent an hour this afternoon in the undignified business of playing with two tame bears that are chained to a tree on the lawn. We had a lively time of it, as they are sometimes disposed to act rudely and be too ardent in their 'hugs.' Still, they are very well behaved and sociable bears." As with his visit the summer before, however, this trip was over quickly, and he again left New Hampshire for his work with the *Times*.[4]

Once again, on assignment, Cross first went to New York City, writing, "I detest that city it is a perfect den of thieves—worse than the old temple the Savior cleaned out one day with a horsewhip. Young man if you had studied your Bible as I have, you would know all about that circumstance." Although not a deeply religious man, he was a voracious reader and could randomly quote passages from the holy book. Cross next went to Philadelphia: "I can sit on the hotel piazza and watch the beautiful women as they promenade for hours at a time. I had heard before of the loneliness of Philadelphia girls, but it is half not been told to me."

Cross found himself bound to visit several of the city's prostitutes, calling them "infernal." He indulged himself in "fingers" of rum, and had a difficult time sleeping due to "scratching bed things." There were many sights to take in, including battlefields, a subject that so fascinated him. This time he went to Germantown, the site of a brutal clash in October of 1777. He remained there nearly two weeks, writing, "Of all the cities in the west, I love old Philadelphia the best. Their wealth and shining flag unfurls and waves it over pretty girls." After returning to Baltimore and Washington to finish his business from the last session of Congress, Cross again returned to Cincinnati.[5]

Cross quickly picked up where he had left off with his writing, filling columns with his summer visit to New Hampshire and also investing significant time in a new fictional piece. Titled "The Young Volunteers," it proved to be his most famous prewar work. Those who have read the story are often struck with the fact that Cross wrote it as a vision of how he saw the future, specifically his experiences commanding the Fifth New Hampshire in the Civil War, due to the mention of many elements that eventually occurred in Cross' life. In reality, "The Young Volunteers" was not his view of how he saw the future. Cross was not a Nostradamus. Rather he was fictionalizing a historical event; the similarities with future events must be looked at in relation to any prophecy after it has occurred. The story was based in large part on the talks Cross had as he grew up in Lancaster, speaking with the veterans of Company H, Ninth United States Infantry, about their experiences fighting at Churubusco, Molino del Rey, and Chapultepec during the Mexican War. The specifics of the story involved the experiences of three Concord printers, Henry F. Carswell, Ezra T. Pike, and John C. Stowell, who worked for the *New Hampshire Patriot* and died for their country in a foreign land.

Working in Washington as a reporter, Cross commanded national attention through his political coverage (courtesy Lancaster Historical Society).

Cross wrote his piece as fiction, the story of two printers from northern New Hampshire who found glory and death fighting for their country south of the Rio Grande. In his opening paragraph, Cross described the main characters, who, like himself, worked for a newspaper: "Printers are peculiar men; they have a tinge of melancholy in their natures, a sort of deep conviction that this world is a monstrous humbug — they have found it out — there's no sincerity, no confidence in it." The rest of the story details the recruiting, service, combat, and death of the Ninth in Mexico. Having been active in the militia for nearly ten years, Cross spoke highly of the citizen-soldier over the professional regular, a man who joined to serve his country in her time of need, not as a career. Tom and Harry stood firm, fired low, and behaved with cool and resolve under fire until they died in the storming of Chapultepec in very similar circumstances to the three men from Concord. Although Cross wrote several more stories in the years leading up to the Civil War, "The Young Volunteers" was his most remembered story, a work of historical fiction that based was in fact.[6]

With another story published, Cross resumed his busy schedule of traveling, politicking, and militia musters. The Know-Nothings did well in the election that fall, which raised his spirits. In mid–November 1854, he went with the Guthrie Greys to Chillicothe, Ohio, for a multiday excursion. The company "had a glorious time of it," but Cross doubted the company would be invited back to the city. The Greys went on "a big spree and played off the bowled sugar boy in high style," to which he, in his usual manner of drinking to excess, "contributed in high style."

Although President Franklin Pierce was a native of New Hampshire, Cross found no respect for him, calling the president "granny." When Pierce refused to intervene in foreign affairs, instead trying to keep the peace in a nation on the brink of war, Cross became disgusted, writing, "We are to have no war with France after all. It's a burning shame that we cannot raise a row with some nation and knock smithereens out of them." A fire continued to burn in Cross to have a fight; he desperately wanted a war so he could live the stories he dreamed of. On occasion, in his writings, he crossed the line between delusion and reality, hoping the tales of military glory would one day come to life.[7]

While Cross wanted a war, Henry Kent was beginning a peaceful life in Lancaster. He graduated from Norwich University in 1854 and wanted to pursue an engineering career. Kent was torn between staying in Coos County and pursuing his dreams elsewhere. In the end, Kent stayed in Lancaster and opted for another career. The *Coos Democrat,* the organ of the county party for fifteen years finally grew silent. James Rix finished his term in the New Hampshire senate, but he was gravely ill and stopped publishing the paper. Kent purchased the press and equipment, and began issuing the *Coos County Republican* in its place to support the growing movement in New Hampshire. He also did job printing and sold paper goods in his father's shop. Following in the footsteps of many prominent men in Lancaster, he became a member of the North Star Lodge, Free and Accepted Masons. In addition to this busy schedule, Kent and a friend from Norwich also operated a survey business on the side, planning a survey of the entire landmass of Coos County. The activities of his friends at home continued to nag at Cross, even after four years of absence. He wanted to be present at home during the holidays, but knew he could not. Lancaster and New Hampshire itself grew far distant. Cross was a continual wanderer, in search of the next story to report on. The story, however, was not in Coos.[8]

With the American Party fighting for its survival, Cross began spending much of his spare time preparing for the presidential election of 1856. Franklin Pierce was failing, as the country grew closer to war. The *Cincinnati Times* was in the process of printing a special edition to be circulated around the nation to explain the viewpoints of the Know-Nothings, an edition Cross was placed in charge of. He planned to send many copies home for Kent to circulate among the people of Coos County, asking Kent to process the papers. With this important act underway, he also began yet another lengthy journey. In St. Louis, Cross met three friends from Littleton, New Hampshire, who, just as he himself had, found opportunity in the West running a messenger service. In almost every letter, Cross wrote constantly for his friend to join him in his adventures, claiming "glorious times." Kent had a growing newspaper and other business to attend to as Cross continued his wanderings.[9]

From St. Louis, Cross traveled to New Orleans for a few hours, thence to Mobile, Alabama, on a tour of the southern states. In Charleston, South Carolina, Cross heard of the spring elections in Cincinnati and wrote, "I am fearful our ticket got a back handed blow from the combined forces—Greeks, Germans, +c." He felt that the Irish defrauded the election, illegally voting several times, while mobs of immigrants threatened to tear down the *Times* office, only being repulsed when the staff armed themselves for the assault. There were several murders and bloody fights. The American Party lost by only three hundred votes. Although the party had lost this election, Cross still pinned his hopes on 1856.[10]

In the Deep South for the first time and face to face with a culture radically different from that of the North, he wrote of his feelings, and his fear of New Hampshire Republican John P. Hale, an ardent abolitionist, gaining a Senate seat:

> I do not like the South at all. It ought to be numbered among the heathen lands of the earth. Hale must be kept out of the Senate by some means for if he is elected the whole of the South will rear and plunge out of the traces; and I wouldn't complain. I don't want to see any more *Abolitionism* brought in to the order. An Abolitionist is a lunatic and nothing else. I am opposed to the extension of slavery, but consider its immediate abolition a chimera, an impossibility, an insane idea. Metcalf's letter of acceptance was crammed full of "niggerism." That better, with the election of Hale, would use up the order South of Mason's + Dixon's line. I am satisfied from this touring through the Southern States, that if you and I live to be fifty years old we shall see a Dissolution of the American Union. It is a dreadful thing to contemplate, but it is inevitable, unless you can hang, or otherwise get rid of the fanatics of N. England.

While the old Democratic Party as Rix and Cross knew it still hung on in much of the Granite State, many of the younger generation, such as Henry

Kent, were switching and becoming members of the Republican Party embracing its message of halting the expansion of slavery into the new territories. Although Cross believed the dissolution would occur when he was fifty, it was much sooner than he could realize.[11]

Returning to Cincinnati in May of 1855, Cross resumed his local duties but continued to write his fictional war stories under the pen name of Richard Everett. During his time in the Carolinas, Cross visited the Revolutionary War battlefield at Charleston, South Carolina, where in 1776 a small force of Americans turned back a British invasion fleet, which became the subject of one of his stories. As the American flag fell, brave volunteers shimmied up the pole to restore it. Of Colonel Francis Moultrie, the fort's commander, Cross wrote, "Amidst the din and fury of the battle, Col. Moultrie coolly walking about, smoking his pipe and superintending the defense with watchful eyes — now directing a cannon, and now assisting to convey some wounded men to a place of safety." Furthermore, Cross visited the sites of Eutaw Springs and Guilford Court House. In both battles, the Americans scored important but not quite complete victories over their British enemy. Cross never failed to write of the virtue and invincibility of the American soldier. After describing the half-starved, nearly naked condition of Nathanael Greene's army on the eve of Guilford Court House, he wrote, "But in the hearts of these noble men burned the fires of liberty. They did not complain, but marched eagerly to the fight." Still afraid of the threat of civil war, he portrayed Greene, Washington's second in command, as a liberty loving New Englander who came to the aid of the South in her time of need. Although many knew that "Richard Everett" was actually Edward Cross, New England native and Know-Nothing, his stories were popular and were reprinted in Utah, New Jersey, North Carolina, and Mississippi, among others.[12]

Again, during the winter of 1856, the *Times* sent Cross to Washington to report on national affairs. The year proved to be pivotal to Cross and the cause he supported. Slowly losing power since their gains in the earlier elections of the decade, the American Party was putting much effort into the presidential contest that fall. Cross lost all faith in Pierce and believed that the American Party candidate was the only one that could keep the nation out of civil war. In New Hampshire, the economy was changing from farming to mechanization, overnight in many areas. Many of the mills were dependent on southern cotton. Despite this, many people were flocking to the Republican Party and its message of abolition, leading Cross to write, "This antislavery agitation is all useless — all a damned humbug to gull votes from fools. Have nothing to do with it my boy." With the Democrats languishing, Kent, like many aspirants, saw the Republicans as their chance to succeed. In January, Cross faced "cold, irregular meals, exposure, late hours +c" that brought about "constipation of the bowels," which kept him in bed for a week. Cross believed that he did not receive proper medical attention, having been bled and given cups of tea to cure his ills. In the end, he did rebound from the illness and continued his reporting. He enjoyed a high social circle, at one point spending one hundred and fifty dollars on brandy for a delegation of Hungarian diplomats.[13]

In February of 1856, Cross became the *Cincinnati Times* correspondent to the first Know-Nothing convention in Philadelphia. Running the fragile line between North and South, the party leaders skirted the issue of slavery to focus on their major concern of immigration and Catholicism. This split represented the last major opportunity for the American Party to capture a majority of the vote. At the convention Cross simply observed as the major party leaders, mostly from New York, and the Border States tried to work on a compromise. As Cross hoped, Fillmore became the party's candidate: "He made an excellent President and will do so again." The convention was not without controversy, as some delegates left protesting the nomination. With the convention over, Cross returned to Washington to resume his duties, while planning his next move to support the party.[14]

From the seat of power in Washington, which he referred to as "the meanest place outside of Napoleon, Arkansas," Cross was "disgusted with this useless and endless slavery question." Despite their being the best of friends, he severely disagreed with Kent, who wrote that slaves were "shrieking for freedom." Recently elected Senator Hale began reading anti-slavery petitions again on the floor of the Senate, thus breaking the twenty-year-old "gag rule" that had helped keep peace in Congress. Although Cross had a passionate hatred for slaves and their white abolitionist sponsors, he did not see the expansion of slavery as having any benefit for the nation. The American Party and its members North and South supported the party platform, being anti–Catholic and anti-immigrant; however, on the slavery debate, its members split fiercely. This inability, combined with the Republicans' national platform, was fracturing the movement that Cross firmly believed in. Many members were leaving the ranks for the Democrats or the Republicans, which he blamed for the loss of the momentum enjoyed earlier in the decade.

In Ohio, Salmon P. Chase, an ardent abolitionist, won the governorship, defeating the American Party candidate in a landslide. Cross felt that the party was selecting the wrong candidates for the positions they contested. Despite his belief in the party Cross never stood for election. He believed that Ohio was the nation's hotbed of abolition, and from there it was spreading throughout the nation, even into Coos County. He hoped, knowing what was ahead, that Kent and his friends were "keeping up the military spirit" in Lancaster, his old home. Although the artillery company's old three pounder could not be of much service in any modern conflict, trained soldiers were at a premium in New Hampshire.[15]

Cross was a conservative in how he felt the politicians should spend the federal treasury. He believed in no outlays for the poor and needy, as they should be able to fend for themselves. When it came to internal improvements such as investing in railroads, turnpikes, and canals, Cross believed strongly in them, urging that the funds be given directly to the states, as they knew best how to spend it. When it came to national defense, he believed the nation should spare no expense, such as paying for new rifle-muskets to arm militiamen to replace their ancient flintlocks, or the building of a new steamer for the navy. Because his grandmother was widowed by his Revolutionary War veteran grandfather, Cross supported the increasing of pensions for widows of Revolutionary War veterans, writing, "This is a very important act, and as it will no doubt pass." Besides his duties of writing a daily letter back to the *Times* and meeting with the delegates from his adopted state, Cross took on other tasks.

During the 1856 session, Cross received nearly one hundred and fifty letters from strangers asking for help in obtaining congressional publications and autographs of selected members. He did draw the line, however, when one woman from New York "wrote a very polite note stating that she was making a collection of autographs, and wished me to procure and send her the signatures of all the Foreign Ministers, Charges, Consuls &c. residing in Washington! This exceedingly simple and modest request was mildly, but firmly denied." On his way home to Ohio at the end of April, Cross spent some time in Annapolis, Maryland, observing the naval academy and the new steamer *Merrimac,* named after a major river in New Hampshire. He wrote, "The Merrimac is a splendid ship, in every respect. She has no superior afloat. Her armament is forty 18 lb. guns, and two pivot shell guns of tremendous force and long range." During the tour of the vessel Cross took part in a mock drill, inspected the Marine detachment onboard, noting their lack of modern weaponry, and ended with a dinner of champagne and oysters with the vessel's officers.[16]

Back in Cincinnati after another restless term in Washington, Cross began to prepare for the election. Working long hours at the *Times* office, he became an editor, and his salary was raised from 800 to 1,100 dollars per year. The difficult work, combined with the ever increasing hours, had an effect on Cross: "I have lived principally upon iced claret punch, sherry cobblers, juleps, and other cooling compounds for a long time. This style of subsistence is not calculated to promote fat, and therefore I am in such redressed condition as to put a reputable fence rail to shame." With hundred degree days a daily occurrence, he longed to return to Lancaster, and go with Kent and other friends on their yearly fishing expedition, but he had too much work to accomplish. Cross hoped Kent could express some trout to him in Ohio. Even after so long an absence, Cross continued to "long for the East, visions of the mountains of Coos rise up before me like the mirage to a desert traveler." The Greys also constituted a large part of Cross' time, and he traveled to Lebanon, Ohio, during one ten-day encampment. He joined the Odd Fellows but wanted to take his Masonic degrees in the North Star Lodge in Lancaster. Despite the campaigning and writing he was doing in support of Fillmore, Cross knew that the Republicans, now running a presidential candidate in the form of explorer and senator John C. Frémont. would carry Ohio. He placed his hopes in Kentucky, where he went on business frequently.[17]

Through the remainder of the fall, Cross, now the chief editor of the *Times*, continued to stump the Midwest for the American Party. He made nearly thirty speeches against Fremont and the Republicans, even as Henry Kent, now a law student, was in Washington with Senator Hale championing the Republican platform of stopping the spread of slavery. It was a difficult fight, even as Cross knew that his party was losing the battle. President Pierce lost his bid for renomination against Pennsylvanian James Buchanan, a former senator, secretary of state and ambassador whose platform was to end sectionalism and restore the nation under a conservative national government. Like the rest of New Hampshire, the once solidly Democratic realm of Coos County was now Republican, and the party leader in the county turned out to be Henry O. Kent. Cross was mortified to learn that the people of Lancaster were sending clothing and money to support Free State settlers in the Kansas Territory, writing, "Bleeding Kansas! Humbug!" The violence continued to draw even those unsure of their stance towards the Republican Party, taking more votes away from the American Party. By the first week of November, it was over. Fillmore carried only Maryland, and to Cross' chagrin, despite his best efforts to bombard Coos County with pro–Know-Nothing papers, only four people in the entire county voted for Fillmore. The editor rewarded them each of them with a free year of the *Times* for their support. Republican Fremont did well, capturing New Hampshire. But despite his effort, Buchanan was going to the White House, and Edward Cross was unsure what to do next, his months of hard work over, destroyed by the issue of slavery.[18]

With the great crusade of 1856 over, the American Party disintegrated almost overnight, its members returning to the Republican and Democratic ranks. Although there was strong support to curtail immigration and the spreading of the Catholic faith, the American Party could not stand divided over the issue of slavery. Without a party to support his political beliefs, Cross was a lost soul. He contemplated studying the law, traveling to England, and returning to Lancaster. In the end, he went back to Washington to cover the new term of Congress, where the Republicans were now in power. It was over six years since Cross left Coos County to make his mark on the world, which he had succeeded in doing to some extent. By 1856, after years of writing how much he wanted to be home and pleading with his friend to join him at the *Times,* Cross finally came to a realization about his best friend and the future of the nation:

Republican Senator John Parker Hale was a radical abolitionist who agitated against slavery in the 1850s and was utterly despised by Cross (Library of Congress).

True, I love New England well — dear to me is native state with its eternal vestments, and its swift river — but the west is my future field of action. Sometimes I think I shall return to dwell under the shadow of our ancient mountains, but each day the boyish charm grows fainter and fainter as new associations cluster round the heart and ties of interest and friendship grow stronger and stronger. You will do well to stay where you are. New Hampshire needs all her active, intelligent young men to stand by her in the days of her age. If you are fond of politics Coos is a good field to begin in. Representative, Member of Congress, the Senate! Your course is clear. God grant you may follow it faithfully and well. You have all the elements of an able man, Henry. I do not flatter you an atom. I expected you would be candidate for the Legislature this spring, and such a position would be better than the clerkship reliability. I know Coos people have an especial culpability to young men — but you must make yourself feel and if you have the *power* you can have the honor and the profit. Now Henry, don't you leave our Old Mountain State. You are one of her coming men; I know it, and the people of Coos know it. But my dear fellow don't be a demagogue. Stick to one faith. I tell you the next Presidential battle will be fought between the American Party and the Foreign Party. The slavery question is settled by the doctrine of squatter sovereignty — settled forever! There will *never* be another slave state admitted to this Union. Kansas free Minnesota free Oregon free. *Three* new free states in one year! What more in God's name can the party ask? Now he must come back to the American question. Now the levies shift between the American party and the Foreign Party and we can whip the Democracy, and on no other issue! You may gain fitful state triumphs, but if they smelt is sending to Congress such a delegation as New Hampshire now has, Providence save the old commonwealth from another Republican victory.[19]

Despite making excellent money working as the chief editor of the *Cincinnati Times,* Cross, even as late as June 1857, was chagrined that they never paid for any of the services he performed during the election. With the contest of 1856 over, that of 1860 was already beginning to shape up to be an event that forever changed the nation.

Although Buchanan was a northerner, he believed, much as Pierce did, in upholding the Constitution, which protected slavery. Cross' fears about the nation coming apart over the issue of slavery came one step closer in March 1857 when the Supreme Court ruled on the Dred Scott case, stating that blacks did not have any rights as citizens and slavery could be expanded into the new territories. Cross agreed with the justices findings, writing, "I think the Supreme Court decision perfectly correct, and at least, perfectly constitutional. Negroes are *not citizens* and never should be. This is a white man's government." Kent did not support his friend's views about the issues, to which Cross was hoping to engage in a "debating expedition" the next time he visited Lancaster, which occurred in August of 1857. The year before, Ephraim Cross had returned from his self-imposed exile in Quebec to pay off his debts, but he still was in financial trouble, as he sold off huge tracts of Cross family land to cover his expenses while working odd jobs, and giving in to an ever increasing drinking problem. During this visit Cross brought along some friends from the West to join him. It was his last visit home for over two years.[20]

With the American Party now deceased, Cross faced a difficult decision. To join the Republican Party meant supporting abolition, and the politicians in New Hampshire who believed firmly in the cause. The Democrats stood for a strong union, bowing to the southern states to prevent civil war by upholding the Constitution, which was interpreted to uphold slavery. In the end, Cross returned to the Democratic Party, but it was not the party of Andrew Jackson and James Rix. In July 1858, he wrote, "Sick of all Old Buck + the crowd of Harpers that harry around him — but just as far from Abolitionism as ever." He again spent the winter of 1858 in Washington, where he grew lonesome and depressed, writing that it "was hard + confining." His mother became his only source of news from home during this dark time as he contemplated his next move.

To pass the time, Cross became part of a séance circle, and reported, "I tell you my boy *theres something in it!* I have investigated for the past year and am convinced of the beyond. Mr. Rix is one of my particular spirit friends. I have many good talks with him. You know I am not very easy to humbug, so go ahead, we only know enough of this world to be aware that we know nothing." This was the beginning of a lifelong fascination for Cross with death. At several points in his life over the next few years he developed a deep sense that he was about to die when he entered a dangerous situation, often worrying those who knew him by the sense of foreboding.

In Lancaster, Henry Kent seemed to be having a career that Cross envied. He ran a successful newspaper, was able to visit and be with friends, fish and hunt when he wanted, had female companionship, was connected with the right politicians who could appoint him to positions of prominence, such as a clerkship in the New Hampshire house, and as the leader of a survey party to determine the New Hampshire and Maine border. He spent nearly eight years of his life in Cincinnati. During that time, he traveled the nation, growing into a respectable editor, militiaman, and political radical. Despite these accomplishments, Cross again felt the desire to wander. This time, however, the wandering led to serious consequences.[21]

CHAPTER FOUR

Tubac

Of my fusillade with Mr. Mowry you doubtless heard. — E. E. CROSS, AUGUST 25, 1859

Sixteen months after the election of 1856, Edward Cross was a broken man. The American Party was dead, and now as a Democrat he was having a difficult time understanding the administration of James Buchanan, as the issue of slavery continued to drive the nation closer to war. He tried to resume his preelection life of writing, editing, and militia duties, but during the winter of 1858 he fell into a deep depression. Cross needed a new story, a place where he could once again become the central figure in his own world. This drive to be in the lead took him from Lancaster to Cincinnati, and then all over the United States. After nearly a decade of traveling the country as a reporter, he was ready to turn in a new direction, and like thousands of other young men in the 1850s he decided to head west.

In July of 1858, Cross, now twenty-six, decided on his future; he took a promising position in Arizona. The Treaty of Guadalupe Hidalgo transferred nearly half of the Mexican territory to the United States, placing the southern border in the New Mexico Territory along the Gila River. In 1853, a ten million dollar appropriation from Congress known as the Gadsden Purchase secured nearly 30,000 square miles south of the river for the building of a southern transcontinental railroad. Although poor for farming, Arizona contained rich holdings of silver in its mines. In 1855, a small group of pioneers from Cincinnati, calling themselves the Sonora Mining Company, under Major Samuel P. Heintzelman traveled to Tubac, a dusty mining settlement near the Mexican border. They did well in their operations. Now, in 1858, a group of Cincinnati businessmen began recruiting for another expedition to Arizona, as the Santa Rita Mining Company.[1]

A former Episcopal minister and newspaper publisher named William Wrightson had already participated in the Heintzelman expeditions and had most recently published the *Railroad Record* in the city. Wrightson planned to return to Arizona and wanted to establish a newspaper there to promote the interest of the company and to attract more business ventures from Cincinnati to the region. The only press available in the city was an old cast iron Washington hand press not much evolved from the original Gutenberg press. It was an expensive operation to bring a press, type, ink, and paper west, so Wrightson collaborated with the Sonora Mining Company to purchase the supply, and hire someone to run the paper. The position paid a salary, in addition to a share in the mine. There were many candidates in Cincinnati to operate the paper, but Wrightson knew whom he wanted, Edward Cross.[2]

Cross instantly accepted the proposal and began preparing for the life-altering adventure. He settled his accounts in Cincinnati, and he wrote what he believed might be a final letter to Henry Kent, who always received paternalistic advice and guidance from his older friend that for the most part he did not heed and lived his own life. Kent's life views, especially in politics, were tremendously different from those of Cross, but unlike many others, the two remained very good friends:

> Going now to a distant part of the county, perhaps never to return, let me assure you, my old friend, of my cordial friendship and good wishes. You have a fine future before you. Good men — talented men are rare in the old Granite State. Stay by her in her old age, as it were, where her children are scattered. My destines for the present is in the other fields of labor. I shall watch your career, although I may not witness your success.
>
> By a paper which I send, you will see the write I intend printing. Joined to a mining company. I got to set up a printing press in the new land of the South West. It is a venture of some magnitude, but well suited to my roving disposition. Do not forget to write me now + *then*.[3]

The journey across the continent was going to be an arduous adventure, even for Cross, accustomed as he was to the rough political world.

On July 26, 1858 Cross and three other comrades, each armed with a revolver and Sharps rifle and carrying the 30,000 dollars worth of newspaper and mining equipment, including a steam engine, began their journey to New Orleans, where they linked up with the other members of the expedition. In describing the credentials of each man, the *Times* wrote, "Mr. E.E. Cross is well known as a ready and forcible writer of the press." Although many readers of the paper hoped to join in such a venture, with the promise of easy riches, the *Cincinnati Times* offered a word of danger to the mission: "Their adventure will be more pleasant to describe than to realize. They will have hard fare, hard travelling, hard knocks with the Indians, and very likely a hard fortune in the end." Despite this prophetic message, Cross was ready.[4]

Although Cross severed his well-paid editorship at the *Times*, he continued to serve as a correspondent, providing readers around the country with updates on the expedition through a series of nearly thirty letters to the paper. He hoped to attract new readers to the paper by "describing each section of the country and its characteristics as I pass over it." The party began by traveling down the Mississippi River to New Orleans. Along the way they docked at Napoleon, Arkansas, which Cross always considered the "hardest place I ever saw." The inhabitants were a miscreant lot of murderers, robbers, thieves, and drunkards. Cross described them as a "sallow, hard-up, miserable race."

The party arrived in New Orleans in the midst of yellow fever season and boarded a steamer to take them to Texas. Finally, after a long delay, the ship began its journey to Galveston. It was the first time Cross had gone to sea, and he became violently ill. "Sea-sickness, like death, is a common leveler. As the wind freshened, and our vessel caught the full roll of the waves, most of our passengers began to undergo the dreadful penalty extorted by King Neptune from all who venture upon his dominions." Deathly sick from throwing up, Cross and most of his companions spent the night sleeping on deck, under the stars.[5]

Arriving in Texas, he became shocked at the prices of fruits and vegetables, thinking that the state had long been a breadbasket but discovering that most of the farmers grew cotton instead. The party hired mules, ten wagons, and a party of Mexicans, described as "strong, swarthy, banditti-looking fellows, expert with the lasso," to assist moving their equipment, including the press, towards Arizona. Many of Cross' letters back to Cincinnati involved describing the local inhabitants and their habits to people who would never see them. The Rio Grande Valley was largely inhabited by Germans, whom Cross found to be industrious but unlike the farmers in Coos County, who took every advantage of the short growing season. The Texans only planted cotton, preferring to import fresh vegetables from the North. Because of the small size of the party, every man had to do his share. Cross became the "chief cook of mess number two," feeding his seven companions with beans and bacon for every meal, washed down with "coffee of sufficient strength to sustain a small brick-bat."[6]

By the middle of September 1858, the Santa Rita Party arrived at San Antonio, site of the legendary Alamo clash some twenty years earlier. Cross thought the town resembled Quebec City. Always fond of visiting battlefields, he spent time seeing the places where heroes such as Davy Crockett, James Bowie, and others fought. The party added Mexican food to its menu, in addition to large frogs, shot in a nearby pond. It was here that Cross experienced Mexican culture for the first time. He was not too fond of it, writing of how the children played together naked, and the peculiar habit of eating peppers "strong enough to blister the tongue of a Christian." The women were "short and dumpy." His strongest opinions were reserved for Mexican men, whom Cross believed were exceptionally lazy, being used to working for only a few weeks a year and sleeping during the afternoons, whereas New Hampshiremen toiled from sun up to sundown on their farms and factories. Still bitter about Catholics, Cross believed that the church had failed the Mexicans, as it they simply preached the Bible rather than helping its fellow men to improve their lives.[7]

Always interested in military matters, Cross was shocked to find out that there were only two regiments of Regulars in Texas. He believed the Regulars lived a life of hardship and should have thanks from the American people: "exposed to hardships and dangers, the position of a frontier officer is far from being enviable, and they are entitled to much more credit and honor than they receive from our people." Comanche raids were a frequent occurrence against small parties such as the Santa Rita Mining Company, which now included twenty-two Americas and ten Mexican teamsters. To combat the threat, the party brought along a large arsenal of twelve Burnside breach-loading rifles, six double barreled shotguns, ten .54 caliber "Mississippi" rifles, twenty-seven Colt revolvers, eighteen Bowie knives, and nearly 2,400 rounds of ammunition. "With this armament in the hands of men accustomed to the use of firearms, we believed ourselves strong enough to protect the train against any Indian attacks."

Despite the fact that most of the men were civilians, they quickly adapted to military tactics, seeing Cross as a leader among them. Each night the men, in pairs, had to perform guard duty to protect the valuable equipment, and the even more valuable pack animals that carried it. Despite often being tiresome, Cross always was on his feet, writing, "This guard duty is somewhat onerous and withal dangerous, as the Camanche has a crafty trick of creeping upon sentinels and either shooting or stabbing them. A knowledge of this fact is not calculated to soothe a man's feelings as he paces too and fro upon his post, in a country full of hostile Indians." Although the party contained plenty of ordnance, water and food became scarce along the way. The company filled their canteens at every available opportunity and took the chance to forage off the land for venison and rabbit. Traveling in a military formation, with Cross often in the lead, they traveled across the western desert towards El Paso.[8]

Nearly two hundred miles west of San Antonio the party advanced into desert terrain quite different from the lush mountain valleys of Cross' youth. Edward was not the only Cross brother in Texas at this time. His younger brother Richard remained in the First Cavalry and was engaged in protecting the frontier but did not see his older brother at the time. The flat expanse of the desert awed Cross, as did the new flora encountered. "I believe every bush in Texas has a thorn in it," he wrote. Tarantulas, ants, ticks, rattlesnakes, horned frogs, and water moccasins all became features of the landscape. Each member of the party took a turn killing the snakes that threatened them, but for Cross, it was a difficult process. Afraid of the reptiles when he arrived in Texas, the close encounters still did not move him. "I own up to a fear of serpents, and although from seeing so many, I am somewhat less fearful than before, it is impossible to shake off that feeling of horror which the sight of a snake always occasions."

While the snakes presented a problem, so too did the weather. Even in late October, it was still scorching hot by day, one freezing at night. One evening, a brutal storm hit the column, turning the dry desert into a mud hole, than it changed to a hailstorm that spooked many of the horses. While the Mexicans in the party began to pray for it to end, the Americans drank to calm their nerves. Lightning began to strike, and one of the bolts found the tall editor from New Hampshire: "I felt a sudden blow upon my right foot as if struck by a sledge hammer, a fearful shock of electricity and was conscious of being pitched violently to the ground. As I was falling, the thought that I was struck by lightning flashed through my brain and I knew nothing more. I am told that for half an hour I lay insensible and then a delirium came on which lasted all night." The party paused for nearly ten hours until Cross, suffering from severe back and leg pains, was able to walk and mount again; for him it was yet another close call with death.[9]

By November, as the party neared El Paso, the weather began to turn and snow affected the wagon train. Despite his having grown up among "the wintry hills" near the Canadian border, the cold affected even Cross: "The cold, although not steady, nor frequent, is very severe — the North wind, especially cut to the heart, and no amount of clothing will warm the heart when once chilled through." Horse races, antelope hunting, and the constant threat of Comanche attacks became the daily ritual of the party. Finally, on November 10, after a forty-five day, 600-mile adventure, the party arrived at El Paso. To celebrate this point in the journey, Cross stayed at the Rocky Mountain Hotel, enjoying a decent meal and a peaceful night without having to stand his turn on guard duty. After devouring a breakfast of biscuits and eggs, he explored the town, enjoying some El Paso wine, and onions, which in some cases weighed over twenty pounds. Crops such as grain and grapes thrived in the region due to carefully dug irrigation ditches. Interested in the over three hundred years of cultural history in the region, Cross was shocked to discovered that a group of Missouri volunteers had plundered a records office and destroyed the written history of the El Paso region prior to 1847, records he believed would have been very beneficial to writing a history of early Texas.[10]

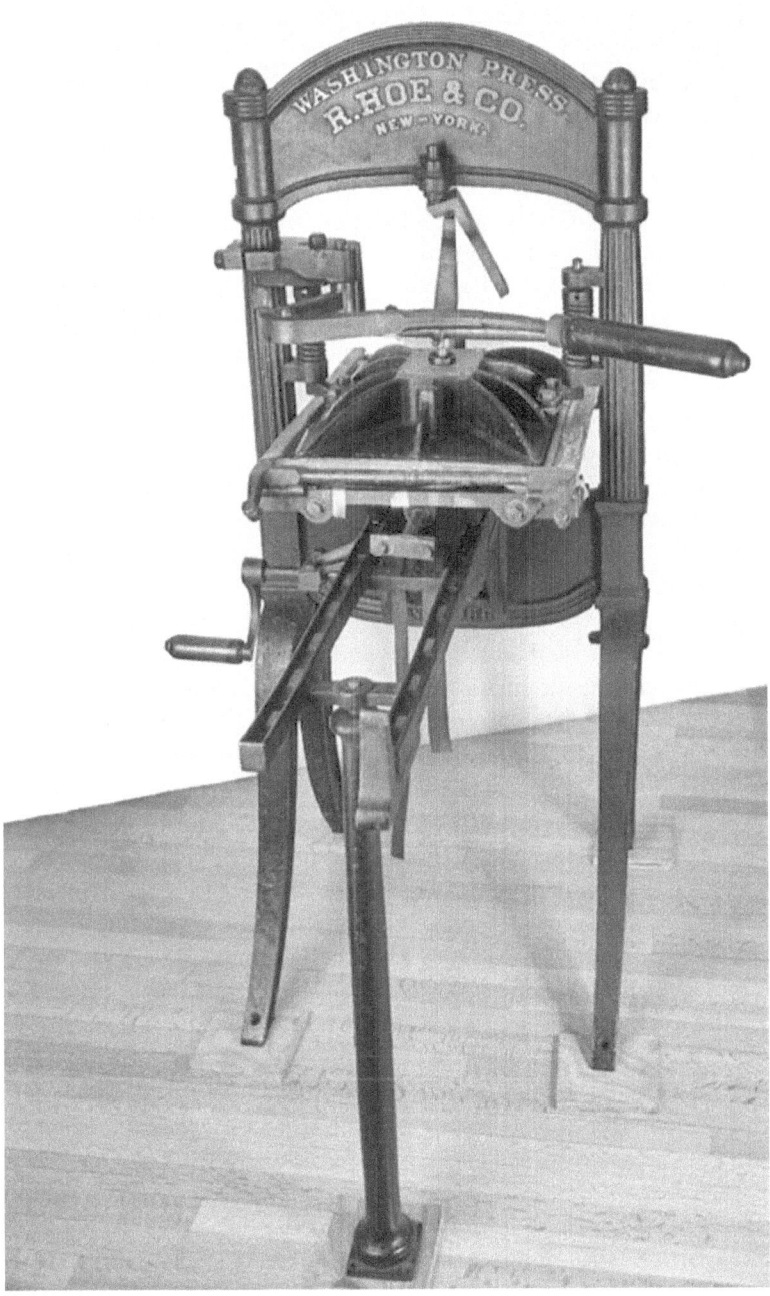

Cross brought this Washington Press to Arizona, where it almost cost him his life (author's collection).

Throughout his life Cross always displayed a blatant hatred for anyone other than white Protestants, but he now turned his attention to a group that was, in his opinion, the worst of all, Catholics. At the cathedral in El Paso, Cross climbed into the crumbling steeple and observed a monstrous bell that had arrived in Texas from Spain in 1620 and had been used for generations to call the local inhabitants to worship. Seeing an opportunity, Cross "surreptitiously pocketed the tongue and carried it as a curiosity." Upon hearing of the act, "the natives so resented this sacrilege that Cross's life would not have been safe for a moment among them." Proud of his actions, he wrote about the act in one of his letters to the *Cincinnati Times,* offering this excuse for his actions: "If there was any sacrilege in the act it must be charged to a spirit of veneration for the time-honored edifice, and not to a vulgar desire of plunder, nor intentional desecration." Although trying to justify his actions, it was just another in his long line of actions against minority groups Cross did not approve of.[11]

On December 1, the Santa Rita Mining Company crossed the Continental Divide and a week later reached the Gila River. Here they began to protect themselves against another enemy, the Apache. Cross wrote, "No Indians are more vigilant, wary, and active than the Apaches. Mounted on their fleet horses, and armed with their long bows and keen lances, they sally forth from their strongholds in the hills on expeditions of war and plunder." Despite freezing cold at night, the party dared not light any fires lest they give their position away, while in the far distance, they could see their enemy gathered by their own fires. On several occasions, the party was fired on and returned fire, but fortunately no member on the journey was injured by the natives. The mules and horses of the party were beginning to break down, and even their riders were beginning to feel the effects of the journey. Finally, on January 3, 1859, after a six-month adventure, Edward Cross arrived at his new home in Tubac, Arizona, part of the New Mexico Territory.[12]

Settled in 1752 as a Spanish presidio, Tubac was a small settlement of 150 Indians, Mexican peasants and white miners located just north of the Mexican border. One member of the Santa Rita Mining Company wrote, "Tubac is a paradise. It is situated in a beautiful valley surrounded by mountains. The valley and hills are covered with timber — mesquite and cottonwood of a large growth. The health here is fine, the water good, and there is plenty of good wholesome food." To the north of the town lay the silver mines that the Santa Rita Mining Company hoped could bring them riches. Northeast was Tucson, the only other settlement of any size, and nearby was Fort Buchanan, the sole military post in Arizona with just a small force from the First Dragoons to guard the rich silver mines and the settlers. To the west, the nearest settlements were in California, while all around, the Apaches were a constant danger. As part of his contract, Cross moved into a small "hacienda" on the outskirts of town. As the Santa Rita Company began making claims and erecting the equipment to find the ore, Cross was confident that the mines produced 1,000 dollars per week. While he owned a share in the mines, his sole job was to begin setting up the various pieces of equipment to produce the paper.[13]

In his last letter to the *Cincinnati Times,* Cross described the territory and the operations his party was engaged in. He estimated there were nearly 8,000, mostly native, inhabitants in Arizona, of which only nineteen were "American ladies." Because of the small Regular force, Cross did not go anywhere without his revolver, knife, and rifle, writing, "There is no presence of law, no sheriffs, judges, juries, and courts. Every one goes armed, and acts as his own court, jury, and executioner, using his weapons whenever he sees fit — preserving his own life and taking the life of any other person if deemed necessary." To add to the heightened state of alert, a fight erupted in front of Cross and a friend, resulting in one man's being killed in front of the new residents. Because of frequent intermarriage between whites, Indians, and Mexicans, Cross considered Arizona "a bastard nation" where the natives were loyal to no nation. The Mexican women were keen to offer themselves to American men; those who married simply divorced each other by moving out of the house. Cross knew his writings would shock many readers in the East, but he felt bound to write what he saw. He became impressed at the thriftiness of the poor peasants hired by the Santa Rita Mining Company to work in the mines, some twelve miles north of Tubac. For a wage of ten to fifteen dollars per month, including rations, they performed many hours of labor. Cross considered them "the best miners that can be employed." Prices in Tubac were terribly expensive, including sixteen dollars for a barrel of flour, and two dollars per pound of coffee. One thing not in short supply was whiskey and tequila, which fueled many of the fights and murders in the area. Having given his readers a lasting look at a dangerous, action-filled journey across the nation to Arizona, Cross finally severed his connection with the *Cincinnati Times* as he began to create the first newspaper in Arizona.[14]

While Mexican laborers conducted the majority of the mining work north of Tubac, Cross had an equally arduous task in printing his newspaper, which he called the *Weekly Arizonian.* As the paper's sole employee, Cross not only had to report the news and write editorials, but also spend the eighty plus hours per week required setting up type, printing and drying the five hundred copies that were printed each week, and then distributing them. Like most papers of the time, the *Arizonian* was a small, weekly, four-page, four-column sheet. It mostly contained old news gathered from passing stages carrying the eastern papers and many advertisements from Cincinnati business owners seeking to make a handsome profit from settlers ordering goods from Ohio and then waiting nearly six months for them to ship overland via the "jackass mail." In addition to printing the paper, the press was the only one for hundreds of miles. As such, and to make additional income, publisher Wrightson also advertised job work, giving Cross the extra tasks of printing posters, pamphlets, ledgers, legal documents, and other necessary papers. It was a thankless, backbreaking effort for Edward Cross, but one he was well suited to perform.[15]

Production of the *Weekly Arizonian* began on March 3, 1859. The small sheet was similar to the *Coos Democrat,* only devoted to the news in Arizona. The paper was much like the editor, blunt and to the point. Cross reported on Mexican politics with the same fiery passion he had given to the American Party, and he criticized Congress for not sending additional dragoon companies to Arizona. In his opening editorial he wrote, "In politics our opinions are fixed, and when the social requirements of our state demand it we shall speak our sentiments freely and fully." Cross did not have great faith in his product: "The reading population is small and the expense of publication great. It is not, therefore, with very bright prospects of pecuniary return that we begin our labors." Although he printed 500 copies of the paper each week, the majority of the population around Tubac spoke Spanish instead of English.

The dusty street of Tubac, Arizona, was the scene of the Mowry-Cross duel (Library of Congress).

Cross gave "bundles" of his creation to stages bound for California and the East in the hopes that their editors might send papers to the office, and also to spread the news of what was occurring in the territory. A weekly feature of the paper was a long column describing the various crimes committed by the Apaches, Mexicans, and whites against each other in the area surrounding Tubac. Most of the crimes were property related, such as the constant stealing of cows, donkeys, and horses. In one two-month period, six whites were murdered around Tubac, including two recently discharged Regulars on their way home to Pennsylvania. As soon as one week's paper was printed, Cross had to start work on another.[16]

Because two of the largest mining parties in the Arizona owned the *Arizonian*, and his salary was tied directly to the output of the Santa Rita Mine, Cross spent an inordinate amount of time writing about mining operations in Arizona. His object was two-fold: first, to attract more white settlement to the territory, and second, to increase the federal presence in Arizona by creating a judicial district and increasing the number of troops at Fort Buchanan to protect the rich ore and miners. Cross' writings were filled with figures and numbers of the yield of the mines, which had been producing since Arizona was a Spanish possession. Cross hoped that by increasing its support in Arizona the United States treasury would gain the silver to support the economy. Most important was to separate Arizona from New Mexico as a political entity to gain the same federal officers as any other territory. As a man with a lifelong desire to fight, he wanted Congress to wage war on the Mexicans to gain the state of Sonora, to establish a water route into Arizona. He praised the agricultural and mineral impact it would have on the territory. Much to Cross' lament, Congress voted not to go to war. At the same time he wrote passionate editorials for the annexation of Sonora, Cross also dealt with the mundane duties of selling advertisements for Colt revolvers, rifles, flour, molasses, and other staples of life at high rates.[17]

Although the paper took most of his time, Cross did have time to write one brief letter home to Henry Kent, by now a successful newspaper editor in his own right with the *Coos Republican* and a major on the adjutant general's staff of the all but defunct New Hampshire State Militia. In long-sought-after letter from Lancaster, Cross received the interesting news that his friend was married. His reply to the news is some of his best writing and shows his caliber as an author:

Hacienda de Santa Rita
March 13th, 1859

My dear friend,
   By a letter from mother, long delayed on the road, for the reason that it made a trip to California + other foreign *parts*—I receive the gratifying intel-

ligence that you are married! Mortifying, I say, for what is life without a *woman's* love to hope and struggle for? Full well do I know the lonely dull + desolate periods which mark the existence of one who has no dear object around which to garner up the treasures of his heart. Let me offer you my sincere congratulations + dearest wishes for your happiness, both of you, now and in the future — the congratulations of an old friend and schoolmate, long separated, but none the less the friend of your boyish days. You have, I presume, married Miss Rowell, although mother did not tell me. Let me present my most respectful remembrance + express my regret, also that some four thousand miles offered something of an obstacle to my witnessing the ceremony.

As for me, I am passing over to the roll of old bachelors—fast becoming a withered post-bitten cabbage-stalk in the garden of the world, in the interesting position of caring for nobody, while nobody cares for me — a misanthropic wander up + down the broad aisles of the world, having, like the old gentleman in the Bible, no "abiding city!" However I intend to appear among you some day like the ancient mariner returned from his voyaging, though I trust not with the same bad fortune that haunted that worthy individual.

I see you are an "editor man" and I am glad to hear it — it is a business to which you are especially adapted to which you are new to succeed. I am at my old business + have just issued the first paper ever published in this region — a copy of which you will receive by favor of Providence + the mail, sometime between now and the 4th of July. Our territory is not organized- the bill having been badly beaten. Still, we have hope, for, as the Mayor of Chicago remarked — Truth *squashed* to earth will rise again. There being no American Party, I am a Douglass man — can't go Seward + hate Hale. Do let me hear from you, as in old times. Again with the cordial regards to yourself + wife (How odd it sounds to think you have a wife) believe me — Yours truly

Edward E. Cross[18]

It was going to be many months before Kent heard again from his friend, as he had other, more pressing, business to attend to.

Continuing with his editorials for the annexation of Sonora, Cross was rewarded for his efforts in producing the *Arizonian* by receiving several papers, bringing such news as camels running away from their owners in California and the murder of an ex-congressman in New York City. Running a major paper without any staff, Cross produced a respectable sheet. Even as early as the April 14, 1859 edition of the *Arizonian,* Cross' hard work was beginning to pay off. In an open announcement to his readers, the editor was proud to quip: "Thanks.—Many papers in the States and some in the Territories notice the "Arizonian" in terms kind and complimentary, and wish us all manner of good fortune. For such compliments, coming, as some of them do, from old friends—we thank our brethren of the profession, collectively, and individually, being much encouraged by their flattering reception of our humble sheet. By and by we intend to publish some of their good opinions."[19]

According to one writer, Cross "presented a surprisingly good balance of local, national, and international news coverage." When easterners doubted the silver mining capability of Arizona, he invited them to come to the Sonora Mining Company's office and view an 889.38 ounce bar of silver, the result of three days' work in the mines. In proudly announcing the success of the mines, Cross wrote, "This is tangible evidence of successful silver mining, and even with only one quarter of the amalgamation works in operation the company will hereafter turn out at least two such bars as the above per week."

Part of Cross' work in his weekly editorials was aimed directly at readers back East. In one particularly spirited column, in April 1859, Cross attempted to paint a picture of the grim reality of frontier life. Having grown up in New Hampshire, he was used to the heroic stories of the Indian as a "noble savage," a master of bush craft who welcomed the "pale face" as a friend, showing him the ways to survive in a hostile wilderness. He wrote, "The halo of sentiment which popularity commends the savage is false and ridiculous." While he respected the Apaches' ability to survive in the hostile environment of the desert, he painted them as little more than a savage band of murderers and horse thieves who killed any stray traveler to take his money, weapons, and horse. As the weeks went on in Arizona, the columns of the paper contained tales of murder and robbery, often at the hands of the Apache. In one instance, a dragoon was so badly bludgeoned that he could be identified only by his clothes. Cross felt that a campaign against the Apaches was needed to end the threat, but Captain Richard Ewell of nearby Fort Buchanan commanded fewer than 100 men and could respond only to threats near the fort.[20]

While Cross wrote his spirited sheet, he also began to agitate. Cross was a warrior and enjoyed fighting whomever he could. Whether it be police officers in Cincinnati, the Apache in Arizona, or Charles Browne in the *Democrat* office, he was a warrior without a war. Sylvester Mowry, a native Rhode Islander and West Point graduate, wrote many of the early reports that came out of Arizona. After serving several years on the frontier in the Third Artillery, Mowry, a first lieutenant, resigned and took up permanent residence in Arizona in 1857. Purchasing the rights to the Patagonia Mine north of Tubac, he became wealthy and served as the territorial delegate to Congress, but he did not take a seat owing to a perceived deficiency in the election.

In early 1859, Mowry, with two years of knowledge and experience living in southern Arizona published a spirited article in the *Journal of the American Geographical and Statistical Society*. Mowry praised the area as "a most beautiful fertile region." He claimed several hundred people resided in Tubac alone, and that the farms near Fort Buchanan contained fields full of wheat, corn, and beans. Mowry downplayed the Apache threat, claiming they numbered only 2,000 people and mostly preyed upon Sonorans instead of Americans in Arizona. Mowry wrote that the silver was plentiful and easy to mine. He praised the superb weather of Arizona, claiming cold was not a factor and water was plentiful in many places. In essence, he wrote his piece to stimulate interest in white settlement in Arizona and increase the chances of its becoming a fully recognized territory and thereby increasing Mowry's own power in the region. While the article gained favor in the East, the paper went to Tubac and, for one man, created an uproar.[21]

Cross read the Mowry article and became incensed. Every aspect of the geography and people of Arizona that Mowry claimed as true, Cross believed to be false. Despite having been in Tubac for only a month, he decided to act. Cross believed that Mowry had a virtual monopoly on the news coming out of the Southwest. He hoped to change this through both the *Arizonian*, and his own writings to papers back East. For some reason Cross felt the need to rebut Mowry's statements and tell the public what life was like in Arizona. He began the crusade by writing to *The States,* a Washington D.C. Democratic Party newspaper. In an article published in late February 1859 titled "The Humbug Exposed," Cross wrote that there were fewer than 200 white settlers in all of Arizona. "Every body that can get away is leaving, and fresh fools arrive constantly, *allured by the false reports of published newspapers.* As an agricultural country it is worthless." Crops could barely grow in the poor soil, while "provisions and clothing command the most extraordinary prices." While the silver mines were successful to an extent, it was backbreaking physical work, requiring special machinery to extract the ore. In writing the letter to *The States,* Cross lit the fuse to a powder keg. Throughout his adult life, Cross had lived a colorful story, sometimes almost the stuff of fiction. In his story, Edward Cross was the main character; in the chapter about Arizona there was room for only one storyteller. Cross always wanted a fight, and in Sylvester Mowry he found one. Mowry, who never met Cross, could not believe that someone challenged his knowledge of Arizona.[22]

The day following the letter's publication, written under the penname of "Gila," Mowry, who was in Washington still pushing for the recognition of Arizona, wrote a spirited rebuttal to *The States.* In a point by point column-length article, Mowry fought back against Cross, again writing, with some exaggeration, that there were 700 Americans working in the mines around Tubac alone, while over 10,000 lived in the territory. Mowry continued to claim the abundance of rich farmland in Arizona and the flowing veins of gold and silver in the Santa Rita Mountains. As he argued the same points he originally posted in his writings and speeches about Arizona, he also began to take aim at the man who wrote "The Humbug Exposed": "The person who wrote the letter you publish has never seen enough of Arizona to write intelligently about it. It is useless for any man to attempt to break down these facts except in the cowardly manner of an anonymous letter. Had he been writing the truth he would not have been afraid to give his name."[23]

Nearly three months went by before a copy of Mowry's letter arrived in Tubac and Cross wrote his own reply. Although he went to Arizona based on a job offer, Cross wrote, "I had been a careful reader of Mr. Mowry's fabulous productions regarding this country, and supposed them correct. I found, however, that many of his assertions were not true, and that all were exaggerated." Cross went on to state each point that he held against Mowry, especially on the issue of Arizona as a farming community, stating there was no water and very poor soil. Cross had "no desire to disparage the territory," but only wanted that the facts, as he believed them to exist, come out. In ending his letter, Cross added fuel to an already volatile situation, by answering Mowry's jibe about who wrote the first letter: "The hanging question I will cheerfully submit to the citizens of the country, if to expose humbuggery, falsehood, misrepresentations, imposition, and fraud, carried on for two years, entitles a man to Mr. Mowry's hanging operation. I confess I am a fit subject; but from the opinions every day expressed towards the gentleman by the few Americans hereabouts who know his course, I apprehend that he is eminently more deserving, and more in danger of lynch law than myself. Respectfully &c. Edward E. Cross." Mowry realized that he had to leave Washington and return to Arizona to confront the threat that Cross posed to destroy his vision of the territory's future, which depended on increased population.[24]

Arriving back in Tucson on July 2, 1859, Mowry finally received a copy of *The States* containing Cross' article. Now he knew whom he was facing and the source of the letters. While the two had never met before, Mowry was familiar with the *Arizonian,* receiving copies while in Washington. Mowry again rebutted Cross' arguments from the first and second letters, while stating his belief that Cross was paid by the Sonora and Santa Rita Mining companies to write the articles, as the mine owners wanted to control the political future of Arizona. As they had the only printing press in Arizona and Edward Cross' talented pen, Mowry believed they were highly effective in ruining his bids for Congress. Mowry thought that Cross should leave Arizona at once, having failed the people through his paper and his attacks against Mowry, who, according to himself, was the legally elected representative. As Cross attacked Mowry, the former officer wrote, "The fact that I have raised him to the level of a gentleman, by demanding of him personal satisfaction for the scurrilous language he has used towards me presents my showing him in his true light." The letter did not reach Washington for some time. Now only fifty miles from his adversary, Mowry sent a note to Cross demanding satisfaction, a public apology or a duel.[25]

When faced with retracting his comments or facing someone under fire, editor Cross was prepared to use force to back up his point. He responded that he wanted to face Mowry in a duel. As the challenged party, Cross could select the weapon to fight with. Instead of following the custom of the old South, where single shot, muzzle-loading pistols were the norm, he decided that the frontier required something extreme. As weapons for the duel, Cross selected a pair of breech-loading, .54 caliber Burnside carbines, a rifle he declared "excellent for frontier service," to be fired at sixty yards. Mowry arrived in Tubac on July 7 and promptly went through the ritual of selecting his second, George D. Mercer, while Cross selected John Donaldson, a United States customs official. Despite being a former army officer, Mowry objected because he had no experience using the Burnside and felt that sixty yards was too far a distance, despite the fact the rifle was accurate up to 300 yards. Mowry finally relented, allowing the Burnsides, while Cross compromised and allowed forty yards to be the target range. For the next few hours both men practiced firing their Burnsides, which fired a lead slug that weighed an ounce from a brass cartridge. Cross fired at a large cactus, taking aim at the leaves with good effect, while Mowry "made havoc with a small cottonwood tree." Both men were excellent shots and for many of the observers who were gathering, including nearly all the whites in Tubac, it was clear that someone was going to die the following day.[26]

The following day in Tubac's main and only street both men met with their seconds and the Burnside carbines. That the newspaper argument got to this point was no surprise, as Cross was stubborn in his opinions. Now, however, he was going to be looking down the barrel of a rifle to back them up. Finally, at 5:00 in the evening as a strong wind kicked up dust in Tubac, the two men met for the first time. Gathered around were nearly thirty spectators, each armed with a revolver and knife in the event the duel turned into a larger fight. Most of the spectators worked for the Sonora or Santa Rita Mining Company and supported Cross; for them Mowry was an outsider who sought to exploit Arizona for his own ambitions. Both men entered the street with their seconds as the breechblocks of the Burnsides were opened, a cartridge loaded and a percussion cap placed on each, then handed to the combatants. Cross and Mowry promptly counted the forty paces, turned and fired at each other.[27]

Because of the high wind, both men missed on the first round. The seconds reloaded, and both men fired again. Cross missed, and Mowry's ball cut across his adversary's right ear, but neither man fell. Mowry called out to a bystander, "Rather close work, is it not?" Again, after the second shot, both men handed their weapons to the seconds, who reloaded. Cross and Mowry walked forty yards again and fired. The third round missed Cross, but he hit Mowry across the chest, ripping his coat. Just as it appeared the duel might not produce a result, the seconds reloaded once more and the two foes prepared to engage yet again. Cross leveled his Burnside, pulled the trigger, and again missed Mowry. At the same time, Mowry aimed and heard only the snap of the percussion cap instead of the crashing sound of the weapon firing. Mowry still kept his Burnside aimed at Cross, which led some in the crowd to believe he would prime again and fire on the editor, who held an unloaded weapon. This led some to draw their pistols and threaten to shoot Mowry if he fired on Cross.

Downrange Cross stood perfectly calm, waiting for the result. Mercer, the second, then proceeded to Donaldson, claiming that under the ancient code of dueling Mowry was entitled to another shot. Cross answered that he accepted, but his second demurred, stating the round could kill Cross, who did not reload. Donaldson finally relented as Cross, handed him his rifle. The tall Granite Stater calmly folded his arms across his chest and waited for the result. The crowd began to get excited again, believing that Mowry was about to murder Cross who stood a scant forty yards away. Sensing their reaction if he did so, Mowry fired his weapon into the air and declared himself satisfied. A bystander remarked on Cross' conduct during the affair: "Cross had stood, with heroic valor directly facing him, not knowing that he could rely upon his generosity to decline firing upon an unarmed foe, fully expecting death, and yet not a nerve trembled — not a single evidence of fear was displayed."[28]

A former artillery officer, Sylvester Mowry was incensed by Cross' editorials and demanded satisfaction: Cross chose Burnside carbines at close range (Library of Congress).

After handing their weapons to the seconds, both men crossed the range and went through the formalities of shaking hands, although neither man was willing to call the other a friend, having stood firm and proved their points. After the duel, a keg of Pennsylvania whiskey was tapped for the spectators, "which melted before the fierce attacks like snow before the midday sun. The last traces of ill feeling were dissipated in the glow of ardent spirits." In the next edition of the *Arizonian,* both Cross and Mowry issued a public apology to each other. Cross wrote that he "withdraws the offensive language used by him and disclaims any intention to reflect upon Mr. Mowry's veracity or upon his reputation as a gentleman, in any publication he has made in reference to Arizona." Mowry was satisfied with the apology and "takes pleasure in withdrawing the imputations against Mr. Cross as a man of honor and veracity," in his July 2 letter to *The States.* Both men concluded their apology with, "Any difference of opinion which may exist between them in reference to Arizona is an honest one, to be determined by the weight of authority." With the fight over, Cross tried to resume his life in Tubac, printing his paper, but as yet unknown to him, the duel had changed his life.[29]

The Mowry-Cross duel held the attention of the entire country when the news finally appeared, traveling slowly west to east. It was the type of news worth reporting, two men standing up and willing to die for their beliefs, and it came to speak for the entire way of life on the frontier. Papers across the nation carried varying reports of the duel. In Concord, the *New Hampshire Patriot* wrote of Cross: "It must be admitted that he exhibited a courage credible to his State and honorable to himself." In Texas, a captain in the Eighth Infantry wrote a poem about the fight and mailed it to Cross, who enjoyed it. Cross himself wrote little of the duel, only briefly mentioning it in a letter to Henry Kent, calling it "bad shooting, but the wind saved us." He enclosed the apology published in the *Arizonian,* and hoped his family and friends in Lancaster learned the truth of the matter.[30]

While the news of the duel spread through the country, a reporter in Cleveland, Ohio, thought it was time to bring up the past and play a joke on Edward Cross. Ever since he had fought Cross in the *Coos Democrat* office in 1848, Charles Farrar Browne remained active in the newspaper business, first as an editor and now as the comical writer "Artemus Ward," for the *Cleveland Plain Dealer.* After the duel, Browne wrote that Cross' dogs were barking wildly at his hacienda, so a party of Mexicans drew their knives on the dogs. Cross came out, and "told them to let the dogs alone. The Mexicans fell on Cross and cut him to pieces. Thus goes the story. You know they do that sort of thing in Arizona." Just as quickly as word of his duel spread throughout the nation, so too did rumors of his murder by Mexicans, spurred on by the pen of Artemus Ward. When Cross received the news, he was not too pleased, writing, "If Fungus Browne wrote that infernal lie I'll have a bit of satisfaction that he will remember to his dying day." Henry Kent did his best to suppress the rumors, writing that Cross remained alive and well in the *Coos Republican*, but the story circulated for some time until Cross returned to New England.[31]

The week following the duel in Tubac, Cross was in for some shocking news. For the sum of 2,500 dollars Sylvester Mowry, the very man he just fought, purchased the *Weekly Arizonian* "in order to avoid any further unpleasantness" between the two. In addition to this, the press, the only one in Arizona, was a very powerful tool. Mowry hoped to use the press as a Democratic Party organ to both stimulate interest in Arizona and to further his own politics. Although the *Arizonian* was Cross' purpose to being in the territory, the paper was actually owned by publisher William Wrightson, who, in conjunction with the Santa Rita and Sonora Mining companies paid both for the press to be brought to Arizona and to support its operation. The high cost of supplies such as paper and ink, and the low number of paid subscribers led to the decision to sell the *Arizonian* to Mowry, who took the press back to his headquarters in Tucson.[32]

Cross quite literally had the last line in the matter, publishing a spirited final editorial in which he summed up his experiences as the man who edited Arizona's first newspaper. "During the period I have edited the Arizonian, it has been my object to labor for the best interest of Arizona, honestly and faithfully — Time will prove the right or wrong of my exertions. At present I would not alter a line that has been written. Conducting a newspaper in a frontier country is a perilous, precarious, and thankless task; it has been especially so in this case. Against many difficulties and discouraging circumstances, I have sought to furnish a readable paper, and I trust with some show of success." He mentioned the experience in a letter home to Kent, stating, "I have left the Arizonian sold out. Couldn't stand it — too many fights — might as well try to issue a paper in the hot place where gates stand open night + day." Cross watched on as his press was loaded into a wagon to be taken to Tucson, and then he went to stay with friends near the mines to "rusticate."[33]

In the fall of 1859, after recovering from his ordeal with Mowry, and with his pockets lined with cash from his mining venture, Edward Cross decided to return East to the mountains of New Hampshire.

CHAPTER FIVE

Mexico

I'm off tomorrow to the mines.—E.E. CROSS, FEBRUARY 4, 1860

After a two-year absence, and after nearly losing his life defending his principals, Cross began his journey back to Lancaster in September of 1859. He paused for a few days at Fort Fillmore near La Mesilla, New Mexico, to visit his brother Dick, now a sergeant in the First Cavalry, but soon he was on his way to join the elite Corps of Engineers. From the fort Cross wrote, "I was never in better health or spirits + hope to eat my Thanksgiving dinner with the old folks at home." Closely following the path overland he had blazed the year before, Cross quickly arrived in St. Louis, on October 5, 1859, and was promptly "full of good spirits," noting he drank a bottle of Longworth's Sparkling wine. Cross' arrival in St. Louis was a noted occasion that finally squelched the rumors he had been killed by Mexicans at Santa Rita.[1]

In one of the ironies of his life, Cross had an interesting dinner guest one night in St. Louis—none other than Sylvester Mowry himself. Although Cross still hated the man, he felt Mowry was best suited as the candidate to represent Arizona in Congress and gave him support in his last edition of the *Arizonian.* Now both men, known throughout the country, were seen "in peaceful intercourse," walking around St. Louis together. Both men visited the Merchant's Exchange, speaking about their adventures in Arizona and together displaying a large mineral collection. After closing some business in the city, Cross was again on the move east, and arrived back in Lancaster for Thanksgiving 1859.[2]

Back in the East, Cross also took time to write extensively to the secretary of war, complaining of the problems faced by the small military force garrisoning Arizona. While entire brigades of the small 16,000 man Regular Army garrisoned relatively peaceful California and Texas, only scattered companies of dragoons, mounted riflemen, and infantry were in the Department of New Mexico. Of these, Captain Ewell's dragoons comprised the entire force in Arizona, and no reinforcements were in sight. Throughout his life, Cross had an eye for military affairs, even without a formal West Point or Norwich education. He was a born leader who had a passion for planning military events. Surveying the Arizona frontier, Cross knew good sites for military posts and drew up a complicated series of forts and posts in Arizona, going so far as to describe the territory and how many companies should be stationed at each one. He wrote, "Military posts should be located in the Indian Country where sudden and effectual blows may be struck home upon the Indians whenever they commit depredations, their ranches destroyed, their women and children seized."

Cross believed that the army's policy of sending patrols in pursuit of the Apache after a raid was ineffective and useless. Instead, he believed the dragoons should adopt a scorched earth policy, burning their villages and crops and capturing the natives and holding them prisoner: "A rigorous, persistent campaign ought to be maintained against the Apaches until they beg for peace, and are willing to settle on a reservation." The army took no action on his suggestions. Cross' passionate hatred for all those who did not fit his narrow ideas of what an American should be continued to reverberate in the Apache country. Unlike the civil streets of Cincinnati, where he could engage only in the occasional bar fight or political attack against German and Irish immigrants, in Arizona Cross always had his rifle and pistol ready to strike.[3]

Finally arriving in Coos County, Cross for the first time in years was able to spend the holidays at home. Besides enjoying his time with family and friends, he had two important matters to take care of. Ever since he turned twenty-one, Cross had wanted to join the Free and Accepted Masons but was never home long enough to join the organization. Writing to Henry O. Kent, his sponsor, Cross was able to petition the Grand Lodge of New Hampshire to grant him a dispensation to receive the three degrees— Entered Apprentice, Fellowcraft, and Master Mason — at the same time. On the night of December 6, 1859, Cross joined the order as a member of North Star Lodge Number 8 in Lancaster.[4]

In addition to fulfilling a lifelong desire Cross finally acted on his mother's behalf. From the time the Coos Bank failed nearly ten years earlier, his father continued to pay off the family debts by working menial jobs and selling off much of the family real estate, leaving only eighty acres of Richard Everett's original holdings. Ephraim Cross' drinking was having a severe strain on his ability to support his wife and two children, Frank and Helen, who remained at home. A lien was placed on the Cross homestead, and a foreclosure was about to occur, as Ephraim still owed nearly 800 dollars to his creditors. Edward Cross, wanting to preserve the family home as a place for his mother, who was nearing sixty and unable to travel much, paid off the 800 dollar debt out of his earnings from Arizona. Now taking legal possession of his former residence, he made his father sign a note to pay him back the funds. In addition to this, he set up an account of nearly 200 dollars at Richard Kent's store, enabling his mother to purchase food and other goods as needed. After only a brief stay in Lancaster, Cross decided to return to Arizona to oversee his stake in the mines and ponder his future.[5]

After tarrying for a few days in Hopkinton, Massachusetts, visiting a "Miss York," Cross visited Washington, D.C. Here the nation was again preparing for yet another presidential contest. The previous October, John Brown's failed raid on the federal arsenal at Harpers Ferry, Virginia, had again catapulted the issue of slavery into conscience of the nation; words were no longer the only weapon used. President Buchanan's weak stance in turning Brown over to the Commonwealth of Virginia and Brown's subsequent hanging polarized the North. Even those who did not care before on the issue took an interest in it, spurred on in part by Senator John P. Hale. Cross remained an ardent Democrat, and in the early course of the election he supported Senator Stephen Douglas of Illinois, who favored compromising on the issue of slavery in order to keep the nation from splitting apart. Again for Cross' beliefs however, the Democratic Party, much like the American Party four years earlier, was split along the issue of slavery, almost insuring the Republican candidate, Abraham Lincoln, the presidency.[6]

Cross arrived back in St. Louis on February 4, 1860, and promptly began making plans to return via the familiar overland route to Tubac. He had had a falling out with the Sonora and Santa Rita Mining companies. Instead, he took a position as an "agent," with the St. Louis Mining Company, which owned the Boundary Mine in the Santa Rita Mountains. The next eighteen months of Cross' life are, from the historical perspective, the darkest. Few letters and no diary entries survive from him during this time, but those he was associated with in Arizona and Mexico during this period mentioned him on occasion.[7]

By the middle of March 1860, Cross returned to Arizona, where the lawlessness continued, and the Apaches were on the warpath again. The Mexican miners continued to find deep veins of silver ore in the Boundary Mine, which was also furnishing gold at the rate of twenty dollars an ounce. His share, nearly a third of the Boundary Mine, earned him nearly 7,000 dollars in 1860 alone. Without the *Arizonian* consuming his time Cross had little to do in Arizona except attending to the mine. He spent much of his time at Fort Buchanan, a military post near Tucson and home to a squadron of the First Dragoons under Captain Richard S. Ewell, whom Cross befriended.[8]

Lynch law prevailed in court due to the absence of a functioning territorial government. Cross was often asked to act as the presiding "judge" during his Tubac visits to overlook cases ranging from thievery to rape and murder. Because of this responsibility, and as a symbol of respect, Cross was given the honorary title of "colonel" by locals and was frequently referred to as "Colonel Cross" in the San Francisco papers that followed his adventures. Captain Ewell wrote, "They murder, each other (Americans and Mexicans), on this and the other side of the line without the slightest remorse." Cross closely attended to the duties, and earned respect among the miners for his fair judgments. In August 1860, Cross, as the representative of the St. Louis Mining Company, met with other mine owners to draft a code of conduct for their Mexican laborers, who were constantly threatening to rebel and caused many of the murders in the area. They tried to satisfy the workers by increasing pay and rations to prevent additional crimes.[9]

Between his ventures in the mines and sitting as a judge, Cross rode as a volunteer with Captain Ewell's dragoons as they chased the Apache and Mexican outlaws. During one expedition, Cross and his party tracked one band for two weeks, going without food or water for three days before descending and attacking the Apache camp, scattering the party, and killing several of them. In May 1860, Ewell wrote "we are in the midst of all sorts of trouble here now" after the kidnapping of an American mother and her daughter. With many miners making considerable wages and nothing to spend it on but whiskey, there were many "frolics." Cross' participations in these events gained him valuable knowledge of military operations. Although he held only the equivalent of an eighth-grade education, Cross always performed exceptionally well in on-the-job learning, from apprenticing at the newspaper to teaching himself how to write, and now working with the Regulars in active combat operations.

Taken when he returned to Lancaster in the winter of 1860, following the duel with Mowry, this prewar image of Cross reflects the years of hard living he endured in the West (courtesy Lancaster Historical Society).

Between his years of service in the artillery company and in his militia adventures in Ohio, and now patrolling the plains as a volunteer, Cross had the equivalent of a military education. He could read tactics and understood how to employ them under fire, he inspired with his presence, and above all, he was a natural leader. The battles with the Apaches were small engagements, with the natives raiding fringe settlements and then being pursued by the dragoons and their civilian posse, led by Cross. The Apaches engaged the dragoons at long range before blending back into the harsh environment or turning into Mexico. Ewell was given a daunting task, and, despite his and Cross' urgent pleas to the secretary of war for additional companies, none arrived. Cross wrote, "Great satisfaction excites throughout this part of Arizona for the liberal allowance of troops. We hope for more security + better days."[10]

One night while he was on campaign, a party of Apaches descended onto the Boundary Mine camp north of Tubac. Here they murdered a half-dozen white miners and torched the camp, destroying the mine and all of its equipment and costing Cross nearly 10,000 dollars in lost wages. In addition to this, they set Cross' hacienda ablaze. All of his private papers, his journals, his poetry and political papers, his rich observations of Arizona, and most important to him, his mother's letters were destroyed by the fire. The loss was a severe one for Cross, whose entire life's work was destroyed in an instant; only the printed columns in forgotten newspapers, and the letters sent to Henry O. Kent remained.[11]

After several months of chasing the Apaches, in January 1861 as the United States descended towards civil war, Cross decided that a cause across the border in Mexico needed his attention. From the time of Mexican independence in 1821, the nation's two factions had been fighting for control of the government. In 1857 the conflict became the Reform War as the Liberals and Conservatives fought for control of Mexico. Cross aligned himself with the Liberal Party and its charismatic leader, Benito Juarez, who sought to create a republic and limit the power of the Catholic Church. The violence was rampant throughout Mexico and frequently spread across the border into Arizona. Cross attached himself to a brigade commanded by a General Riveira, who recruited many of the Mexican miners from the Tubac area to join the Liberal cause, and invaded the state of Sonora to fight the Conservatives. Although the Americans who went south, including Cross, fought for the rights of Mexicans, an ulterior motive existed: to coax Sonora into the Union by force to gain a port on the Pacific for Arizona. Ultimately, the campaign to capture Sonora for the United States failed, as the Americans became involved in a bloody Mexican civil war.[12]

Reveira deployed his forces along the Pacific coast at Guaymas, some 250 miles south of the United States border. Cross received a commission as lieutenant colonel, devoting his time to fighting the Yaqui tribe. He also negotiated contracts between the Liberal government and American merchants peddling their supplies. Among the items he purchased for himself was a beautifully embossed Mexican-style saddle, and a cartridge box and revolver that were always on his belt. During one of the expeditions into the interior, Cross' party came under fire and he was hit by a ball to the ankle, leaving a scar but not injuring him to any extent. The colonel's duties mostly had him acting as a dispatch rider, riding long distances over the desert quickly to deliver messages and supplies, experiencing the thrill of being involved in a real war. He did have some difficulties on occasion with the men under his command and fought two duels, one with revolvers and the other with sabers and coming out uninjured both times.[13]

Sometime that long summer, still campaigning south of the border, Cross received word that the war he had longed feared between the North, wanting to preserve the Union and liberate the slaves, and the South, wanting to maintain the institution of slavery, had erupted. Cross promptly resigned his post at Guaymas and proceeded overland to San Francisco. He arrived on July 1 and booked passage to Panama; on his way home to New Hampshire to fulfill a lifelong dream.

At San Francisco on July 3, 1861, Cross immediately went to the Wells Fargo office and borrowed two pieces of paper to write two of the most important letters he ever wrote. The first he addressed to Governor Nathaniel Berry of New Hampshire. He wrote, "A citizen of New Hampshire, having had considerable experience in military affairs, I tender my services to the state of my nativity in this day of peril, to take any position which may be assigned me." He also wrote home to an old friend, Colonel Henry Oakes Kent, assistant adjutant general. With the mustering of troops in New Hampshire, Kent was one of the few men still on duty with the Adjutant General's Department and assigned to organize recruiting efforts in New Hampshire's Third Congressional District, which included Coos County. Knowing his friend was in a high place, Cross solicited him for aid in obtaining a commission, hoping to raise a battalion of dragoons from Coos County: "I am a ready for the wars — have been offered a captaincy in a regiment of Mounted Rifles in this state but declined. Have written to the Governor offering myself for any position but prefer mounted service. You may say I am coming but not for what end."[14]

Over 3,000 miles away, in the Granite State, Governor Berry was preparing to activate yet another infantry regiment, the Fifth, which needed a competent commander to lead it. Cross had prepared his entire life for this moment — to follow in the footsteps of his childhood hero, General John Stark, and lead New Hampshiremen to glory in a great war.

CHAPTER SIX

"At once entered upon my duty"

> The Fifth is the best organized, officered & equipped Regiment yet raised in this State. — COL. E.E. CROSS, SEPT. 15, 1861

A perilous month-long journey across the Pacific from San Francisco to Panama, followed by a train ride across the isthmus and then another leg by steamer, placed Edward Cross in New York City on August 3, 1861. Two days later, he arrived in Concord, New Hampshire. Through the intervention of Kent, Cross had a meeting the same day with Governor Nathaniel Berry, the state's somewhat aged Republican leader who, in addition to leading the day to day operations of the state, was swarmed by men seeking commissions in the regiments being raised. Berry spoke to Cross about the manner the state raised volunteers, and the condition of military affairs in New Hampshire. Returning to the state of his nativity, Cross had an aura about him. The duel with Mowry had made him famous throughout the nation, while his subsequent adventures on the frontier and his strong writing skills added to his fame, as many read of his travels. He was able to offer some suggestions to the governor on the matters discussed, and then he promptly left for home, high in the hills of Coos County. As the tall man from Lancaster left the state house that day, he knew that the meeting had been beneficial for him, and he believed he was about to become the lieutenant colonel of the unit then being raised, the Fourth New Hampshire Volunteers.[1]

Like many states throughout the North in 1861, New Hampshire suffered from a lack of competent military leaders. The abolishment of the enrolled militia in the 1850s severely delayed the state's ability to respond quickly to President Lincoln's call for volunteers in April 1861; it took nearly a full month for the First New Hampshire to depart for the war. While competent company grade officers could, and often did, learn from on-the-job training, field grade officers, especially competent men to command the regiments, were in short supply. The few West Pointers from the state such as Captain Joseph H. Potter of Concord and First Lieutenant Haldimand Putnam of Cornish were still serving on the frontier with their Regular Army units. Mexican War veterans such as John Bedel, Thomas J. Whipple, and John H. Jackson were already serving in the Second, Third and Fourth New Hampshire. A smattering of Norwich University graduates such as Henry Kent held positions in the adjutant general's office, while others such as Charles Long of Claremont worked throughout the state at training camps assisting to drill the volunteers. With few trained military officers available, Berry and the executive council, a unique New Hampshire institution of five individuals who advised and consented to all appointments the governor made, needed to find men who knew what they were doing. If nothing else, a competent commander was the most important part of the equation. New Hampshiremen were volunteering in great numbers, but someone had to lead them.[2]

Governor Nathaniel Berry of New Hampshire commissioned Cross colonel of the Fifth Regiment of New Hampshire Volunteers (author's collection).

In reviewing Cross' credentials for a position in the New Hampshire Volunteers, Governor Berry and the executive council could not have helped but be impressed. While he lacked a traditional West Point or Norwich University education, Cross had perhaps more active field service than any other man in the Granite State. He served in the old Forty-Second Regiment, rising to the rank of lieutenant, also serving in an adjutant's position in an Ohio unit. Throughout the decade prior to the war, he practiced military tactics and studied with Regular Army and Mexican War veterans who had prior combat experience. During the three years preceding the Civil War, Cross took part in active combat operations against the Apache in Arizona, survived his own firefight in Tubac, rode with the First Dragoons, acted as a posse leader, and took part in the Reform War as a lieutenant colonel in Mexico.

While these credentials were impressive enough, Cross did have a serious strike against him in the state. While much of New Hampshire transformed in the 1850s, from the Democrat Party to the Republican Party, Cross did not. His writings from the *Cincinnati Times* freely circulated, and his position on issues such as slavery and immigrants was widely known. Although the state was largely Republican, a strong Democrat minority still possessed a voice in the general court. By appointing a Democrat such as Cross to a high position, Governor Berry not only gained the experience of a veteran campaigner, he also appeased the opposition. On August 14, 1861, the New Hampshire Executive Council unanimously voted to give Cross the rank of colonel and command of the Fifth Regiment.[3]

After his interview on the fifth, Cross passed an anxious week at home with his parents at Lancaster, waiting for news from Concord. A letter from Secretary of State Allen Tenney arrived on the seventeenth, inviting Cross to a second interview on August 22. He promptly left Lancaster and went back to the capital. Although Cross wanted to muster a battalion of cavalry from Coos County, New Hampshire was raising only infantry regiments. During his second meeting with the governor and the executive council, Cross received something that he had wanted his entire life, a military commission.

This was not a time for the glamour of the parade ground, but rather a real commission, raised for a real war. Berry offered Cross command of the Fifth Regiment of New Hampshire Volunteers, a unit then in the process of recruiting throughout the state. Despite wanting the command, Cross did not accept immediately. Instead, he demanded the right to appoint the regiment's commissioned officers, and to "organize and fit the Regiment to suit myself." Berry promptly agreed, for the most part keeping his word in the weeks and years ahead. Several days later, as Cross was in the process of beginning to organize his affairs, he received his commission as colonel, dated August 27, 1861. He immediately purchased the new uniform of his rank, a knee-length tunic with two rows of seven eagle buttons each and a gilt silver eagle on a light blue background sewn onto each shoulder, designating him as a colonel of infantry. Cross immediately removed to the east side of Concord and opened up Camp Jackson, the rendezvous of the Fifth New Hampshire.[4]

Although commissioned to lead a regiment, in late August 1861, there was no Fifth New Hampshire to take command of. In each of the state's ten counties, men who were interested in becoming officers in the new regiment began the process of recruiting their neighbors and enlisting them to serve three years in the army. Some of the officers took out advertisements in local newspapers, trying to use Cross' fame to gain recruits. Charles Hapgood, who recruited in Hillsboro County, wrote in the *Farmer's Cabinet*: "The Fifth will be a Regiment of Light Infantry commanded by Col Edward E. Cross, late of

Six: "At once entered upon my duty"

Arizona, whose reputation as a military Commander and Gentleman is unsurpassed."

Unlike the prior four regiments from the state, which recruited largely from the urban centers of Manchester, Nashua, and Portsmouth, the Fifth was the first to recruit largely from outside the industrial centers of the state, with the majority of the recruits coming from the many small farms and industry centers in the western and northern parts of New Hampshire. They represented a mixture of men from nearly every age and occupation in the Granite State. Not all the men who recruited soldiers for the Fifth received commissions. Cross wanted "good competent men" who brought in recruits, not men who owed their commission to political patronage.[5]

While only the surgeons who performed the rudimentary medical exams on the enlisted men could pass or reject enlisted men for the Fifth, Cross did have a wide range of discretion when choosing who received commissions in the regiment. Through connections, he was able to secure the discharge of his brother Richard, who had reenlisted in the Regulars and still had four more years to serve. After meeting his brother in Texas, First Sergeant Cross traveled east to Fort Monroe, Virginia, and took part in the security detail protecting Lincoln during the inauguration. After this detail, his company of engineers went to Fort Pickens, Florida, until Cross' brother, with Henry Kent's assistance, secured Dick's discharge and a promotion to first lieutenant in Company H of the Fifth.[6]

Other officers that Cross put his faith in included Edward E. Sturtevant, the first man to volunteer from New Hampshire in April 1861. Sturtevant's first

As a token of his appreciation to the officers under his command, Cross presented copies of this photograph to them for Christmas in 1861 (courtesy Lancaster Historical Society).

lieutenant was James Larkin of Concord, a coach painter but one who quickly learned the soldier's trade. Captain John Murray of New Castle was a Mexican War veteran, decorated for heroism at Chapultepec. From Littleton came William Adams Moore, son of a wealthy doctor and a veteran of the Fifth New York Zouaves, while Claremont sent Norwich graduate Captain Charles Long, who spent the early part of the war drilling recruits in Sullivan County. Unfortunately, Berry saddled Cross with some officers who held promise, such as Lieutenant Elijah W. Johnson, a Norwich graduate, and Captain Ira McL. Barton, a First New Hampshire veteran, but who proved to be incompetent and worthless.[7]

In selecting his field and staff officers, Cross had even wider latitude, unlike those who had recruited men expecting a commission in return. Cross wanted Edward J. Conner, a West Pointer who had seen service on the frontier, for his lieutenant colonel. Unfortunately for Cross, the appointment instead went to Samuel Langley, the sickly adjutant of the Second New Hampshire who fought at Bull Run. For major, Cross selected William W. Cook of Derry, who was active in the Massachusetts militia. He wanted Henry O. Kent to become his adjutant. Instead, Kent decided to remain on the staff, performing the equally important job of forwarding New Hampshiremen to the front. Although Kent from Lancaster would not serve, another childhood acquaintance in the form of Dr. John W. Bucknam became the regiment's assistant surgeon.[8]

Cross made his headquarters near the old state fairgrounds in the east of Concord, naming it Camp Jackson after "the illustrious soldier & statesmen." Given power to raise and equip his regiment, and without the proper staff to compete the many small tasks needed in camp, he promptly began issuing contracts for provisions, uniforms, boots, accoutrements, and the other items needed to outfit the thousand incoming recruits, who began to arrive on September 28. Two days later, Cross left for Washington to procure arms for his men and to transact regimental business. He stopped in New York and purchased an ornately engraved Colt navy revolver, a cavalry saber, and other necessary military equipment for himself. With the entire Fifth Regiment encamped at Camp Jackson, Cross and his carefully appointed officers began the tedious process of transforming Yankee farmers, laborers, and mechanics into a disciplined military force.[9]

The Fifth had less than a month at Camp Jackson to learn the rudiments of a soldier's life before they were required to leave the state. The men impressed Cross, including Company B from Coos County. Of them he wrote, "I never saw men who sooner adapted themselves to military law." Thomas Livermore was among the men who wanted a commission in the Fifth. A veteran of the First New Hampshire, he gladly accepted the role of first sergeant of Company K. Livermore was impressed with Cross from the moment he arrived at Camp Jackson, writing, "The colonel, whose reputation had excited my curiosity, was seen busily engaged around the camp in every department, now directing the quartermaster, now receiving new detachments, now superintending drill, and now trying a horse." Following a strictly laid down schedule from their commander, the men had a rigorous day of training as they learned how to properly turn and maneuver, first as individuals then as companies, until finally the entire battalion could respond to Cross' command. The colonel knew that strict discipline was necessary; the men suddenly realized that their lieutenant or sergeant who might once have been a coequal on the farm or factory was now in command and was to be obeyed and respected as such. Although the men were citizen-soldiers, Cross knew the regiment had to drill hard and be held to the strict standards of the United States Army Regulars. He was able to instill in his regiment the same level of tenacity, fearlessness, and courage he himself possessed. When others ran away, the Fifth New Hampshire stood firm and fired low. Little did they or Cross know that one out of every five of these men would never return to the Granite State.[10]

Dr. John W. Bucknam grew up with Cross in Lancaster and served as the Fifth's surgeon. There was nothing he could do to save his friend from death (author's collection).

In the final week of October, the War Department ordered the Fifth to the front. Cross became furious at not having more time to prepare his men, gain additional supplies, and recruit additional soldiers; he nearly resigned in disgust, and was finally given four additional days to ready his men. As the regiment prepared to leave, Cross issued a detailed fourteen-point general order detailing how the men would proceed, what was expected of them, and how his officers should act, including chronicling how their uniforms were to be worn and what rations were carried. A member of the Fifth later wrote, "The attention to details may seem trivial, the discipline may seem severe, yet in this direction alone was the future success of the regiment." The same day, Cross finally announced the 150 men in the regiment who earned a warrant and became noncommissioned officers. Although the rank was not as prestigious as a commission, many of the men were proud of the recognition as they received a personally signed warrant from Colonel Cross.[11]

On the morning of October 28, the entire regiment, 1,012 strong, formed a hollow square as Governor Berry and Adjutant General Anthony Colby presented Cross with the United States colors and a beautiful regimental flag of dark blue silk featuring an American eagle on one side and the seal of the State of New Hampshire on the other. Both flags bore the inscription, "Fifth Regiment, New Hampshire Volunteers." The national colors bore plenty of room for the men to inscribe with the battles they knew would come. Cross took the flags and handed them to the color sergeants. First Sergeant Livermore was there and never forgot Cross' remarks:

> In a clear voice which all could hear he made a speech considerably different in tone from those of roseate hue which recruits were accustomed to here [*sic*]. It has ever been in my memory because it proved so true, and was in the manly tone of a soldier who knew whereof he spoke. The import was that we took those colors to fight under; that it was not to be play and glitter of glory altogether, but that we might expect to leave many of our numbers on the fields where we were to uphold them; and that we should brace ourselves with the resolution to maintain their glory and our honor even at the cost of life and limb.[12]

The following morning, with the Fifth's band playing the traditional military air of "The Girl I Left Behind Me," the Fifth boarded the rail cars for the front. For Cross it was one of the most important days of his life, the culmination of everything he strove for. He wrote, "For myself, I never felt better. That morning I bid farewell to my mother, & having been inured to partings, felt calm and happy. My face might have shown weariness but not sorrow." As a young man, Cross had read Homer's classics and dreamed of war; now he was finally off on the odyssey of his life.[13]

After a two-day journey from Concord, the Fifth arrived at the front at Bladensburg, Maryland. Here they went to a brigade under Brigadier General Oliver O. Howard, a Mainer, whose command included the Fourth Rhode Island, Eighty-First Pennsylvania, and Sixty-First New York. Unlike the Rhode Islanders, the Pennsylvanians and New Yorkers would always be by the Fifth's side. Cross respected Howard, considering him a brave soldier, but he believed Howard's practices of ordering prayer before marches and battles to be strange, the colonel referred to Howard as a "crank," while the general called Cross "a very able officer." After organizing the regiment into the brigade Cross and his men prepared for a mission into eastern Maryland, to Marlborough in a Union effort to "protect" the polls from southern infiltration in the uneasy border state on November 2. A heavy rain the day before made the journey especially difficult for the raw regiment. Held in reserve during the voting, the fifty-mile march gave Cross the time to shake his regiment out and train. After the muddy, wet ordeal of the Marlborough march, the Fifth returned to camp near Bladensburg. In its first mission, the Fifth did well, with the colonel writing home to the governor: "It was hard for the first trial, but the men did nobly." General Howard complimented Cross and the Fifth by writing, "Colonel Cross did his duty well in marching and disciplining his command." It was the first of many compliments for the New Hampshire regiment and its leader in the years to come.[14]

With their first real mission over, the Fifth continued in the Bladensburg camp, with two hours of company drill in the morning and three hours of battalion drill in the afternoon. Strange commands such as "change front, forward on the first company" and "by the right of companies to the front" that appeared as passages in Hardee's Tactics soon came to life as the men learned to respond to the commands as one by voice and bugle. While these drills were important for the Fifth to maneuver properly under fire, Cross placed great emphasis on the ability of his men to quickly load and fire their Enfield rifle-muskets. Under ideal drill field conditions, the men could deliver three rounds a minute. However, on the battlefield, with incoming fire, fouled muskets, and the chaos of the situation, it often broke down to one to two rounds a minute. Cross pushed his men hard to fire as fast as they could. In an antiquated system that frowned upon target practice, the colonel was able to obtain on several occasions both live and blank cartridges to add to the realism of the drill. Cross also put great faith in the use of the bayonet, with the men learning the complicated French drill system of George B. McClellan, the commander of the Federal forces massed near Washington. Cross and his senior officers held classes in the evenings for the company officers and first sergeants to learn tactics and regulations, which they had to repeat verbatim for the colonel upon command.[15]

Although he presented himself as a figure of authority, Cross genuinely cared for the men under his command, teaching them how to make small shelters from their blankets, writing home asking for the women of New Hampshire to knit socks and mittens, and being worried that they did not have enough rations to eat. For those who held ambition and potential, Cross always found room for them in the ranks of his noncommissioned officer corps and was constantly able to fill commissioned vacancies with a superb grouping of competent young men who idolized their colonel. While he commanded a ten-company regiment, two companies were Cross' favorites: Company K, known as the regiment's "pet company," and Company B out of Coos County. When Frank Heywood, the son of a wealthy farmer from Lancaster, died in late November, Cross remained by his bedside, closing his eyes as he passed. After Cross visited a photographer in Washington, he gave each of the officers a copy of his image, signing them as a token of affection for those under his command. In addition, Kent sent complimentary copies of the *Coos Republican,* which the colonel gladly gave to the men in Company B. With firewood scarce near camp, Cross allowed his men to take the "top rails" from nearby farmer's fences. The "New Hampshire men were expert woodmen," wrote General Howard and they considered each rail left the "top rail" until soon none were left. Although he tried to make camp life and the rigors of a soldier's career easier on his men, Cross often lost his temper at the least infraction, spilling over into a violent boil raging from a tongue.[16]

Although he believed slavery to be wrong, Cross thought it would die out of natural causes but to agitate against it would only inflame the situation. The North elected Lincoln on a platform to stop the spread of the institution, but as the war progressed, Lincoln realized that ending slavery was the only way to bring the nation back together, much to Cross' angst. Moving into Virginia, the Fifth encamped at the Volusia plantation where many of the soldiers, fresh from the granite hills could see the effects of the peculiar institution firsthand. Although Republicans were running the war, Cross, a Democrat to the core, believed their policies were in the process of destroying the nation rather than reuniting it. In a letter to Kent, a true Republican supporter, "This attempt to make an abolition war is got to make trouble if not stopped. A little more attention to soldiers and less to Negroes is what is wanted. If not we shall get whipped." Cross gave the most venom to New Hampshire's senior senator, John P. Hale, a radical abolitionist and a man with political connections in the Lincoln administration who was in a well-placed position to help those who supported the Republican platform. Now a senior officer in the United States Army, Cross simply could not silence his pen. He was a thickheaded man who believed he was always in the right, and he wrote home, "Do give old Hale hell. He is a fanatic. We don't want to make this an abolition war, don't crowd us into it."[17]

In December of 1861, the Fifth was assigned to a division commanded by General Edwin "Bull" Sumner. A veteran dragoon officer, Sumner trained his men as foot cavalry, to push through at all costs, destroying the enemy through fire, and maneuver. A superb tactician, it was Sumner and officers such as Howard and Cross who molded the men of the division, soon to be redesignated as the First Division of the Second Corps, into a competent fighting force that carried it through the next three and a half years of combat. The brigade to which the Fifth was assigned was designated the First, still under Howard, while the Fourth Rhode Island was replaced with the Sixty-Fourth New York. Soldiers in the Sixty-Fourth looked in envy at the Fifth.

While they had a good colonel, they knew that the New Hampshiremen were better led, as seen from the hours of time they spent on the drill field perfecting movements that only a few months before did not make any sense but were now second nature. A member of the Fifth wrote, "Beyond a doubt this thorough discipline, constant drill, and practical education, were the principal causes, other things being equal, of the excellent qualities afterwards exhibited by the regiment."

Cross ensured that everyone in the regiment, from he himself down to the corporals, knew the tasks of the man above them in rank, they taught their positions to those below them, so all knew how to act in line of battle when commanders became casualties. While the long hours of drill tired many arms and upset those who did not understand by ordering them to perform extra drill under the direction of their sergeant, it was vital in order not only to discipline the regiment but also to learn the fundamentals of how to handle their rifle-muskets when they entered combat. With General Howard often absent from the command Cross, as the senior colonel, was in command of the brigade "half the time," learning how to command and control four regiments on the drill field. Under arms for less than three months, Cross was proud of his regiment, writing home, "The Fifth regiment is hard to beat."[18]

Throughout the remainder of the winter at Camp California, the Fifth trained hard, Cross knowing that the spring would soon bring a campaign that would test the mettle of his regiment. Regular inspections were also a large part of Cross' mission to instill discipline and morale in his men. On Sunday, the colonel personally inspected each man in the regiment, insuring they complied with his notions of what a soldier should appear to be. Private Miles Peabody of Company K complained: "Our brasses have to be all polished up, guns cleaned, boots brushed, and everything in the neetest manner, or stand on a barrel head the rest of the day." Sickness was a continual factor, with measles, typhoid, and dysentery afflicting the men. For many of the men, the disease struck hard because they had no immunity. Cross, long used to a hard life on the frontier, remained immune, continually claiming he had never been in better health and while giving medicines his mother had sent him to help several officers recover from camp diseases.

Camp life continued unabated, with First Lieutenant Cross building a stockade to keep prisoners in and teaching the men the fundamentals of military engineering, such as constructing fascines, gabions, and other engineering specific equipment. First Sergeant Livermore served with Lieutenant Cross and remembered: "Cross had obtained very severe ideas of discipline; he was not illiterate, and although erratic was a good officer." Cross would prove to be a competent company commander, but like his father and brother he enjoyed whiskey and gambling. During the winter, the colonel insisted his regiment have the best material and it remained the best regiment in the division, Cross wrote to Kent: "I want you to come out and see a model Regiment where there is no drunkenness, no rows—where the men are well fed, clothed, and made to walk up square to martial. I don't think the men like me, but the War Department & the Generals have a different opinion." [19]

During the months at Camp California, as the Fifth came together as a unit, the officers and men of the regiment developed differing opinions of their commanding officer, some that would change with time and others that were set too deep to expire. By those that Cross chastised and punished, he was seen as a tyrant, a petty man who saw his position as a means to insult and punish others while rewarding those he favored. But for many in the regiment felt that Cross was an experienced man in military matters and the ordeal that they undertook on the drill field or in dealing with the colonel being off would prove the regiment once it entered combat. Some, like Sergeant George S. Gove of Company K, feared that the hard training would always place the Fifth in the position of greatest danger. "If we do go into a fight he will put us ahead I reckon." Little could Gove have realized how accurate his prediction would be.[20]

Cross could be cordial to some, inviting officers into his tent for drinks after hours, but be physically violent to them the next day. For others he was a man who always gave favors while shunning those who did not meet his high standards. In February of 1862, his youngest brother, Frank, joined the Fifth at Camp California as a private. Two views of Colonel Cross are given by the enlisted men of the Fifth, one by Private Peabody, who wrote, "Our Colenel does not prove as good as was expected. He is very quick tempered." Sergeant Lee Sears of Company D, soon to be promoted from the ranks only to die at Fredericksburg, wrote, "Our colonel is a good soldier. He is a perfect gentleman, and one of my best friends." Many in the Fifth, both officers and enlisted men, were equally divided in their opinion of Cross.[21]

While Cross cared for his men in camp, he was ruthless to anyone who breached military discipline, believing that those who could not comply with the rigors of army life could have no place in the Fifth New Hampshire. Most of all, Cross hated those who deserted the regiment, which broke the esprit de corps that formed among men who marched shoulder to shoulder into a hail of lead. These deserters not only abandoned their comrades they also took with them government equipment and often paid the advanced bounty. In order to join the Fifth, recruits had to be at least eighteen and have parental permission, but many lied about this in order to enlist. One of these recruits was Private Orastus J. Verry of Company F, a resident of Swanzey. Verry forged his parent's signature on the enlistment paper. When the father found out his son had already been mustered in, he wrote to Cross attempting to have his son discharged as a minor.[22]

The colonel refused at first, claiming, "If he is discharged, with equal reason might one-half our army be discharged." Verry's father then approached Representative Thomas M. Edwards of Keene, a Republican congressman, who interceded with the War Department and had Private Verry discharged as a minor on December 18, 1861. Cross immediately counterattacked by filing charges against the younger Verry, claiming he was a deserter, took government funds under false pretences, and carried off government property. Congressman Edwards, still representing his constituent, again contacted the War Department and attempted to have the desertion charges removed. The action enraged Cross, who wrote a very pointed letter to the congressman: "It seems to me, *Sir,* with all due respect, that at this crisis of our national affairs, Members of Congress would do better service by attending to public business than to spend time and energy in getting able-bodied men discharged from the service." The letter from Cross was published in several Republican newspapers throughout New Hampshire and was yet another log thrown on the fire of those who were beginning to despise Cross.[23]

When Cross attacked members of Congress, he received a very blunt and direct order from Lorenzo Thomas, the adjutant general of the United States Army. While others would tolerate Cross' stubbornness at times, Thomas would not, writing, "A proper zeal for the service might have prompted you, on receiving the Secretary's order, to give your reasons for thinking the discharge 'a fraud upon the government,' but your persisting in regarding him a deserter after the renewed order of the Secretary, is an assumption of authority, and disobedience of orders without excuse."

Lieutenant Colonel Samuel Langley was a burden placed on Cross' style of leadership and resigned after being sick for months (U.S. Army Military History Institute).

Despite receiving the sternly worded letter, the only warning he ever received, Cross continued in his battle between the administration and his regiment, believing that only he had the final voice in matters relative to the Fifth New Hampshire. Colonel Cross was set firm in his opinion of deserters when he said, "Deserters are the worst sort and ought to be shot."[24]

Having had considerable experience acting as judge, jury, and executioner during his time in Arizona, Cross served on several courts-martial during the winter, giving out convictions for those involved with drunkenness in camp, arguing with officers, and refusing to perform duty; such punishments typically involved marching around with a knapsack filled with bricks or having one's pay reduced. In most regiments, the field and staff officers typically had too little time on their hands to contend with the individual enlisted men, letting the company commanders manage their own companies. Cross was a micromanager and often wanted to control the affairs of individual soldiers in his regiment. Under regimental orders, only men who held a medical condition as diagnosed by one of the regimental physicians could be excused from drill or picket duty. When Captain Ira McL. Barton, the incompetent commander of Company E, told three of his men they could be excused from duty, Cross went into one of his wild outbursts, especially when Barton tried to write off an excuse being given by Dr. John Bucknam. Barton tried to defend his point, but Cross promptly returned the letter, demanding to know who excused the men; he never found the answer.[25]

Although Cross could not control the actions of individual enlisted men, Governor Berry gave him wide latitude in selecting the Fifth's officers. Even though Cross believed his initial grouping of company officers was the right mixture of experience and talent for his regiment, the time at Camp California proved otherwise. In addition to several incompetent company grade officers, his field officers as well were proving troublesome, Lieutenant Colonel Langley constantly being ill and Major William Cook's drunkenness in camp always under discussion around the campfire among the men. In late February 1862 Cross decided to enact changes in his regiment. As part of a general reorganization of the Army of the Potomac, as General McClellan's force was now called, any officer could be brought before a brigade board of review to question their qualifications for command. Cross saw this as an opportunity to rid his regiment of incompetent leadership, and he selected for dismissal Captains Richard Welch and Edmund Brown of Lancaster, in addition to First Lieutenants Elijah W. Johnson and James B. David.[26]

In company drill, Welch was unable to master even the simplest of commands, forgetting how to deploy his men and rally them as a line of skirmishers, instead leaving the practical instruction to First Sergeant Livermore. Welch also used his first sergeant in off-duty hours by making him write love letters to married women in Washington he was interested in. Sergeant Gove of the company wrote of his captain: "He was mean & dishonest & was dispised by the men & all the officers in the regt." Although Brown was a Lancaster native, and the popular commander of Company B, he did not meet his fellow townsmen's standards and left the regiment as well. David was a veteran of the First New Hampshire, but he could not make the transformation from enlisted man to officer, and Johnson was a Norwich graduate. They could not properly drill their men, and Cross was disgusted with the way David and Welch frequently fraternized with the enlisted men of their company.

Although both officers and enlisted men came from the same stock, an invisible line separated the two. On several occasions, General Howard chastised Captain Sturtevant for being too friendly with the men in his company from Concord, but he always knew when to put duty first. General Howard gave the examinations, which consisted of the same basic tactics of company and battalion drill that the officers had studied all winter long. If these were not mastered on the drill field, the companies would fall apart when they came under fire. A ten-company regiment depended on cohesion, one weak chain would destroy it, and Cross knew he had to have good officers in command. The board found the men incompetent and forwarded their discharges to the War Department on the grounds of being unfit to command.[27]

Brown and Johnson accepted the board's findings and returned to New Hampshire, while Welch and David, both Republicans with friends in high places, tried to seek reinstatement in the Fifth. They traveled to Washington in early March to visit Senator Hale and the three representatives from New Hampshire. What inflamed the officers perhaps more than anything else was the fact that only those Cross wanted to appear before the board were sent. In addition, the colonel knew that Welch and David were both strong Republicans. Further complicating the situation against Cross was the fact that the men included was his appointment of Richard Cross to captain and command of Company K, in addition to several other officers known to be favorites of the colonel.

The two officers visited Camp California after their meeting with Hale, trying to intervene with the commander. Cross entered the house both officers were in and said the whole of the New Hampshire delegation could not reinstate them, specifically calling Senator Hale a "God damn fool." The two subalterns attempted to persuade Cross to let them back into the Fifth New Hampshire. Cross drew his sword on Lieutenant David, who was unarmed, threatening to run him through. David had no weapon, so Cross took off his belt and wanted to box David, who continued to repeat he did not come to fight the colonel. The colonel went on to add that he considered the West his home and did not care how those in New Hampshire viewed his actions. Cross finally tired of arguing with the two officers and left in disgust after he "abused us shamefully," according to Captain Welch. When Cross left, an intoxicated Major William Cook, who behaved well on the picket line but was constantly drunk while in camp, entered and saw the two men. Cook yelled out they were part of the "cult of damn black Republicans," literally throwing David out of the house and injuring his face.

The two officers returned to Washington and explained their confrontation to Senator Hale, who was enraged at the treatment sustained by his constituents, and wrote to Governor Berry: "From all that we have learned thus far, we incline to the belief that these two officers have been discharged *from sinister and unworthy motives.*" Despite the senator's investigation, Berry took no action against Colonel Cross or Major Cook. To inflame his already tender relationship with New Hampshire's Republican delegation in Congress and at the state house in Concord, Cross, blunt as ever, wrote to Secretary of State Tenney in March 1862: "Welch and David can *never* come back, as they are *trying* to do. I won't have either of them, & they cannot be forced on me. I have blocked the game in Washington." At times, Cross apparently did not care how others saw him, not realizing he was already destroying his chances for promotion.[28]

The time at Camp California solidified the Fifth New Hampshire Volunteers into an effective regiment. Disease, the rigors of picket, and the tireless hours of drill bonded the men together in remarkable ways. Throughout the winter of 1861–1862, Cross endeavored to produce a regiment that met his own high standards of efficiency and discipline. The results were sometimes controversial, such as the sacking of several well-connected officers, but, as he knew, it was for the betterment of the Fifth. If one could not handle his company on the drill field, then in combat he would utterly fail. While he was extremely popular with his men, the colonel's temper, fueled by alcohol, came out more than it should have, affecting both officers and men, while his never ceasing pen continued to harm his reputation in New Hampshire. Despite the controversy, many in the Fifth knew that their regiment was above average, and their colonel was the reason why. Writing twenty years after the war, one Fifth officer wrote of Colonel Cross and what he embodied in the Fifth New Hampshire: "He was a man of fine of personal presence, iron will, great energy, courage in difficulties, bravery in danger, experience in the field and knowledge of men and things. He was the prime factor in making this most excellent material into one of the best organizations in the army."[29]

Although he produced a fine regiment, Cross' Fifth New Hampshire was still incomplete. Reviewing the regiment one day on the parade ground, General Sumner, the Second Corps commander remarked to the colonel, "The Fifth New Hampshire Volunteers needs only one thing to render it the best of regiments—that is a baptism of fire." This event, a watershed in the regimental experience, was coming soon along a small stream in northern Virginia.[30]

CHAPTER SEVEN

Baptism

I hope God has caused this war to kill off the Abolition Party. —COL. E.E. CROSS, JULY 14, 1862

After months of training at Camp California, the men of Howard's Brigade and the rest of the Army of the Potomac were now ready to march south in the hopes of crushing the rebellion. General McClellan began his spring campaign in March 1862 by sending probes into the Shenandoah Valley and northern Virginia to test his men and prepare them for his own planned campaign later in the season, to attack Richmond from the peninsula running between the York and James rivers. The Confederate forces around Manassas began to fall back to Richmond as the triumphal Second Corps took possession of the captured works. The redoubts and fortifications that the Rebels built impressed Cross, who took pleasure in spending time in the hut of his old friend Richard Ewell, now a Confederate general, using his stationary to write letters with. By March 15, the bulk of the army had returned to Washington, while two divisions of the Second Corps pushed on from Warrenton to the Rappahannock River.[1]

Crossing cold streams in late winter, Cross used the band to play the regimental march, "One-eyed Reilly," a rowdy British marching tune, to encourage the men to struggle onward as they occasionally saw Rebel cavalry. When one private threw a fit, laid down in the road, and refused to do his duty, the colonel kicked him and almost ran him through with his sword. On the morning of March 29, Howard sent his men forward in pursuit of Jeb Stuart's cavalry. As the column pursued, Stuart's artillery began to open up. As the Fifth New Hampshire watched the shelling, the Sixty-First New York began to break and was soon "driven." The shelling continued for some time, but none of the rounds hit any members of the Fifth, except for throwing dirt over the Coos County Company. The colonel wrote, "Three shells struck close to us—one spattering the dirt over me and my horse. The men were cool, marched steadily, kept well closed up, nor did the terrible screaming of the balls & the bursting of the shells seem to frighten them." General Howard began to worry that Cross' men were too far advanced, as the shelling began to get more accurate, one shell striking within feet of the colonel. Howard sent a staff officer to order the Fifth back. The officer told the colonel of Howard's request to double quick out of range, to which Colonel Cross countered, "Does the general *order* me to double quick?" "O, no," came the answer, "he thinks you had better do so." Cross was not going to pull his men out of a fight because of a few artillery rounds and called out, "Then I'll be hanged if I march double-quick by that battery," and the regiment continued to watch the spectacle, maintaining their ranks without being injured. Cross slept that night with the knowledge that his Fifth New Hampshire had done well in their baptism by fire.[2]

The Fifth came under fire for the first time, earning their first battle honor, "Rappahannock," which the colonel promptly had painted on the regimental colors. The baptism of the Fifth made Cross extremely proud of his men, and he wrote to Henry Kent, who had recently won his first term in the New Hampshire House. "I feel better now I have seen the men under fire & know they can be depended on." Cross hoped to use his friend's new found power to erect a large arsenal in Concord and expand the role of the active militia at home. To Secretary of State Allen Tenney, he wrote, "My Regiment behaved *nobly*, never faltered, never flinched, but marched deployed, and fired, with perfect coolness." After every battle, he never failed to write glowing remarks about his men, hoping to gain the attention of the New Hampshire newspapers. Although a minor, forgettable skirmish by the standards of events to happen later that year, Cross always remembered the affair on the Rappahannock as the baptism of his regiment, the test that showed him that his months of hard training finally paid off. His men were able to stand their ground under fire.[3]

After the reconnaissance to the Rappahannock, Howard's Brigade and the Fifth returned to Alexandria to join the rest of the Army of the Potomac on the Peninsula, sailing down the Chesapeake to Yorktown, then under siege. The bombardment of the Confederate works enlivened the colonel, who thought it compared favorably to the firepower of the battle in the "Star Spangled Banner." With his regiment in the field, Cross again showed his devotion to the soldiers of the Fifth, keeping the saddlebags on his horse Jack full of small supplies such as bandages and medicine to care for his men. At Yorktown Cross found his men detailed from combat operations to the engineer brigade, and as the Fifth began assisting in building corduroy roads, gabions, fascines, and other material needed to mount a successful siege. During an inspection of the regiment, a Regular Army officer told Cross he commanded "the most

A stickler for regulations, Cross wore this fancy overcoat during the winter months (Gettysburg National Military Park).

perfect Regiment of Infantry he ever inspected." The Rebels abandoned Yorktown without a fight, but the participation of the Fifth earned it another battle honor.

On May 5, the Fifth led Richardson's Division on the march, Cross writing, "We blundered on, the mud perfectly awful, & mixed up with tree tops, logs, brushwood, with now and then a deep hole full of water." As the Fifth proceeded up the Peninsula, supplies began to get low as disease and privation began to take their toll. On occasion, the colonel would not move his men without obtaining enough supplies to fill their haversacks. Even forty years after the campaign, Private Norman Corser remembered "we had a Colonel who knew his business."[4]

While many in the regiment felt that Cross was the supreme reason for the excellence of their unit, to others, particularly the minority of Republicans and the older line officers, the colonel was a liability. He was a drinker and a hothead who never failed to speak his mind, someone who lacked self-control, as demonstrated by his removal of Welch and David. Some feared his lack of control might lead to recklessness in combat. Captain Edward Sturtevant, a former Concord police officer, wrote to his former chief: "There are many things that should be different in this Regt. and I think improvement should commence with its commanding officer." Sturtevant was a brave officer who, like the colonel, preferred battle to dress parade, but he too hoped Cross' temperament to his subordinates would improve.[5]

As Cross approached Richmond, he began to develop the sense of foreboding he experienced before every battle, that it might be his last: "Somehow I have an idea that this god abandoned spot is to be my future residence. It matters little." The colonel had confidence in his men, but knew the threat that lay before them. In a letter to his father, the colonel wrote, "The position of the Rebel Army is very strong, being covered by the muddy country in front + flank. But all depends upon whether we can get our artillery to bear on them. If we can, they are gone." The scenes of camp life, with parades, glamorous uniforms, and orderly lines of advance, gave way to dysentery, death, mud, and mosquitoes. Still, Cross loved the hard life of a soldier. The lowlands of Virginia were terribly different from the mountains and forests of New Hampshire, causing many to fall ill. "Amid the pestilential vapors and miasma of the swamps many of the men grew sick, and several died." For some the war seemed, without a battle to come, to be about over, leading a few to suggest that Richmond would fall without a fight. For an aggressive man like Cross, this news was damning as he waited anxiously to take his men into combat.[6]

On May 25, McClellan sent two corps across the Chickahominy River to a railroad crossroads called Fair Oaks. As there was only one bridge crossing the river, he needed additional spans to reinforce the position at the station. The First Minnesota began building a bridge across the Chickahominy on May 23, but abandoned the project after finding the task impossible due to the swamp and muddy terrain. Heavy rains swelled the Chickahominy to flood stage as both sides maneuvered for battle. General Sumner knew the men to build the span, Edward Cross and the Fifth New Hampshire. Without a bridge across the Chickahominy, the Union forces would have to countermarch over fourteen miles to cross.

With many of the men in the ranks from northern New Hampshire proficient with the axe and long used to cutting cords of wood to allow them to survive the harsh New England winters, Cross ordered them further upstream to cut as much wood as possible and float it down the river into position. The men, working in water up to their chests, built cribs of heavy timber, sinking them into the river then laying "stringers" on top before finally placing the cut logs on crosswise to complete the project. Both officers and men, including a large contingent from the Sixty-Fourth and Sixty-Ninth New York worked feverishly on the project to allow the Army of the Potomac to cross into action. While the work was built by the men of the Fifth New Hampshire, it was largely a product of the two Cross brothers. Colonel Cross personally supervised the details, detailing men, ensuring the materials were on hand, and rallying the soldiers to complete the task, while former engineer sergeant Lieutenant Cross gave practical instruction and supervised the engineering aspect of the Grapevine Bridge, as Sumner named the creation.[7]

The New Hampshiremen were proud of their accomplishment, with J.W. Bean writing, "In 48 hours, a bridge nearly 1,200 feet long and bridging two channels had been built, without a nail, spike, bolt, or a piece of sawed plank." Bridges built by other regiments floated away, but the Fifth's stood as a product of Yankee ingenuity designed by Colonel Cross. As late as the 1920s the surviving veterans of the Fifth continued to defend Cross and their accomplishment, especially when veterans of the First Minnesota who began the project tried to claim they, instead of the Fifth New Hampshire, built the bridge that "saved the army." A reporter from a Boston paper wrote, "This bridge was in one sense the savior of our army. The N.H. men received great praise from all who saw the result of their arduous labors." The *New York Times* referred to Cross as "the best practical engineer in the army." One observer noted that had Colonel Cross been a Regular Army officer he would have gained an instant promotion to brigadier general for the act. Instead, it was the first in a long series of acts that he would be praised for but receive no reward for.[8]

With the Grapevine Bridge prepared, it was finally time for the first major engagement of the Peninsula Campaign. The Confederates struck first, at Fair

The building of the Grapevine Bridge on the Peninsula first drew Cross to the attention of his superiors as an excellent combat leader (Library of Congress).

Oaks Station on May 31, attacking the Union forces under General Silas Casey, whose men were able to hold their position with the help of well-placed Union artillery. Among the casualties was Confederate commander Joseph Johnston, replaced by Robert E. Lee, who regrouped and prepared to attack the following morning, June 1. That night Cross wrote, "The dreadful hour of battle drew near. Silently the angel of death hovered over our camps. The lives of thousands drew near their end. But all unconscious were the victims. The laugh, the song, the soldier's story all were prevalent in our camp." Few men from small towns in the Granite State knew what they were getting into when they joined the Fifth New Hampshire. Colonel Cross had awakened them to what a soldier's life was, but many, including the colonel, never forgot the events of June 1, 1862.[9]

Despite heavy rains, the Grapevine Bridge held, allowing Richardson's Division to advance forward on May 31 and move into a position near Fair

Oaks, the ground already saturated with blood and bodies. General Richardson knew he needed a strong guard that night, and he called on Cross to perform the dangerous duty to act as the alarm of the army. General Howard told the colonel, "I'm going to give you the advanced guard. Hold your position until you are whipped or relieved." As Richardson, a native Vermonter, rode along the Fifth's line, he shouted, "Fifth New Hampshire, remember your granite hills; you will stand firm like your granite hills." The night before the Fifth's first battle was a tense, uneasy time for Cross and the men of the Fifth. Lieutenant James Larkin wrote, "It was so dark we could not tell whether they were friend or foes." The colonel added, "Nothing could be heard but the groans of the wounded." Cross kept his men alert, while two companies under Captain Sturtevant were on picket duty most of the night. He wrote, "To many it was the last of earthly slumber—their last sweet dream of home & friends." After midnight, Cross observed fires to his front and upon seeing them went to investigate. Stumbling into the camp of the Fifth Texas, composed mostly of the German immigrants he encountered on his journey to Arizona, the colonel put on his best southern accent and quickly left. A few moments later, he captured a courier, gathering vital intelligence and, for himself, a Remington .44 revolver and a horse. While others slept, Cross remained awake most of the night, checking his lines, getting ready for the fight.[10]

With dawn, the men prepared a cold breakfast, and Cross called his regiment into line, musketry erupting to their front. The Fifth formed their ranks and deployed as skirmishers to the front of the First Division, sending an occasional shot into the woods, until Howard recalled them. He then moved the Fifth to the rear of his line, as Cross had received a stray ball through his coat. During the initial morning of fighting, Howard held the Fifth in reserve, personally leading the Sixty-First and Sixty-Fourth New York into a series of woodlots near a railroad to engage the Confederates of George Pickett's brigade. Among those hit was General Howard, who lost his arm, as the New Yorkers fell back. Colonel Cross prepared to lead his men into action, and the fighting intensified as the rest of the brigade went in.

At 10:45, Cross, as the senior colonel, was now in command of the brigade. Instead of rallying the remaining three regiments, he decided "with characteristic decision" to take his 800 Granite Staters straight ahead into the woods to fight the Confederates. The Fifth advanced, "coolly, steadily, amid the whistling balls until the rebel line was close at hand, not ten rods off." Cross continued to scream "onward" as the Fifth proceeded into action. marching as if on parade, the regiment moved forward in a straight line of two ranks, with sergeants and lieutenants to the rear and Colonel Cross in front with the color guard. This was the moment he had waited for his entire life, his first time leading a group of men into the muzzles of their enemies' muskets. While the enemy shelled the Fifth from a distance at Rappahannock, Fair Oaks was their first time under infantry fire.[11]

The battleground at Fair Oaks was "swampy," with thick undergrowth that made it hard to keep the well-dressed battle line most were used to on the parade ground, and some struggled to prevent the mud from sucking the boots off their feet. The men of the Fifth continued advancing until they were within "blunderbuss" range of the Confederates. Although their Enfield rifle-muskets were accurate at long distance, Cross preferred to bring his men close into action, to within forty yards of the Confederate line. The same madness that had prevailed in his close-in fight with Sylvester Mowry several years earlier surfaced again. Cross "liked things hot" and brought his men in closer than they should have been. Corporal Charles Hale served in the Fifth's color guard and saw the colonel as a "holy terror" as the Fifth fought its first battle. The Fifth came onto line, knelt down, and began "whacking at the johnnies," every man firing as fast as he could. Cross placed himself behind the two ranks of riflemen, calmly pacing back and forth along the length of his long line, a revolver in each hand, swearing at the men to stay in line and to keep up their fire as the bullets began to clip tree limbs and bring down New Hampshiremen at a fast rate.[12]

Lieutenant William Moore stood with his men in Company E, closely following Cross' order to keep the men in line as the file closers "rallied our brave men to the work of death." Cross saw the opportune moment, as the Virginians appeared to be falling back. With bayonets fixed, the colonel was about to order his men forward to clear the woods. At the same time, a minie ball struck him in the left thigh without breaking the bone as he passed near Company I. Cross, who "raged like a lion through the battle, went down like a pine tree." Moore heard someone shout that the colonel was down, and "surely as I looked around, I saw him lying under a tree bleeding severely, his broad forehead covered with blood." The colonel described his wound: "the ball grazed the main artery and tore the flesh in the most shocking style." As Cross bled on the ground, small groups of Fifth soldiers continued to go to the colonel and attempt to take him to the rear; all the while Cross continued to order them back into line.[13]

He propped himself against a tree, and a piece of buckshot hit his temple, causing another wound and covering his face in blood. Command of the Fifth passed to Lieutenant Colonel Samuel Langley, who had been constantly ill with bronchitis since Camp California. With the Confederates pulling back, Langley ordered the men to hold their ground instead of pursuing. Cross shouted, "Charge 'em like hell boys, show 'em you're damned Yankees. Sorry to say I can't go with you." The battle was over as the Fifth fired a few more rounds into the fleeing enemy. As the Sixty-First New York passed out of the woods, Lieutenant William Spencer saw the colonel "weltering in blood." Several Fifth soldiers managed to secure a stretcher for Cross, but they too were ordered back to the firing line as the Fifth successfully held on against an entire Confederate brigade and caused them to flee.[14]

The Fifth New Hampshire managed to check and repulse the enemy when the other three regiments of the First Brigade were repulsed; it came, however, at a very high cost. To Henry Kent, Cross wrote, "The Rgt did nobly, more than nobly, *gloriously.* We beat back the enemy, but at fearful cost." Accompanying the letter was a list of the casualties in northern New Hampshire, for the *Coos Republican,* the first in a series of sad notices throughout the state. Private George E. Shannon recalled, "Our Regt. was cut up pretty badly." Colonel Cross recorded his casualties as forty New Hampshiremen dead, 187 wounded, and eleven taken prisoner, a costly baptism of the 800 who went into action.[15]

In their first time under infantry fire, the Fifth New Hampshire did well. Cross' training was the reason why, even though "that battle ought really never to have been fought, for it had no purpose, no plan of action, no place in any scheme of operations," according to one Second Corps staffer. General Howard, the injured brigade commander, wrote, "I commend Colonel Cross for the excellent disposition of his command, which I particularly noticed in the morning." The months of drill, inspection, and discipline had finally paid off into something that Cross and his men could be proud of. The regiment was able to live up to the colonel's own motto of "Stand Firm and Fire Low." What three regiments were incapable of accomplishing the Fifth New Hampshire did, pushing the Virginians back. Only Lieutenant Colonel Langley's timid behavior in not ordering the Fifth to charge prevented the regiment from completely driving them from the field. Lieutenant Larkin remembered, "Col. Cross done well, the men stood it well." After the battle, an observer saw the relationship between Cross and the men he commanded: "Stern and strict in his duty, he is a gentlemen of the kindest feelings, and greatly beloved by his men. It was affecting to see the brave fellows crowd around their fallen leader, and listen to their expression of affection and regret." When the thought that Cross' use of "emphatic language" would upset some of the readers, a Cincinnati correspondent who knew Cross from the *Times,* wrote, "Those who know the Colonel best can appreciate his Yankee mannerism. But he acquitted himself gallantly in the fight."[16]

Carried back from the front line, "faint and bleeding," upon a stretcher by members of the Sixty-Ninth New York, an Irish Brigade regiment, it was obvious to many that Cross was severely injured. Lieutenant John Hazard of the First Rhode Island Light Artillery offered the wounded colonel a flask of brandy and asked him "a hundred questions about the fight." As Cross lay upon the stretcher, Generals Howard, Richardson, and Sumner all "sent to the Colonel to express their admiration and bravery and steadiness of his life." Despite being in agonizing pain, the colonel wrote a short note to the men of the Fifth, thanking them for their conduct in the battle and vowing that he would return: "Continue to maintain the noble character you have so firmly established — be cool and brave in battle, vigilant in front of the enemy, and soldierly in your deportment." Sergeant George Gove was hit as well, and when brought to the collection area for the wounded, noticed his colonel circulating among the wounded New Hampshiremen: "Tho badly wounded was never more cheerful talking & laughing with the boys. He said we had behaved splendidly & he felt satisfied."

Besides receiving his own wounds, Colonel Cross had room to worry, as his three brothers were also on the field. Lieutenant Colonel Nelson Cross, a half brother, was the commander of the Sixty-Seventh New York, while Dick and his seventeen-year-old brother, Frank, served in the Fifth. All four Cross brothers survived the fight, but the commander of the Fifth's Company K had been hit. Two doctors Cross knew from the Regular Army in his Arizona days treated his wounds, as he "lay 8 hours in the field until all the badly wounded were carried off."[17]

A wagon took Cross and a wounded lieutenant from Pennsylvania on a jolting ride towards the York River. All the while, Lieutenant Francis Adams, who considered the colonel "a very agreeable companion," attempted to hold Cross down, as the "jolting of the ambulance caused him to use some strong adjectives by way of easing his pain." The doctors could do little but offer alcohol until the wounded went to the central hospital on the York River. From there, the patients

The first man from New Hampshire to volunteer, Edward E. Sturtevant earned Cross' respect as an excellent company commander and major (author's collection).

went to the steamer *Spaulding*, staffed by female nurses from the Sanitary Commission. Cross made an impression of Nurse Harriet Whetten by constantly asking for eggs and barely fitting into his assigned bunk. He passed the time onboard talking with a wounded Confederate officer about the rights and wrongs of secession. A native of the Granite State, Whetten called Cross "the fighting colonel." Overloaded with scores of patients, including many men from the Fifth, the *Spaulding* began a long, slow journey to Philadelphia.[18]

Cross began his recovery in the same Philadelphia officer's hospital as General Howard, who gave Cross great credit in carrying on the fight after Howard lost his arm. Throughout his stay, however, Cross continued to vent frustration and anger that the men of the Irish Brigade, whose operations were widely covered in the New York and national papers, gained fame as the unit that repulsed Pickett's Virginians at Fair Oaks. The Fifth New Hampshire's part in the fight was covered, and even then, briefly, only in the New Hampshire papers, most of which did not circulate out of the county. Not only was he furious about the lack of coverage of the Fifth at Fair Oaks, but he firmly believed the Sixty-Ninth New York was responsible for firing a volley into the backs of the Fifth, causing the "death of my best men" and wounding his brother Dick. The colonel "kicked up a devil of a row about it," writing several letters to the New York papers condemning the Sixty-Ninth New York. In his private journal, Cross fired at General Thomas Meagher, who commanded the Irish Brigade, believing he was drunk and absent from command in the engagement. Of the volley, he wrote, "There was no excuse for this murderous act only stupidity of the grossest act." In visiting the patients in the hospital, Dr. Thomas Ellis noted of Cross' condition, "I was gratified to find him fast recovering from the effect of his wound, but suffering mentally from some unjust statements that appeared in one of the New York papers." The colonel wrote of his experience: "For 28 days I lay in a hospital having a damned hard time of it." When his thigh wound stabilized enough, he went to a hospital in New York, but he desperately wanted "to join my beloved Regiment." Still "laid up," by July 1 Cross arrived home to Lancaster for two weeks to regain his strength.[19]

While he enjoyed praise for his role in the Battle of Fair Oaks, Cross was less complimentary about his commanders. "In this battle the Generalship on the part of the federals was wretched. Instead of shelling the woods with 30 pieces of artillery, as we could readily have done — we allowed the rebels to choose their own ground — ambush themselves and wait for our attack — nothing but the indomitable bravery of our rank & file and live officers, saved us from defeat," wrote Cross. While he commended the performance of Howard, he ripped into General Meagher for being drunk and Richardson for not bringing up additional artillery. Fair Oaks was a turning point for Cross' criticisms as well. Never one to back down, he began to readily scorn those he believed did not match his own prowess on the battlefield; few commanders lived up to the standards Cross set for himself. With a strong belief in his capabilities as an overtly competent battlefield commander, Cross had a good eye for combat leadership and never failed to crucify those who failed under fire.[20]

Back on the Peninsula, the Fifth remained on the frontline, picketing and engaging in an occasional firefight with the Confederates. All the while, Richmond lay some ten miles away, and McClellan refused to move. On June 25, the Confederates counterattacked and drove the Union forces away from Richmond in a series of battles known as the Seven Days. The absence of Cross in the Seven Days was severely felt by some in the regiment. Many were pleased that Major Cook, the regimental drunk and also wounded at Fair Oaks, was gone; but the somewhat competent Lieutenant Colonel Langley, ill since mustered in, left the regiment for good on the morning of Malvern Hill, passing command of the Fifth to Captain Edward Sturtevant. Lieutenant Charles O. Ballou of Claremont recalled, "Since our brave Col was wounded, the regt has been going to the devil as fast as possible. When I see other officers shirking their duties, leaving them to be performed by those who are not afraid, it makes me indignant, and I have half a mind to throw up my commission." The fact that thousands waited for their discharge because of illness enabled Cross to relieve the regiment of several officers who survived his spring purge but proved themselves worthless at Fair Oaks. The Fifth behaved in the same manner at White Oak Swamp and Malvern Hill as it had at Fair Oaks, but Cross' absence was felt by all.[21]

Recovering from his wounds in Lancaster, Cross enjoyed two weeks of respite from the horrors of war. One resident remembered the wounded colonel arriving home with a small Confederate flag and, "never lacking in the sense of the dramatic," threw it down on Main Street and then proceeded to jump on it several times. Despite being off duty, Cross wore his uniform the entire trip and walked with a cane. Although he had climbed Mount Washington before, Cross and several friends used his warhorse Jack to pull a wagon up the newly finished stage road leading to the summit, stopping for a photograph on top. He was able to enjoy a final fishing trip on the Androscoggin River with Henry Kent and several friends during the muggy, mosquito-filled time he was home. Kent always remembered the outing as the final adventure he had with his friend: "Of that trip, one evening is silhouetted against the sky of my memory forever — a wild camp under the tall trees, the rushing river, a blazing fire, the sparks trailing up the stream on a strong warm wind, Col. Cross sitting cross-legged on the ground, a red silk handkerchief bound around his head, patting the 'Juba,' crooning darkey songs and narrating Arizonian and Mexican experiences trenching on the marvelous." It would be the last peaceful time in Cross' life, and the last time he saw his beloved home.[22]

With his two weeks in Lancaster over, Cross returned to Concord to collect recruits for his regiment. Still he felt he was not physically fit to return to the army and requested an additional twenty days to recover in New Hampshire. He used the time to add nearly fifty additional reinforcements for the Fifth, sought commissions for officers in his regiment, tried to arrest deserters, and attended political rallies and speeches, trying his best not to let his opinions boil over into rhetoric. He looked forward to returning to the army but felt an old enemy — abolitionists — contributed to the Army of the Potomac losing the Peninsula Campaign. In a letter to an old friend from Arizona, Cross wrote. "The infamous conduct of the abolitionists in keeping reinforcements from McClellan is arousing a fierce spirit of revenge in the Army of the Potomac. I hope God has caused this war to kill off the Abolition Party- we are heartily sick of 'highly intelligent contrabands' and I have them booted out of camp." Such letters Cross addressed only to those he could trust, fearing the content would leak out into the public view. For him, however, his actions spoke as loudly as his words.[23]

Finally, on August 10, Cross, Dr. William Child, the new assistant surgeon, and recruits for the regiment were on their way south. Cross wrote, "My wound was painful and troublesome, but I resolved to bear it, though my endurance was severely taxed." On the steamship *Cahawba,* off Fort Monroe, the colonel became violently ill with seasickness, much as he had in the Gulf of Mexico years earlier. Back in camp on August 23, the colonel could see what his absence did to his men. He "received a hearty welcome" but "found everything in a very disorganized state — discipline broken, and a general confusion. Ten minutes after my arrival I had commenced reforms." Soldiers were barefoot, uniforms were in rags, and there was little food. While Sturtevant, now the Fifth's major, managed to handle the regiment well in combat, he was not the administrator that the colonel was. There was no time to search for new supplies, as the next morning the Fifth boarded a steamer north, finally leaving the Peninsula.[24]

CHAPTER EIGHT

The Fighting Fifth

Put on the war paint and give 'em the war whoop!—COL. E.E. CROSS,
SEPTEMBER 17, 1862

The army Cross returned to was radically different from the one he had left in June 1862. The once cheerful, battle-ready force that had advanced towards Richmond in May 1862 had by August been replaced with a demoralized, dejected, and ragged band of survivors. Defeats at Oak Grove, White Oak Swamp, Beaver Dam Creek, Gaines Mill, and Savage Station had been hard for many to accept. Many blamed Lincoln for withholding reinforcements from McClellan, who in actuality was responsible for the defeat in the Seven Days because of timid leadership, retreating instead of standing firm and fighting Lee. Reluctantly, Lincoln began to send troops from McClellan's command to northern Virginia. He put John Pope in command of Union forces around Washington, as he began a new offensive in northern Virginia. In essence the government had stripped McClellan of his authority. General Sumner continued to command the Second Corps, while Richardson remained in command of the First Division. New to command however was Brigadier General John Curtis Caldwell, a Mainer and a school principal before the war, who led the Eleventh Maine at Fair Oaks and now found himself in charge of the First Brigade.[1]

In New Hampshire, Governor Nathaniel Berry again called for volunteers, this time raising five new regiments for the front under a call from President Lincoln in July 1862, immediately following the defeat in the Seven Days. While the men of the Fifth enlisted the year before for a one hundred dollar bounty, men now came out of the granite hills for bounties nearing $400 in some of the smaller towns in the mountains with few able-bodied men left. With fewer than 300 men in the Fifth, many hoped that the regiment would be brought back up to full strength; but only the few recruits Cross brought with him arrived. The colonel pleaded with the governor for recruits for the Fifth, claiming they would quickly learn the ways of the old veterans, but the governor demurred. For Berry, raising new regiments allowed him to offer commissions to those who patronized the Republican Party. While no recruits came to the Fifth, what was worse for those officers, such as Captains John Murray and Charles Long, who performed well on the Peninsula, was that no Fifth officers were promoted into the new regiments, much to Colonel Cross' angst: "I have in the 5th Rg't officers and men that deserve promotion, having earned it by long & arduous service in the field, and brave conduct in battle." Despite his pleadings, the only officers promoted were those to other companies in the Fifth. Cross would allow no outsider to hold a commission in his regiment.[2]

While the men of the Fifth welcomed Edward Cross back to the ranks, another member of the family was on his way back to Lancaster. Frank Cross, the youngest of the three brothers at seventeen had joined the Fifth, in February 1862, as a private. Serving on the front line in the ranks, Frank had survived unscathed through Fair Oaks and the Seven Days. In Edward's absence and unwilling to be Frank's guardian any longer, Captain Richard Cross tried to orchestrate the transfer of Frank to the Sixty-Seventh New York, under command of his half-brother Nelson, in July. Army regulations forbade the transfer of enlisted men between companies and regiments without the president's approval. Because he was a minor, and through the influence of his three brothers who were commissioned officers, two of them colonels, Frank Cross received an honorable discharge from McClellan's headquarters and went home to Lancaster to continue his education.[3]

After clearing Federal forces off the Peninsula in August 1862, Lee knew that the Army of Northern Virginia had to take the initiative. The Rebels began their campaign in mid–August, scoring victories at Cedar Mountain, Second Manassas, and Chantilly, as the Union forces from the Peninsula moved north in support. Cross found Pope's forces even more demoralized then McClellan's army, strung out along the road: "It was a shameful sight." As a testament to the trust placed in the Fifth by their commanders, Cross' men, in addition to two other regiments, held the picket line alone on September 2, 1862, near Chantilly, and the next day were the last Federals to leave Virginia, and did so in a driving rain.

By September 5, Lee's men had invaded the North, crossing into Maryland, hoping to score a decisive victory and win European recognition. President Lincoln as well knew that the moment called for action. The only way to reunite the nation was to destroy the thing most responsible for starting the war, slavery. Once a Union victory was securely in Lincoln's hands, he would issue the Emancipation Proclamation. The stakes were never higher than the fight in Maryland in the late summer of 1862.

Reluctantly, Lincoln put George McClellan back in command, which Cross supported, and sent the Army of the Potomac marching north and west from Washington in pursuit of Lee. To celebrate the return of their leader, Cross organized "a grand pow wow over it." In their ragged condition, the Fifth began marching from Washington on September 5, foraging through the countryside, which Cross also supported. Although little food was available, he managed to kill a pig with his sword.[4]

After discovering a copy of Lee's battle plan on September 13, McClellan pushed his men hard to the west. The result was a Union victory on September 14, as the Army of the Potomac cleared the South Mountain passes. They pushed the Confederates through Boonsboro, towards a small town wedged between Antietam Creek and the Potomac River, Sharpsburg. Cross' men were not called up to fight on the fourteenth, but the following morning General Joseph Hooker, in command of the Union's right wing, called up his reserve, the First Division, Second Corps. Hooker told Richardson that "there would be a fight or a foot race" as they chased the remaining rebels towards Sharpsburg, and he wanted the division in front.

Marching down the slopes of South Mountain into Pleasant Valley on the National Road during the early morning hours of September 15, Richardson ordered Cross and the Fifth to the front of the column, and the soldiers from New Hampshire began chasing after a tired band of troopers from the Fourth and Ninth Virginia Cavalry. Throwing four companies forward under Major Edward Sturtevant, the men began a running shooting battle with the Confederates. For Cross, it was almost a game, as his regiment, the eyes and ears of the army, moved forward at will, shooting at the Confederates they came into contact with, who more

A school principal from Maine, General John Curtis Caldwell commanded the Fifth's brigade and later division. His style of leadership was not approved of by Cross (Library of Congress).

often than not after a week of starving in Maryland gave up and surrendered.[5]

Together with a large force of cavalry, Cross passed through Boonsboro, then into Keedysville. By 2:00, after a tough seven-mile running fight, the First Division, with Cross still in the lead, arrived at Antietam Creek. The remaining Confederates in their path retreated to the opposite side of creek as the bulk of the Army of Northern Virginia began to arrive on the field from Harpers Ferry to take positions in farmers' fields, woodlots, and sunken roads. Still seeing Rebels across the Antietam, the Fifth continued the fight at long-range distances with their Enfield rifle-muskets. As the Fifth engaged in the firefight with the Confeder-

Thomas Livermore served ably under Cross and left behind an excellent record of that service (U.S. Army Military History Institute).

ates across the stream, a ball tore off one of Cross' shoulder straps, barely missing his arm and a major injury. The colonel observed one of his men running vigorously past to shoot at the Rebels. "My young friend," said Cross, "if you don't want a hole through you, you had better come back." At that instant, another bullet hit the soldier's hat, causing him to retreat towards Cross. A shell also struck near Cross, who, to his men, seemed oblivious to severe wounds in action. Instead of pushing Richardson's Division across the Antietam in attack, McClellan ordered a halt. Instead of going across the creek to attack the disjointed forces, McClellan, cautious as always, waited until all his divisions were present. The Confederates as well continued to receive reinforcements from the disjointed pieces of their army.[6]

The Battle of Antietam began at 5:00 in the morning of September 17, 1862, as Union forces attacked along the northern flank of the Confederate line. Through a cornfield, woodlots, and along the Dunker Church ridge, it was attack and counterattack as both sides brought up reinforcements, leaving thousands dead and wounded in the corn and woods. Orders initially held Richardson's Division in reserve, the men watching the firestorm occurring across the creek, waiting for their turn to go in. Federal artillery along the hills east of the Antietam began to open up. Cross began to perk up — these were the moments he lived for. The men began to cheer like "mad" as "Colonel Cross frantically shouted to our artillery to put the shells into them."

Across the creek, the shelling was incessant as farm buildings burned and the fight raged. Out of range, the men felt safe near McClellan's headquarters at the Pry house. Cross was invited into the house and formally introduced to McClellan, whom he described as being "in good spirits though thin and careworn." Cross was among the majority of soldiers in the Army of the Potomac who admired McClellan. The two men shared the same firm Democratic politics, a fear of the administration, and knew how to drill, equip, and discipline men. The similarities ended there. In combat, McClellan did not know how to command soldiers under fire, while Cross excelled at it.

McClellan ordered Sumner to take two of his divisions across the Antietam at 7:20 A.M., in the wake of a fierce counterattack that nearly drove the First Corps off the field. Sumner selected Sedgwick's Second Division and William French's Third. Sumner's instructions were to keep one division— Richardson's—back until a division from the Fifth Corps could relieve it. Meanwhile, at 9:15, Sumner led Sedgwick's men to disaster in the West Woods, where the Confederates flanked them, and the division lost half their strength in fifteen minutes. The Fifth Corps troops finally arrived, freeing up Richardson's men to march to support the Union line.[7]

Cross' men crossed the Antietam as the roar of the cannon intensified. The colonel "never felt better in my life" as he told his men they were about to destroy the enemy. Sergeant George Gove, going into the fight with Company K, remembered: "Our boys went into it with a will." The Third Division, under General French and the First Division were to have followed Sedgwick; but mistaking some Twelfth Corps troops advancing to the south for the rest of the Second Corps, French wheeled his men south towards a sunken road. This was a narrow farm lane some half mile in length that concealed two brigades of North Carolina and Alabama troops under D.H. Hill. French's men, mostly green troops, launched a bayonet assault against the road and were repulsed, losing heavily several times before they began a long-range firefight with the entrenched defenders.

By 10:30, with the Third Division spent, it was time for the corps reserve, the First Division, to enter the fray. Seeing their plight, Richardson sent in the Irish Brigade under Thomas Francis Meagher to the east side of the road to add support as the First Brigade advanced to the right, preparing to deploy to support the Irish. The Fifth New Hampshire formed the left flank of the division, a very critical spot in the line and one that General Richardson trusted to his best regiment. As the First Brigade came onto line, the Irish went in. Their green banners dropped as one bearer after another fell, while their large "buck and ball" muskets had some effect on the enemy below. At the same time, the men in the First Brigade, including the Fifth New Hampshire, began to look around and could not locate General Caldwell, their brigade commander, who in the moment of crisis was not present with his men. Lieutenant Thomas Livermore and others believed that the general was hiding behind a haystack with his staff to the rear.[8]

As the Irish Brigade fought to the Fifth's front, Colonel Cross paced anxiously in front of his men, hands clasped tightly behind his back, and told them what he expected of his regiment in the coming fight: "You have never disgraced New Hampshire; I hope you will not this time. If any man runs, I want the file closers to shoot him. If they do not, I shall myself. That is all I have to say." Cross knew his veterans from the Peninsula would not run; the message was "to encourage any individuals who might fail." As the men rested on a slight rise behind the sunken road, waiting to go into action, artillery shells exploded overhead. A sergeant recalled, "Shot shell, grape & canister were poured into us like rain & we gave them the same in return. The roaring of cannon the screaming & bursting of shell, the continuous battle of musketry & mingled with it all the shrieks of the wounded made it a scene I shall never forget." The fragment struck the colonel in the head and shredded his hat, and he began to bleed from his forehead. With his hat gone, Cross reached into his pocket, pulled out his red handkerchief, and tied it around his head, making the tall New Englander a conspicuous target clad in crimson. The men of the First Brigade saw the Irish faltering to their front, but received no orders to deploy from Caldwell, even as General Meagher himself rode up seeking aid; the commanders of Caldwell's regiments could not act without orders from above.[9]

Seeing Meagher's Irish slaughtered like French's men, General Richardson rode up looking for Caldwell to take his men in. The men in line shouted he was behind the haystack, and would not come up. As Richardson rode up to the New Hampshiremen, he shouted, "God damn the field officers. Get your asses up there." Spotting the red-swathed colonel from New Hampshire, the general ordered Cross and the Fifth, 319 strong, to advance and relieve the Irish Brigade. For Cross, it was the moment he had been waiting for, the uncaging of a lion who was about to enter the fray. Cross unsheathed his sword, drew his revolver, and ordered his men forward at the double quick as they ran to support the crumbling Union line. Stumbling over a tattered rail fence the Fifth approached the scene of action below as the colonel shouted out they were going to "whip the enemy."[10]

Many authors have written that the Fifth New Hampshire performed the complicated maneuver of breaking "by the right of companies to the front by the right flank march" at Antietam. In doing so, Cross' men would have performed a very complicated series of maneuvers resulting in the ten companies of the regiment forming a column, dashing through the ranks of the Irish and then re-forming a solid line of battle to their front. While the Fifth New Hampshire and Colonel Cross were certainly capable of such of a move, having practiced it countless times on the drill field, the colonel did not execute the command. With Cross at its head, the Fifth simply pushed their way past the battered Irish to get into line. There was no time to execute anything else, as they had to get into position immediately. Once the Irish were in their rear, the line was quickly dressed as the New Hampshiremen prepared to engage. A sergeant in the Twenty-Ninth Massachusetts always remembered the image of Cross, his red handkerchief wrapped around his bleeding head, sword in hand, leading the Fifth New Hampshire as they came over the crest and onto line to relieve the Irish Brigade, which suffered over 50 percent casualties, as they fell back.

Cross directed a volley into the ranks of the North Carolinians to his front, which, with the concentrated fire of the Sixty-First New York to the right, created a flanking effect through a raking fire on the lane, causing the Confederates to panic and flee. The Fifth moved down into the sunken road, described as "a bloody place" by recently promoted Sergeant Charles Hale, stepping over the bodies of the Alabama and North Carolina defenders as they clambered up the opposite bank to the high ground in the rear.[11]

To the Fifth's front, two divisions of Confederate soldiers ran for their lives. General Richardson knew that the end of the Confederacy was in sight and ordered every man possible across the sunken road in pursuit of the fleeing Rebels. James Longstreet, the Army of Northern Virginia's second in command, saw this as well and

Cross' actions in combat earned him celebrity throughout the North, as attested by this engraving, published in *Harpers Weekly* (courtesy Lancaster Historical Society).

ordered his artillery near the Piper farm to begin firing at the advancing Federals, causing a momentary halt to the advance and mortally wounding Richardson. Division commander Daniel Hill managed to rally a force of some 200 Alabamians and North Carolinians who had been defending the sunken road and now led them in a counterattack to stop the Second Corps troops from advancing further towards Sharpsburg, where they could cut off Lee's line of retreat. A bullet tore into one of Cross' men, who ran up to the colonel announcing, "Oh, Colonel, I am wounded." Cross quickly replied, "It's the fortune of war, my young man." The colonel taught his men never to leave the line of battle unless seriously wounded, and even then to ask permission from a commissioned officer.

As the rest of Caldwell's Brigade continued to advance, the Fifth drifted further to the left and suddenly found itself alone. A young lieutenant ran up to the colonel and told him the Rebels were about to flank the regiment as Cross, peering above the ranks, saw five Confederate battle flags in the distance. It was Hill's rallied command. The colonel realized the importance of the situation. The Fifth New Hampshire formed the extreme left flank of the Second Corps. If the Confederate force outflanked his regiment and reinforcements came up, it would spell disaster for the Army of the Potomac. Alone, unsupported, and without orders, Cross took advantage of the moment and prepared to meet the foe.[12]

Promptly ordering "change front, forward on the Tenth Company, march!" The ten companies of the Fifth, beginning with the men on the left, ran to bring the line on a ninety-degree angle to meet the Confederates head on. Instead of finding the Second Corps' flank open, the Rebels found the Fifth New Hampshire with Enfields loaded and aimed. Colonel Cross remembered the moment: "My boys brought down their rifles as cool as on parade & our volley tore them to fragments." The regiment continued to advance to a slight rise of ground, again to prevent the Confederates from gaining the upper hand. Francis Walker, a member of the Second Corps staff, recalled, "The two lines actually moved parallel to and not far from each other. Cross is ahead, seizes the crest, and pours a volley from his whole front upon the discomforted enemy. This action of Cross has been spirited and timely." It had been over three months since the last time Cross saw combat. Now in command of a veteran force, he along with his men, stood eye-ball-to-eyeball with Hill's veterans, refusing to yield in the deadly contest.

All along the line, "men became almost frantic; guns could not be loaded fast enough; those of the wounded were seized and even the arms were taken from the hands of the rebel dead and discharged at the heads of their living comrades." Sergeant Hale remembered the colonel as "master of the situation" as the New Hampshiremen kept up a steady fire. Cross sent Hale to find General Caldwell as he tended to his shrinking line. The regiment fired by wing. As the right five companies loaded, those on the left engaged; they kept up a continuous fire on the enemy, neither side willing to back down. While Colonel Cross ran the length of his line, issuing commands and keeping his men in line, his brother was just as occupied attending to the men in Company K. When one soldier was struck in the head by a piece of shell, splitting his skull open, the captain "shut the piece of skull down like the lid of a teapot, tied a handkerchief around it, and sent to the rear the wounded soldier, who ultimately recovered."[13]

General Hill continued shifting his small force to the right, trying to find a weakness in the Fifth's line, but he continued to be blunted by Cross and the Fifth. General McClellan himself called it "a spirited contest." At distances of thirty to fifty yards, the men were standing like granite yet again. The colonel continued to move his men by the left and rear, shifting the line from the right to the left to outflank the flankers. A member of the Fourth North Carolina wrote, "The roar of musketry was incessant and the booming of cannon almost without intermission. Occasionally the shouts of men could be heard above the awful din, indicating a charge or some advantage gained by one side or the other." A spent ball hit Captain Cross in the foot, but he stayed with his men. Although his regiment was performing a heroic task in continuing the fight, which had been going on for nearly ten minutes, Colonel Cross knew that the situation was critical. There were no reinforcements in sight, and one-third of the regiment, including nearly half the company officers, were down.[14]

Acting on pure adrenaline, Cross knew he had to do something to inspire his men. Picking up the torn end of a musket cartridge from the ground, he smeared the remaining powder left in it onto his bleeding face, creating a ghoulish, black-looking figure along with his long beard. Cross screamed out as loud as he could to "put on the war paint," and his remaining soldiers followed suit, smearing their sweaty faces with the grime of battle. Dr. Child, helping the wounded on the front line, saw the colonel "incessantly striding along the line [as] he watched every man, and saw every detail of the action. He seemed the very incarnation of war." The colonel recalled the scene in a letter to a friend in Concord:

> My brave boys, knowing that all depended upon promptly checking the rebels, raised the wild Indian yell and poured an awful volley into their ranks. Their center regiment was literally smashed to pieces, and before they could rally their forces, several regiments hastened to my assistance. Then came the most terrific fighting. I had been in seven battles before, but they were nothing in comparison to Antietam. We shot down the rebel color-bearers as fast as they could get up, killed their officers, broke their ranks and piled them in heaps among the tall corn. I never felt better in my life, and if the rebels didn't hear

the Apache war whoop that day it was not my fault, for I yelled it until I was hoarse. My men fought nobly, gloriously; never wavered, never shrank. Not a man but the wounded and dead fell out. My officers also conducted themselves like heroes.[15]

With the faces of the men black with powder, grime, and sweat, Cross then ordered "give 'em the war whoop" as he began shouting like the Apaches he once fought in Arizona. His men quickly followed in pursuit, giving their own strange New England version of the famed Rebel yell. Lieutenant Thomas Livermore remarked, "I have sometimes thought it helped to repel the enemy by alarming him to see this devilish-looking line of faces, and to hear the horrid whoop; and at any rate, it reanimated us and let him know we were unterrified."[16]

Sergeant George Gove stood in the rear of Company K with Captain Cross, passing cartridges to the men and yelling words of encouragement. Always a strong supporter and admirer of the colonel, Gove was a willing participant in this unorthodox maneuver the Fifth was taking in attempting to drive back the Rebels. Two weeks after the battle, he wrote to his sister Julia Parsons, a schoolteacher in the small Rockingham County town of Raymond: "I enjoyed it as I would some game or sport. Our boys kept cheering & yelling all the time like so many wild Indians indeed. I think our yelling scared the rebs more than our balls. We finally drove the rebs out like a flock of frightened sheep. Then how we cheered & shouted. I could hardly keep in my skin." It would be a moment that Gove, like many Fifth New Hampshire veterans who survived, would never forget.[17]

One eyewitness to the spectacle recalled, "The sound rose above that of artillery and musketry, carrying defiance to the foe and encouragement to friend." Sergeant Charles Hale, who did not find any reinforcements, arrived on the scene and recalled the actions of the colonel: "His face was strangely streaked and smeared with powder, and with his orders he occasionally interjected an Apache war-whoop to which the men in the ranks responded." The shouting added to the confusion of the engagement and allowed the Fifth to intimidate the Rebels as their numbers continued to decrease. In the moment of crisis, the colonel was able to command his men in a terrible situation, encouraging them through his own bravery and fortitude to stand their ground as they continued to slug it out with the enemy, neither side willing to back down from the fight as they continued screaming at the foe. Despite taking heavy casualties, Hill's men refused to yield. It was clear the Fifth needed help.[18]

Major H. Boyd McKeen saw Cross' men fighting alone and promptly rushed the Eighty-First Pennsylvania to the side of the Fifth, adding additional firepower to the fray. Directly ahead, the color bearer of the Fourth North

Carolina went down. Severely wounded, Corporal George Nettleton captured the trophy, earning a battlefield commission and Cross' praise. With McKeen's support, the Fifth finally stopped the Rebels and ended the threat to the line, as the enemy retreated towards Sharpsburg yet again. While Hill's small battalion did not carry much firepower, it was a formidable force of veteran Confederate infantry that could have caused severe havoc to the First Division's flank, causing a rollup, as had occurred just a few hours earlier in the West Woods. The Fifth happened to be in the right place at the right time to prevent such a movement from occurring.

Colonel John Rutter Brooke brought his brigade up to replace Caldwell's command. New division commander Winfield Scott Hancock ordered a halt to the advance, as McClellan withheld the needed reinforcements. The soldiers of the Fifth, their faces still besmeared with powder and their throats hoarse from the continued shouting, returned to the Roulette farm with other Second Corps units to reequip and prepare to reenter the fight, but Hancock held them in reserve. The colonel ordered another roll call: nineteen men were dead, and one hundred more wounded.[19]

With the battle over, Cross and the men began the difficult task of picking up and recovering from the traumatic fight. That night, the battered, exhausted regiment slept among the dead, Cross writing, "The battle field was several miles in extent & in some places the rebel dead lay in two ranks, & in files, the most awful spectacle ever presented while the wounded strewing the earth at every step were fast dying for want of attention. O' it was a dreadful *dreadful* battlefield." Never a man to rest, the colonel was extremely active the day after the battle, working with Captain James Perry to recover two wounded Confederate officers, who were brother Masons. In addition, he attended to the burial of Lieutenant George Gay, "a brave and respected young officer," who was the first Fifth officer to die in combat. The colonel wrote, "I sat for a long time & held the hand of my young friend — hoping that he might yet evince some consciousness." Cross also made recommendations for promotions to those who distinguished themselves in the fight and used the battlefield to replace the equipment left behind on the Peninsula.

September 17, 1862, was an exhausting day for Cross and the Fifth and he was pleased to see it end, writing, "Gladly did we see the sun go down upon the field of battle & the dull clouds of war roll away to the west." The Battle of Antietam was the first major Union victory of the war in the East, prompting Lincoln, much to Cross' annoyance, to issue the preliminary Emancipation Proclamation on September 22. What Colonel Cross had feared most was now true. It was now a war to end slavery, not to kill off abolitionists, whose voices continued to grow stronger throughout the North.[20]

Beginning with brigade commander Caldwell and extending up to General McClellan, Cross' performance in the sunken road fight garnered widespread knowledge and respect from his superiors in the Army of the Potomac. Caldwell wrote, "Colonel Cross handled his regiment in the most admirable manner, and is entitled to the sole credit of detecting and frustrating the attempt of the enemy to turn our left flank. He displayed in a high degree all the qualities of a good commander— bravery, readiness, coolness, and skill." Division commander Hancock added that Cross' actions "handsomely frustrated" the Confederate flanking movement. Corps commander Sumner did not single out Cross, but mentioned, "I adopt and indorse all the subordinate reports." Even Rebel general Longstreet admitted to Cross' actions, adding him to a short list of Union and Confederate commanders who made "the best tactical moves at Antietam." In a military system without awards for individual bravery, with the praise of the commanding officer often being the most that one could ask for, Colonel Cross and the men of the Fifth New Hampshire earned their place in history at Antietam.[21]

An unidentified Fifth New Hampshire private. Scores of these young men idolized their colonel and died following his orders to never back down from a fight (Library of Congress).

While he received praise from his commanders, Cross was proud of his men's performance at Antietam, seeing it as proof that his hard work and determination in drilling the Fifth was worth the effort. Cross was a superb self-promoter of his own actions, never missing the opportunity to speak with a reporter. He hoped Henry Kent would bring the news to the attention of those in power in Concord. The colonel wrote, "This has been for the Rebels a Waterloo defeat. They struck the wrong crowd when they ran against my brave men." In a letter to Adjutant General Colby, he proudly wrote, "We whipped the rebels awfully. The Fifth saved Richardson's Division from being out flanked." For many, the Fifth's performance at Antietam was the defining moment of the regiment's career in the Army of the Potomac.

Despite the praise he had for his own men, Cross offered scorn to those he felt deserved it, writing. "Gen. Meagher was drunk as usual. Gen. Caldwell did not show himself either brave or skillful & he lost the confidence of his soldiers." While many cited Caldwell as being absent on the field, many considered Antietam to be Meagher's best battle, as he personally led the Irish in the vain attack against the Bloody Lane, he himself receiving a concussion falling from his horse. While the Irish did receive the bulk of the attention in the New York papers, Cross was pleased that his men finally received the praise the regiment was due.[22]

The Battle of Antietam proved to be the greatest day in Edward Cross' stellar military career. It was the only time he remained on the field with his regiment from start to finish. Under his direct leadership, the men were able to respond to the threats around them and defeat the enemy by fire and maneuver. Through direct inspiration, using textbook tactics, the Fifth was able to accomplish tasks that seemed impossible for so small a command. It was the day that Cross went from being the fairly competent commander of a regiment of New Hampshiremen to becoming the legendary colonel of one of the best infantry units in the Army of the Potomac, a regiment now called the "Fighting Fifth."

The image of Cross, a red handkerchief wrapped around his bleeding head, powder smeared on his face, and the regiment screaming loudly at the Confederates, would be remembered by many Fifth veterans as the greatest moment of their Civil War career, and they recounted scores of times at veteran's reunions at the Weirs, and Grand Army of the Republic encampments over the next six decades. Sergeant Hale remembered Antietam as "the most exciting battle of the war, for the Fifth New Hampshire Infantry."[23]

While his commanders lauded the colonel from New Hampshire, Cross did not extend any feelings to brigade commander John Caldwell. Although a native Mainer, Caldwell was not a professional and owed his position to seniority. On the Peninsula, Caldwell had managed to command the brigade during the Seven Days, but at Antietam his performance was dismal, not being in a position to direct his men during their attack on the sunken road. Many of the enlisted men in the Fifth felt betrayed by the lack of higher leadership in the fight, allowing their regiment to fight on alone and unsupported. General Richardson knew of his actions, but his death ended any threat of prosecution. While he could remove incompetence in his own regiment, Cross despised those in power who failed on the battlefield. Unwilling to serve under Caldwell any longer, he wrote a letter of resignation, sending a letter to brigade headquarters on September 27, 1862, stating, "In doing so I desire to state that I take this step because I am unwilling to serve under Brig. Gen. Caldwell, not having any confidence in his courage or capacity." The general held the resignation for two days before returning it to Cross, denying the request to resign, while the colonel, feeling his point was made, did not seek out Hancock's endorsement to leave the service. He believed that simply filing the charges against Caldwell would prove the point that he was not present on the line at Antietam.

To clear his name, Caldwell asked Hancock for a board of inquiry to review his actions at Antietam. The general asked his subordinate to specify the charges against him, but Cross refused, leaving three Second Corps generals, including Oliver Howard, to find a cause for the accusations. The board, after interviewing several members of the First Brigade, First Division, Second Corps, published their findings. Despite the fact that more than a few Second Corps soldiers wrote that Caldwell was hiding in the rear, no evidence of it was brought up in the inquiry. In addition, Cross did not testify before the board. Howard determined that "there is no evidence of Gen. Caldwell's lack of courage or capacity," finding that Cross' charges were without foundation. The board made no mention of Caldwell's conduct on the field, of staying behind, instead concluding that he had done the best that could have been asked in the sunken road fight. General Caldwell filed Cross' letter of resignation away in his desk, and the colonel never again made so bold a movement against those he declared to be incompetent. Caldwell retained command of the brigade, but the relationship with Cross was ever afterward strained.[24]

After the battle, as the Fifth moved into a camp at Harpers Ferry, Cross began to entertain the thought that his actions would earn him promotion. While the building of the Grapevine Bridge and Fair Oaks proved that he could function as a competent regimental commander, Antietam solidified his reputation. Many, including McClellan himself, gave him credit for saving the flank. To add to the situation, after recovering from a severe wound at Antietam, Colonel Francis Barlow of the Sixty-First New York, the man who found the weak spot in the Confederate line and breached the road, was promoted to brigadier and assigned command of a brigade in the Eleventh Corps. Compounding the matter for Cross was the fact that Barlow, while an excellent officer, was commissioned months after Cross, thus making him his junior. Cross had commanded a brigade in action at Fair Oaks. Barlow never had and now found himself wearing stars. The inability to gain advancement was a continued frustration with Cross throughout the rest of his career in the Army of the Potomac.

As usual, it was Kent back home in New Hampshire who received the brunt of Cross' criticisms and news from the front. It was Kent who persuaded Berry to give Cross command of the Fifth New Hampshire, but he could not assist in the quest for a star. Only President Abraham Lincoln could appoint him. Cross vented: "I begin to believe that hard work, hard times & danger don't amount to anything." In another rant, Cross told Kent he was seriously considering leaving the army: "I can get along without the service better than the service can get along without me! If I am not appointed I shall quit the service & go back to the Land of the Hidalgos." The threat was largely idle, as the colonel loved the dangerous and exciting life of a soldier, and had much at stake in remaining in the service, including his reputation and salary. The news that a promotion was coming spread to New Hampshire, with the *Statesman* reporting, "Col. Cross of the Fifth Regiment had one of his shoulder straps shot off at the battle of Antietam. It would be a good fashion in such cases to replace the lost decoration with that of the next higher rank."[25]

While he waited for his own promotion, Cross took notice of some promising individuals in his own regiment, rewarding them for their performance under fire with commissions and warrants. Of officers, he wrote, "Volunteer officers do not have that sense of military responsibility felt by regulars, and they require constant watching to remind them of their duty. I found it far more difficult to make officers than soldiers." For those who sought the colonel's recommendation, he gave it for those he felt warranted it; for others, he would not have his name associated with those who failed him and the men of the regiment. One Fifth officer recalled, "Social consideration had no weight in him when making promotions. His sole concern was to appoint those whom he thought the best fighters or disciplinarians." When First Lieutenant William Moore sought Cross' endorsement to receive a transfer into the Regular Army, the colonel instead rewarded him with a promotion to captain in the Fifth. When Company G lacked in discipline and drill after receiving additional recruits after Antietam, Lieutenant Charles Ballou, a native of Claremont, went from Company K to train Company G. Cross credited him with bringing the company back into shape. Many soldiers were proud to write home of the approbation they received from their colonel, as he rarely voiced his agreement with anything.[26]

After failing miserably as a company commander on the Peninsula, Captain Ira McL. Barton managed to gain a surgeon's certificate and resigned his commission to become a pension agent in Sullivan County. A young officer who owed his position to Republican patronage, he had somehow managed to stay in the regiment, even after the purging in early 1862. Barton wrote frequently to Captain Charles Hapgood, who returned to New Hampshire as well to recruit the Fifth's vacant ranks from an office in Rochester. Barton believed Hapgood hated the colonel as much as he himself did, often urging him to resign. To this, Hapgood, who remained stoic in his duty, wrote, "I do not feel as you do about the Col. I like him. I cant help it, you may call it *infatuation* or what you like. I am alive to his faults and am no apologist for them but since the Regt. left Concord I have had no reason to complain." Besides his affection for Cross, Hapgood also heard the rumors that the colonel was about to become a general, and hoped to obtain what would be the vacant majority.[27]

In camp at Harpers Ferry, the Fifth was able to reequip themselves after the harsh campaigns of that summer. One issue that the colonel would not tolerate was intoxication among the enlisted men, even while dealing with his own problems with the bottle. Dr. William Child saw the reaction that Cross' took: "The refractory conduct of some untamed specimen of a village rowdy or a drunken soldier sometimes seemed to unbalance him with rage, and then with the first weapon at hand he would strike without regard to the consequences." Child attributed Cross' reactions to the justice he saw on the frontier, where one had to act fast and strike quickly to prevent a minor problem from becoming a larger one. While the discipline was severe, it worked to prevent problems from occurring in the regiment, as many knew the consequences of misbehaving around the colonel. For Cross, his own addiction to the bottle was acceptable, but he would not allow others, including his officers, to act in the same manner as he did when intoxicated. When he drank, Cross became little more than a bully rather than the man idolized by his soldiers in battle.[28]

Cross often rewarded his men for their soldierly conduct and neatness by granting them reduced fatigue or guard duty and giving more to those who were not soldierly in their ways. One man Cross often excused was John Lynch, described as "an excellent soldier." Lynch became intoxicated one day while visiting the town of Harpers Ferry and walked across the pontoon bridge into Virginia, returning several days later. While in Virginia, Lynch joined the Regular cavalry, who did not know he was in the Fifth. Returning to Bolivar, the wayward private asked Cross for a discharge. Cross questioned Lynch, asking, "You want to ride — to join the cavalry?" "Yes, Colonel," was the reply. "Well I will arrange that," said the colonel, who made Lynch ride a wooden pole above the ground for two hours. Cross used punishment to reinforce discipline in the men, not to go absent without leave, and to remind them to whom their first duty was, the Fifth New Hampshire.[29]

After an electrifying performance at Antietam and after spending five weeks at Harpers Ferry recovering from the hard campaigns of the summer of 1862, the Fifth New Hampshire and the Army of the Potomac prepared to march south once again on October 28, 1862. This time they were heading back into the heart of Virginia to a city named Fredericksburg, where the tall colonel from New Hampshire hoped a star awaited him.

CHAPTER NINE

Marye's Heights

As God is my witness it seemed to my heart that it was a failure.—
COL. E.E. CROSS, DECEMBER 11, 1862

As the Fifth headed south, again into Virginia, through the Loudoun Valley, the men began, against strict orders from General Hancock, to forage liberally from the countryside. When some Fifth soldiers stole several sheep near Upperville, Cross and his staff shared a meal of mutton with Boscawen native and reporter Charles Coffin. After the meal, the farmer came by looking for evidence of the feast and wanting to search the Fifth's camp. To this, the colonel replied, "My soldiers are honest men. To allow you to do so would be an imputation upon their honesty. They come from the State of New Hampshire. It is a State that produces honest men and great men, the state of Daniel Webster and President Pierce. No, sir, you cannot go through my regiment." The farmer went to Hancock, who did not find the mutton but personally paid the farmer for seventy sheep.[1]

By the beginning of November, as many believed the Army of the Potomac was positioning to strike Lee, President Lincoln decided he finally had enough of McClellan's "slows" and removed him from command, placing Major General Ambrose Burnside in charge of the massive army driving south. A Democrat, Colonel Cross saw the removal of McClellan as yet another of the actions by Lincoln to prevent the army from winning the war. Cross considered the removal "ill-advised," believing McClellan was about to order his men to attack Lee at any moment, when in reality he was stumbling into Virginia without a plan. The Army of the Potomac lined the road to say farewell to their commander, who "carried the heart of the Army with him." Although he was a poor tactician, "Little Mac" inspired confidence in his men. For units like the Fifth New Hampshire, who had trained under him for a year and looked to him as the master of their cause, the news was a blow that many would never forget.[2]

Nine: Maryè's Heights

On the night of November 8, the Fifth spread out along a muddy road, with the officers barely trying to push their men along. Cross, who was still upset about the removal of McClellan, was outraged at the straggling and screamed, "Close up, you God damned hounds. Your company officers are not worth a damn." To prod the men along, Cross ordered his brother's Company K to the rear of the column to bayonet any man who did not quickly fall in. Captains James Larkin and James Perry became enraged that the colonel was pushing his men harder than he should and spoke aloud that they would no longer serve under Cross because of such harsh orders. The actions of Perry and Larkin, even if they were uttered under duress, and in the heat of the moment, was a major turning point in Cross' relationship with his commissioned officers. For over a year, the commander and his subordinates had endured a tumultuous relationship, with the colonel's violent temper and quickness at jumping to conclusions often hindering what should have been a respectful relationship between officers. That officers reacted in the manner that they did was a shock to Cross, who was determined to make examples of them to prevent a further spread of insubordination in the Fifth New Hampshire. Cross demanded the officers either apologize or face a court-martial. Seeing nothing wrong with their actions, the two captains appeared before a military panel, who acquitted them of mutiny.[3]

While Perry and Larkin underwent their ordeal with the colonel, the two officers, in coordination with others in the Fifth who were slighted by Cross, began to draw up court-martial charges against him. The thrill of ridding the Fifth of their colonel, who had caused much distress in Captain Larkin's life, was a moment he had been waiting for. The captain wrote, "Charges have gone in against him and if he has a trial he will be dismissed. I firmly believe he is cutting a big swath just now but he may get humbled if he gets his deserts." General Caldwell was pleased that the officers of the Fifth were taking action against Cross, but he believed the charges the officers filed would not be enough to have him dismissed from the army. Using the same articles of war that the officers of the Fifth were forced to memorize, they charged Colonel Cross with conduct unbecoming an officer and "conduct detrimental to good order and military discipline." The specifications included using "abusive language," ordering the men of Company K to bayonet stragglers, publicly stating that Caldwell was a coward at Antietam, ordering his men to forage for food, and ordering the destruction of private property. While not serious breaches of military discipline, they were, in a culture that valued respect and decency among military officers, a divergence from the normal behavior of a commissioned officer.[4]

Discovering the actions of his subordinates sent Cross into an outrage. During a visit from the paymaster, he attempted to have the pay of Captain

Larkin seized for absence without leave in front of the enemy by feigning illness on the way to Antietam, which prevented him from taking part in the Maryland Campaign. Larkin tried to talk calmly to the colonel, explaining that he really was sick in September, but Cross would not listen to him: "He got mad fairly boiled over he called me every thing he could lay his tongue to and then offered to tear up his commission and throw off his rank and go out and give me satisfaction." Knowing that his relief lay in a judge advocate pursuing the charges, Larkin remained cool, taking the abuse he was long used to suffering. He wrote, "I cant see much chance for his *highness* to stay long in the service." After the outrageous conduct displayed by Cross, Larkin was paid. But for unknown reasons, General Caldwell decided not to permit the charges against the colonel to proceed, allowing him to retain command of the Fifth New Hampshire. Cross believed that subordinates had to respect their commander, no matter what. He wanted the best material in his regiment and was vicious against those who would not comply with the parameters of military discipline; the result turned many, who praised him in combat, against him in camp.[5]

At the same time he dealt with problems with his company officers Cross had to rebuild his field and staff corps. Lieutenant Colonel Samuel Langley, who had been absent without leave for nearly three months, finally resigned in December. This opened up the majority and lieutenant colonelcy in the Fifth. While the logical solution was to promote Major Edward Sturtevant to wear the silver oak leaves, Cross demurred at first. Although Sturtevant was praised for his heroism leading the Fifth at White Oak Swamp and Malvern Hill during the Seven Days and in commanding the skirmish line at Antietam, Cross, for reasons known only to him, did not want Sturtevant, believing the man was happier being the Fifth's major. Although eager for promotion himself, Sturtevant would not accept a transfer out of the Fifth for higher rank. For his second in command, Cross believed that Major Josiah Stevens, who had resigned in July 1862 from the Second New Hampshire, would prove the best fit for the Fifth. "Owing to the small number of men in my Regt there is no particular need of filling the vacancy at present," wrote Cross. If Berry and the Council would not promote Stevens, then the colonel wanted Sturtevant for the position.

With Sturtevant promoted, the majority would also be vacant, which Cross wanted to fill with Captain John Murray of Company D. Though the Fifth's second ranking captain, Murray was a decorated Mexican War veteran, well established in the Portsmouth community, and performed ably and nobly at Fair Oaks, White Oak Swamp, and Antietam. Cross felt that the ranking captain, Horace Pierce, was a good soldier but was lazy and inattentive in his duties. For Cross, Sturtevant, and Murray, the promotions had to wait.[6]

As Burnside was waiting for his pontoon bridges to arrive to cross the river, the Army of Northern Virginia was not remaining idle. After losing over 12,000 men in the Maryland Campaign, Lee had rebuilt his army back to nearly 70,000 men to fight against Burnside's 100,000-man force. Knowing that the Federals would have to cross at Fredericksburg, the Confederate commander set out to build a series of impenetrable defensive points, via a series of hills and swamps in the rear of the city. On Marye's Heights, General James Longstreet, who in his memoirs praised Cross' actions in the Sunken Road fight at Antietam, positioned two battalions of artillery, totaling twenty-four guns, under Colonel E. Porter Alexander, a gifted artillerist. He placed the guns in a murderous position to enfilade the length of the entire Federal line. In front of his position was the Telegraph Road, which skirted the base of Marye's Heights. Years of use had eroded the road so it was now three feet below the base of the hill. In front, a four-foot high stone wall, allowing for a perfect defensive fire, reinforced the wall. Into this road was stationed a brigade of Georgians. Separating Marye's Heights and the city of Fredericksburg was a half mile wide plain that the Federals had to cross in order to reach the hill.

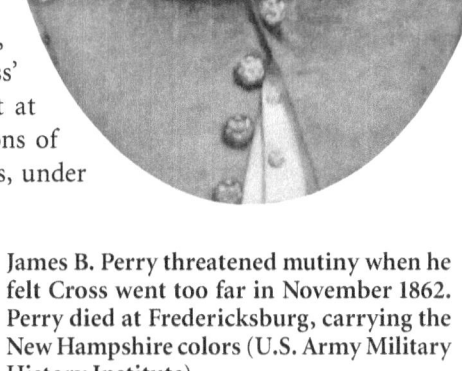

James B. Perry threatened mutiny when he felt Cross went too far in November 1862. Perry died at Fredericksburg, carrying the New Hampshire colors (U.S. Army Military History Institute).

The Confederates built their lines so well that they covered from all angles, and units could maneuver along the line as needed. Colonel Alexander said in reference to his defenses and the attackers, "Scarcely a chicken could live upon that field when we open up upon it." There was no other way to cross in front of Fredericksburg without a direct assault upon the hills and the fortifications. Cross took his field glasses and surveyed the Rebel fortifications that continued to strengthen daily, as Burnside waited for the pontoons. He believed that the army should attack the city further downstream, but upon receiving orders for the direct assault, the colonel was sickened: "As

God is my witness it seemed to my heart that it was a *failure*." Despite his own misgivings, Cross was a soldier and taught his men to obey orders without question, as he would have to do himself.[7]

For Cross the days of waiting at Falmouth proved long and wearisome. He was ill, and his wounds from Fair Oaks and Antietam bothered him. He knew at any moment his next battle could be his last. Perhaps in a deepened sense of foreboding, he prepared his will and arranged his personal papers. He did receive a welcome message from General Sumner, who "told me that he had written to Governor Berry respecting my appointment and also to the President," as Cross hoped for promotion. Because of a carbuncle, Captain Cross was relieved of duty, and Lieutenant Livermore became the acting quartermaster, placing Company K in the hands of Lieutenant Charles Ballou, who the younger Cross severely abused owing to a sharp rebuke from his brother. A welcome respite to the months of hard campaigning and his continued resentment over the removal of McClellan came to Cross on December 10, when a friend in the form of Murat Halstead, a fellow reporter from his days in Cincinnati, arrived at Falmouth to cover the battle. Halstead found Cross living in a small pine cabin covered with a canvas roof, with "a neat and spacious brick chimney, in which a cheerful fire crackled." The old friends talked about life in the army and the prospects of the old campaign before going to a party to celebrate the promotions of several men in the brigade. The experience relieved some of the tension that was beginning to develop as Burnside prepared to order the army forward against the city on December 11.[8]

Early on the morning of December 12, the First Brigade, including the Fifth, marched across the Rappahannock into Fredericksburg. Colonel Cross strained to keep up with his men, barely being able to walk, while having a deep foreboding of the coming events: "Some how I had an impression that I was to be killed or badly wounded, so I made my will, and an inventory of my property packed everything in my trunk, and gave the key to the chaplain. Although greatly prostrated by physical weakness, and my mind overshadowed by the sense that we were marching to disaster." An occasional cannon shot echoed off Marye's Heights as Cross allowed his men to gather tobacco, Cross doing his best to insure that they did not take part in the general looting of the city other Federal troops participated in. After suffering over a hundred casualties at Antietam, the Fifth was going into this fight with 249 riflemen and nineteen officers.[9]

On the morning of December 13, Lieutenant John Duren left the Fifth's camp at Falmouth to go across the river to issue rations and other last minute supplies to the regiment. The artillery on Marye's Heights began to open up immediately, dropping shells into the city as Cross ordered Duren back to the Fifth's camp and ordered his men into line to prepare for the assault. General Hancock called his regimental commanders together, giving them the plan of assault. The division would advance in lines of brigades, supporting each other to storm the hill. It was a simple yet dangerous plan, with the men marching in line of battle in the open under the full fire of the artillery on Marye's Heights to reach the stone wall. When Lieutenant Livermore, detached on quartermaster duty appeared, Cross chided his subordinate to go in with the Fifth, but Livermore demurred, carrying on with his official duties. Colonel Robert

Richard E. Cross was a competent company commander, but his drinking and his brother's death led to his dishonorable discharge from the service (U.S. Army Military History Institute).

Nugent of the Sixty-Ninth New York, who considered Cross "a good fellow and a very gallant soldier, even if a little profane at times," approached the colonel and asked him if he got to Richmond before the Irish Brigade to order dinner at the Spotswood house for the two of them. Cross replied, "in very strong and emphatic terms so and so, Nugent we are" [Cross swore a lot. Nugent wrote his account in the 1880s and used "so and so" as a substitute for Cross' swearing]. He caught a glimpse of General Meagher, who "addressed his troops one of those frothy, meaningless speeches peculiar to the man. There is not in the United States another such consummate humbug, charlatan, imposters, pretending to be a soldier as Thos Francis Meagher." Still an ardent nativist, Cross could not hold back his feelings of hatred for the Irish Brigade, who were to advance ahead of his men and had been dying by their side for the last year. Finally, at 12:30, Caldwell gave the order for his brigade to go in.[10]

Ahead of Caldwell's Brigade a half-mile wide-open plain separated them from their objective. Already the division's other two brigades went in and were slaughtered by the artillery fire and musketry, but some units continued until they were within fifty yards of the wall. Cross calmly stepped in front of his regiment and told his men in a loud, clear voice, "It was to be a bloody strife — to stand firm & fire low — to close on their colors — be steady." Caldwell ordered his men forward to storm the heights, as the Irish Brigade fell back. The regiment deployed into line of battle, crossed a small canal, and began the assault against the hill. Cross, in the center of the regiment, ordered his men forward at the run, shouting, as he limped along, "Forward men, forward!" Immediately the Washington Artillery opened up on the Fifth, killing Major Sturtevant.[11]

A piece of shell then struck in the center of the regiment, near the Color Guard wounding the colonel. Cross wrote, "A large fragment hit me on the breast, a smaller piece knocked out two of my teeth- & filled my mouth with sand." Still more pieces struck his forehead, eye, and hands. "I was knocked clean off my feet, & lay insensible until roused by a violent blow on the left leg." Stunned and with a mouthful of dirt and his own teeth, Cross began to grope around for his Colt revolver, a trusty friend he purchased in New York the year before that was always at his side. On his hands and knees spitting out the contents of his mouth, the colonel looked through the smoke as his regiment continued to advance. He tried to crawl to the rear, but finally resolved to lie on his back and await what he thought would be his death. The wound was believed to be mortal, and Cross' death was widely circulated in several New Hampshire papers.[12]

When Cross went down, his men continued to rush forward, obeying his orders to leave him on the field. With Major Sturtevant dead, a succession of captains led the Fifth. One after another was shot down, including Captain Perry, whose last words were that he had no ill feelings towards the colonel. The major, three captains, one first lieutenant, and three second lieutenants were killed, with ten more officers wounded in some form, in addition to scores of noncommissioned officers, destroying the Fifth's command structure. The national and New Hampshire flags were constant targets. As the bearers fell, others threw down their muskets to keep the banners aloft, only to meet death an instant later. Despite the murderous fire, the Fifth advanced into the firestorm, passing other Union troops who had halted and angling directly for the stone wall. Sergeant George Gove went down, carrying the New Hampshire colors and remembered: "When we got within 100 yds their musketry opened on us from the rifle pits. Then our line melted away like snow." Through the smoke, Cross, barely conscious, could faintly see the regiment as it approached the stone wall. The Fifth seemed to evaporate before his very eyes, finally stopping yards short of their objective, where those still able to function tried to fire at the entrenched enemy. Unlike the sunken road at Antietam, the Rebels at Fredericksburg stayed put. The regiment was close to its objective but could advance no further and pulled back to the safety of the Stratton house. Finally, at sunset, small groups of Fifth soldiers, leaderless and stunned from the slaughter, began retiring back to the city.[13]

With shells bursting around him and minie balls sloughing up the frozen ground, Cross placed his feet to the foe, covered his face with his hands and counted to one hundred to pass the time. In horror, he watched as a shell disemboweled a captain from another regiment who died by his side. He remembered the experience as "the most awful moments of my life." Regiments marched over him, and moments later ran over him in retreat. A spent ball struck his scabbard, stunning Cross who waited any moment for the end to come. Although helpless to stop it, the colonel was disgusted to see officers and men faking wounds to leave the field as the Rebels slaughtered his men. After three hours of lying on the battlefield, Lieutenant Daniel Cross, a cousin from Hanover who was serving on Caldwell's staff, found his injured relative and went to find a stretcher to bring him off the field. Lieutenant Francis Adams, who rode in the same ambulance with Cross after Fair Oaks, watched as three members of the Fifth brought him to the hospital on a stretcher. Adams, like many believed he was dead. At the same time, the lieutenant "noticed a number of the 5th New Hampshire loitering behind and plundering the dead."[14]

During the late afternoon, word reached the Fifth's camp across the river that the colonel was dead. Captain Cross, sitting by a fire, was calm and did not say anything, perhaps knowing that his brother was going to die in action one day. However, when told that Charles Ballou, his first lieutenant was dead, Dick Cross began to break down and cry, despite having argued and bullied Ballou since the Peninsula. Lieutenant Livermore wanted to find the colonel and rode back into Fredericksburg. Spotting a few survivors of the Fifth's charge, he found Cross, "crazed to some extent,"

Lieutenant Daniel K. Cross was a cousin of the colonel who spent most of the war on staff duty and rescued his kinsman from death at Fredericksburg (U.S. Army Military History Institute).

lying on a stretcher in a house. Cross, barely conscious, told the lieutenant to go out and rally the men, knowing the slaughter that had befallen his regiment in front of the wall.[15]

Captain Larkin, was the only surviving officer who crossed the river with the regiment and survived unscathed, brought the Fifth, numbering seventy men, back to Falmouth on December 14. A party brought the seriously wounded colonel back to the Fifth's camp, when a startled soldier said that the colonel was dead. Barely able to move, Cross raised his head and said, "Not by a damned sight." The spectacle of the shattered command was moving to all who witnessed it. Lieutenant Duren, who stayed behind with the supply train, wrote, "When they came on the field they were covered with mud and their faces black with powder and smoke. You could hardly recognize them and their ranks were thined out and many a soldier left his comrad on the battlefield never again to fill his place beside him in the ranks." Cross offered a written apology to Captain Larkin, praising him for his conduct in leading the remnant of the Fifth during the battle. Only a few days earlier, the two had been bitter enemies, and now they were "good friends."[16]

Fredericksburg destroyed the Fifth New Hampshire in the futile, desperate charge to capture Marye's Heights. The colonel praised his men, writing, "Allow me to state here the reason why the loss of my regiment was so heavy was, the men held their ground and endeavored to whop the enemy, instead of skulking or shamefully leaving the field. No soldiers on any battle-field ever exhibited greater bravery or devotion." Sergeant Rodney H. Ramsey wrote home a week after the engagement, describing the destruction brought on the Fifth: "The title of the Battle is Burnsides slaughter house! I shant tell you anything about the Battle only it was nearly a Balls Bluff and our army was badly whipped. We have no regiment now. Co g went in with 35 men 27 of them were killed or wounded." While his regiment lost heavily, Cross was justly proud that they, unlike many others, did not run, and instead continued to follow his order of "forward." The sight of the Fifth's charge garnered the regiment universal admiration, with one member of a Pennsylvania regiment recalling that the Fifth "maintained an excellent alignment" while Cross' command "seemingly disappeared entirely." The battle cost the Fifth New Hampshire fifty-seven dead and 123 wounded in some form, nearly 70 percent of those who went in.[17]

Cross first went to Washington, arriving on December 17, to begin his long recovery. His brother-in-law Dexter Chase went there to be with him. News of Cross' death was circulating in New Hampshire, being published in several papers and leading him to write to his father, Ephraim: "I am not as badly hurt as the papers say." Although writing he was not that injured, the colonel had indeed suffered from massive lacerations and loss of blood and was now missing several teeth. He hoped the wounds would grant him some time home in Concord, but the colonel decided not to go to Lancaster, as "the weather is too cold." Recovering as best as he could, he notified the governor of the disaster that befell the Fifth, urging him to send reinforcements and fill the promotions already waiting in the regiment.

Fredericksburg destroyed the officer corps of Cross' regiment. While it was the duty of the company officers to offer condolences for their subordinates, Cross took it upon himself to write to the families of Captains John Murray, William Adams Moore, and James Perry, all of whom died leading their companies against the stone wall. Despite his poor relationship with Perry, Cross offered a heartfelt message to his widow. The deaths of Murray and Moore affected him more deeply, as their loss represented valuable combat leadership that was irreplaceable. To Dr. Adams Moore, the captain's elderly father, Cross wrote, "No act of my life ever pained me more than to inform you as I did a few days since, by telegraph of the death of your brave son. I loved him for his brave and faithful spirit, his honorable ambition, his kindness and gentlemanly deportment. Deeply have I regretted the disastrous day which stripped my gallant regiment of its honest hearts." The news destroyed the doctor, who died a few months later.[18]

The death of Captain William Adams Moore, only twenty when he was killed at Fredericksburg, greatly affected Cross (author's collection).

The condolence letters to the families of these slain officers reveal the unique duality of Cross. He was a man who genuinely cared for some of those under his command, as seen in the letters to the Moore and Murray families. He deeply regretted the loss of these officers, as they were like sons to him, leading the companies he commanded. At the same time he could be caring and compassionate, one small act such as not saluting properly or making too much noise could cause him to be vicious and off balance to his subordinates. Many of the younger officers in the regiment who came up from the ranks, such as Moore, Livermore, Gove, and others, learned how to behave properly around Cross, holding their tongues and offering the respect his rank accorded. It was with many of the regiment's older officers, such as Larkin and Perry, that the colonel directed the bulk of his anger and aggression.

As in his previous battles, Cross' actions brought in praise from his commanders. Although the battle was a complete failure, the Fifth performed as well as expected under the circumstances, and, together with the Irish Brigade, left their dead closest to the stone wall. Again, General Hancock praised Cross as one of his best regimental commanders: "Colonel Edward E. Cross, severely wounded, behaved in the handsomest manner. The conduct of his regiment was heroic; refusing to yield any ground, his brave officers and men died where they stood." While the colonel often scorned General Caldwell as a poor, incompetent commander, the general offered nothing but praise for Cross yet again: "At the time of the action, he was suffering from an attack of chills and fever, which would have laid most men on their beds. He did not hesitate, however, to lead his noble regiment into battle, and was struck down, severely wounded, while at the head of his regiment, bravely leading his men forward." For the third time, Cross earned high remarks from his commanders, but he hoped this time their comments would lead somewhere besides of a report filed away in a desk.[19]

CHAPTER TEN

A Star

> As an act of justice, I ask that my case be considered and that I may be informed if there is anything against my character that may prevent my appointment.—COL. E.E. CROSS, MARCH 10, 1863

Although severely wounded with multiple lacerations and stunned from the shellfire around him, Cross, much as he had after Fair Oaks, seemed to make a miraculous recovery from the horrors of Fredericksburg, surviving injuries that would have killed others. First sent to a hospital in Washington on December 17 and then to Concord to recover, Cross pondered his chances for promotion to brigadier general. He first began to consider such a promotion shortly after building the Grapevine Bridge and Fair Oaks and he was positive that the Fifth's performance at Antietam would catch the notice of the generals and politicians. The heroic actions of the Fifth at Fredericksburg in nearly reaching the stone wall were sure to bring Cross his star. He firmly believed that, despite having alienated many politicians, he would rise in rank simply due to his actions on the battlefield.

At the time, each state had a certain allowance of appointments for general officers. In the winter of 1863, there was one vacancy for a brigadier general from New Hampshire based on seniority and experience; there were only two viable candidates from the Granite State, Cross and Colonel Gilman Marston of the Second New Hampshire. In May 1861, Marston, a Republican congressman, was placed in command of the regiment. Technically, he outranked Cross, receiving his commission two months before, and had led the regiment at Bull Run, where he received a painful wound. After that, Marston divided his time between his House seat, and the Second New Hampshire, again fighting on the Peninsula and at Second Manassas. He won reelection in 1862. Popular with his men, he was far from the lion that Cross was, and spent much of his time in Washington. Despite Marston's presence, Cross still had an excellent chance of obtaining the star from New Hampshire, based on his battlefield exploits. With only one prize to be awarded, Cross' supporters wrote passionate letters urging President Lincoln and others to nominate Cross for promotion. Even in the ranks of the Fifth, the rank and file knew what was occurring, with Sergeant George Gove writing, "He ought to have a star on his shoulder & would have if he would get the politicians to use their influence. He deserved it more than Marston."[1]

Two weeks after the battle, Major General Winfield Scott Hancock, commanding the First Division, Second Corps, began the process of trying to obtain a star for the colonel by sending two glowing letters of recommendation to the two Republican senators from New Hampshire, the men who could ensure a speedy passage of the promotion through the Senate confirmation process. Little did Hancock know that it was Cross' continued rants and personal vendetta against the politicians of New Hampshire, especially abolitionist John P. Hale, that had prevented his having received a recommendation already from these two men. To Senator Daniel Clarke, Hancock wrote descriptions of the Fifth's performance under his command: "I do not believe there is a better regiment in the world. These men are refined gold. I would trust that regt. now to hold a position that a new regiment of a thousand men would be driven from." He gave the reason for his conclusion as Colonel Cross' actions in disciplining, mentoring, and leading the regiment, ending with, "I consider that Col. Cross has made the regt. what it is. He should be promoted. 100 men is too small a command for him."[2]

The largest hurdle for Hancock to clear was Senator Hale, who was well aware of Cross' activities as a Democrat and his personal hatred against Hale. Hale had especially become infuriated at the colonel when he threw Captain Welch and Lieutenant David, two constituents, out of the regiment in March 1862. Hale's endorsement would prove critical to Cross' case; he had to be won over. In his letter to Hale, Hancock laid out many of the same facts about the Fifth that he wrote to Clarke and added, "If the government will promote such men, fill up, encourage, and cherish such regiments as his we can subdue the South and put down this Rebellion." Hancock sent the letters to Washington, while writing to the recovering colonel that he believed a promotion would quickly be forthcoming.[3]

With General Hancock's recommendations in hand, Cross knew he had to work hard in New Hampshire to secure additional testimonials for his skill and demeanor in order to be promoted to a higher command. He was able to receive endorsements for the promotion from the generals he had both admired and scorned. George B. McClellan, Ambrose E. Burnside, Edwin Sumner, Silas Casey, Darius Couch, Israel B. Richardson, John Sedgwick, William French, Joseph Hooker, Oliver O. Howard, John C. Caldwell, and Hancock had all, at one time or another, given their endorsement for Cross' promotion. Recommendations such as those from Hancock, Howard, Sedgwick, and other generals known for their actions on the battlefield and their work with the administration would help his cause. However, those of McClellan and Burnside, two failed commanders, were not as powerful as they once had been. A leading Democrat and failed general, McClellan had fallen from favor with the Lincoln administration, and Cross' continued attachment to him was suspicious. General Casey, the army's master of tactics whose corps the Grapevine Bridge had saved at Fair Oaks, wrote: "He would make a good brigadier general." In addition to the general's endorsement, several senior officers from the First Division who served with the colonel and knew his performance under fire added theirs as well.[4]

Winfield Scott Hancock was Cross' most vocal supporter and tried desperately to obtain a star for the colonel (Library of Congress).

Although he had the endorsements needed from the commanders in the field, Cross lacked one important factor, support from the politicians at home. In his outbursts and actions, the colonel had alienated nearly every Republican leader in New Hampshire, except perhaps his friend Henry Kent. The men who held power in the state knew of Cross' deeply held feelings of disgust and anger towards the Lincoln administration, and his disdain for the policies of abolition and emancipation. The colonel was suspicious, writing to Franklin Pierce, "I find that everything I said or done as a democrat is known." Although Cross was an excellent regimental leader, and might prove so as a brigadier general as well, being a general carried additional weight of persuasion and power to command. Those in power could forgive some of the actions such as his anger and fights with subordinates, but the colonel had to support the policies of the Lincoln administration to gain promotion. The president, much like Governor Berry, was no longer in a position to promote men to win support from the Democrats. Candidates not only had to be competent military men, they also had to support the policies they were fighting for, namely abolition. Even with his promotion on the line, the colonel still did not believe in the "malice of niggerism."[5]

Those who held the key to Cross' future were divided. He could not be denied a promotion because of his actions on the battlefield, which had garnered nationwide attention, especially at Antietam where the Fifth saved the First Division from being flanked. No one could deny that Cross earned his star there. However, some Republicans believed he was a Copperhead, a northern Democrat who supported the Confederacy. This thought was absurd, as the colonel gave his all in his battles and hated the Confederacy as much as, if not more than, blacks and the Irish. Finally, the Republicans reached a compromise, which they presented to Cross as he recovered in Concord. "If he would only forswear his political opinions and throw his personal influence into the same scale with the Administration," a promotion would be forthcoming. The colonel knew this was his chance and relented.

On January 1, 1863, still weak from his wounds, Cross went to the Republican state convention in Concord that led to the nomination of Joseph Gilmore as the Republican candidate for governor. Gilmore pledged to stand by President Lincoln in this dark time. Amid repeated cheers, he pledged continued support for the war effort and promised that New Hampshire would prosecute the rebellion to the utmost. The blood-stained, battle-torn colors of the Fifth that Cross brought back to Concord in order to receive a replacement set decorated the podium. After Gilmore's speech, it was Cross' turn to address the audience. Widely cheered by the crowd, which included most of the Republican leadership in the state, the colonel insisted the applause was for his men, not him. Knowing he had to hold his tongue, Cross gave a history of the Fifth, as told by the battles inscribed on the national colors. He said, "Those men have carried the flags you see there in front of every fight. They have never, on any field, moved, except toward the enemy, and those flags have never been trailed in dishonor." As he went on, his chest wound began to grow painful, causing him to stop occasionally. Cross would not publicly nominate any Republican candidates, instead ending with, "Gentlemen, I can only thank you for your kindness, and hope that whatever candidates are elected may prove an honor to the State and to the government."[6]

With Cross now somewhat on the Republican side, at least by attending the convention, New Hampshire's congressional delegation finally gave the colonel the endorsements he had been seeking for so long. John W. Foney, the secretary of the Senate, penned a letter to President Lincoln summarizing the battles and wounds Cross received in action, adding, "He is accomplished, and loyal. If his is not a strong case, I do not know one. At any rate I hope my word in favor of Col Cross will not weaken it." Two state representatives endorsed the letter as well as congressman Edward H. Rollins, who added, "I hope that Col Cross may be appointed Brig. Gen." A general and former Republican congressman from Illinois, John F. Farnsworth, added in his own letter, "I have known him + his regiment *well* for more than one year and *do know* that he is one of the *best* officers, and his regiment one of the *best* regiments in the service." A friend from his Arizona days, now New Mexico congressman John S. Watts, added, "His service in the field and his energy and personal courage eminently qualify him for such promotion." Prominently missing among the written endorsements was that of Senator Hale. However, with the ones that he had from the Republican leaders, combined with those from his commanders, Cross felt he would soon have his star. Cross packaged the letters together and added his own to Secretary of War Edwin Stanton: "I ask that my case may be considered, and that I may be informed if there is anything against my character that may prevent my appointment."[7]

While Cross received several important endorsements in his quest for promotion, one that he did not receive was from Governor Nathaniel Berry. Since receiving his commission, Cross had written dozens of letters to the governor and the adjutant general with a constant stream of rants, requests, complaints, and concerns regarding the Fifth New Hampshire. While Berry could not revoke Cross' commission simply because of the discourse between them, he could withhold a letter to President Lincoln. With the Republicans losing ground due to a vocal antiwar sentiment in the Granite State, many saw Cross as a member of the hated opposition, those who opposed the principals of abolition and freedom. To promote such a man would only add fire to the Democratic cause, already burning bright in northern New Hampshire. In addition to this, Berry's constituents were growing restless about the war. In towns such as Croydon, Grafton, and Holderness, scores of young men were dead serving in the ranks of the Fifth. The colonel was somewhat responsible for those deaths because of his persistence in not backing down in a fight. To a confidant, Berry gave his feelings towards Cross by stating, "So profane a man ought not to be entrusted with a larger command."[8]

At the same time the generals and politicians, perhaps begrudgingly, gave Cross their endorsement for promotion, the men of the Fifth tried to add their voices. In a letter to the *Independent Democrat,* three former noncommissioned officers from Company A sent a long letter to the paper listing their experiences with Cross under fire at Fair Oaks and Antietam and his credentials for promotion: "Whatever charges his enemies may bring against him they cannot bring that of *cowardice.* A better man to look after the welfare of his men never wore the eagles. — Every man under him was expected to perform the full duties of a soldier. If they did this nothing more was required of them. Were we to enlist for a score more of times we should under Col. Cross each time." The bond between Cross and the men of the Fifth was tested under fire and each time the men of the Fifth came to realize that, although Cross was oftentimes a pusher in camp and on the drill field, demanding perfection, it was necessary. The attention to detail more than paid off under fire, where his direct inspiration and leadership was enough to hold the regiment together under tremendous pressure.[9]

In Concord, Cross backfilled the promotions of the line officers in the Fifth, and he was able to fill the vacant lieutenant colonelcy and majority. Governor Berry wanted Captain Charles Long, a Fifth veteran wounded at Antietam and now the lieutenant colonel of the almost defunct Seventeenth New Hampshire, to fill the position, but, still heeding his promise to allow Cross to select his own officers, Long was passed over, and Captain Charles Hapgood was promoted. The promotion of Hapgood, despite his being the Fifth's senior captain, raised many eyebrows. While performing credibly in his only battle at Fair Oaks, he fell ill on the Peninsula and went home to recruit, thus missing Antietam and Fredericksburg. Despite his service in one battle, and having no prior experience commanding a battalion, he was now the Fifth's second in command. Captain James Larkin wrote, "That is the way they do things in N.H. the ones that are at home the most get the best offices." While Hapgood earned his promotion strictly through seniority, the awarding of the vacant majority was yet another concern to the officers of the Fifth.

Another engraving, this one of a worn-down Colonel Cross showing the effects of three battles and his constant battle with the administration (courtesy Lancaster Historical Society).

Colonel Cross nominated and received a commission for his brother Richard. The younger Cross was similar to, and different from, his brother. He was a competent officer while under fire, but he did not raise the same amount of inspiration in his men as the colonel did. He was bullish at times, especially rough on his first lieutenant, Charles Ballou, who died at Fredericksburg, and his drinking raised some concern, including several public incidents where his older brother disciplined him. Most of the time, he was allowed to carry on because he was the brother of the regiment's commander. With many officers wanting to leave the horrors of the Falmouth camp for a brief furlough at home, Richard Cross, without suffering any major illness, managed to receive a surgeon's certificate through fellow Lancaster resident Dr. Bucknam to go home for twenty days. Captain Larkin referred to him as "the old scoundrel." Captain Welcome Crafts, who also competed for the promotion, wrote, "Cross is incompetent, intemperate, and wholly unworthy. He is a ranting McClellanite and copperhead." Although now a senior officer, Major Cross owed his position solely to his brother's influence.[10]

In Concord, Edward Cross became acquainted with former president Franklin Pierce, a Democrat who shared the same feelings towards the Lincoln administration. Cross saw Pierce as a military, rather than a civilian, leader and always referred to him as "general," rather than "president." Before leaving for the front, the colonel, still weak from his wounds spent some time in Concord visiting with Henry Kent. His long months of recruiting New Hampshire soldiers for other regiments finally paid off in the fall of 1862, when Berry transferred him to command the new Seventeenth New Hampshire, a nine-month regiment. Kent and his officers, including Charles Long of the Fifth recovered from his Antietam wounds, did yeoman's work in recruiting a full regiment from northern New Hampshire. Unfortunately, for Kent and his officers, the government drafted the vast majority of the men recruited for the Seventeenth to fill vacancies in the Fifteenth and Sixteenth New Hampshire regiments, leaving some 300 men in camp. Cross inspected the regiment and shared his enthusiasm for Kent's command, which unfortunately never fought as a regiment. With his business in Concord over, his furlough expired but his wounds still causing him pain, Colonel Cross left his home state for the last time in early February 1863.[11]

Still severely pained from his injuries, Cross managed to gain additional time on his furlough and spent it in Boston with the Babcock family. During his summer recovery in Lancaster, the colonel became acquainted with the two daughters of a minister, calling them "educated refined & smart." Unable to move for a week, Cross passed his time with the family at Jamaica Plains, hoping to "prospect the diggings." The colonel greatly enjoyed the companionship of women, continuing to write and send them photographs of himself in uniform. He had decided long ago, however, not to "settle down" and marry as Henry Kent had done. The colonel was not willing to trade his adventurous and often uprooted way of life, moving from place to place as his circumstances changed. As a lifelong wanderer, he was not content to stay in one place for a long time and preferred to pay prostitutes rather than form lasting relationships. Despite frequenting brothels in Cincinnati and Philadelphia, he produced no known dependents and saw his mother as the sole beneficiary of his estate.[12]

Colonel Cross' actions in the Battles of Fair Oaks, Antietam, and Fredericksburg, the wounds he suffered, and the weeks of campaigning for a promotion finally came to a decision point on the morning of March 11, 1863. Meeting with Senator John Hale, a man he had hated since his twenties for his antislavery beliefs and continued to agitate against even while a senior officer in the army, Cross hoped would finally give him the assistance he needed. Although the two men were on radically different platforms, it was now clear that Cross, after accomplishing so much, could not be denied his promotion. All he needed was the support of President Lincoln and a Senate confirmation, and Cross would be a brigadier general. That morning, Hale and Cross went to the White House, and the colonel pled his case before the president, who was known for his leniency and generosity. During the brief meeting Lincoln noted, "The Col. says he is the senior Colonel of the A.P. He has been in several battles, has been nine times hit, and appeals to his military record." Cross felt confident at the conclusion of the meeting, believing that Hale's support would finally lead to his promotion. Lincoln promised Cross his star and reassignment as the military governor of the new territory of Arizona. The president forwarded the note to Secretary of War Stanton, never mentioning what he had told Cross, and never saw the colonel again. Indeed, the president never forwarded Cross' name to the Senate for confirmation, instead nominating Marston as the new brigadier from New Hampshire, who was speedily confirmed and awarded the rank rather than Cross.[13]

While the battered remnant of the Fifth New Hampshire struggled to survive the harsh, diseased-filled conditions at Falmouth, many soldiers in Cross' regiment worried deeply about their commander. Having been under his command since September of 1861, most now realized that Cross was the sole reason why their regiment was able to function as it did. When Burnside proposed to advance on Fredericksburg again in January 1863, only to be stopped by heavy rains, the Fifth faced the reality of going into battle for the first time without Cross to lead them. This led Corporal Miles Peabody to write, "This Regt. feels rather down hearted at the prospect, many of them say that they will not go into another fight." The shirkers and cowards had left the regiment through battle, disease, and the colonel himself. The small number of men who remained believed that their unit was the best in the army and they could handle anything the Confederacy threw at them. Cross' absence from the regiment was keenly felt in the ranks, leading recently promoted Lieutenant August Sanborn to write, "I sapose that he will be back here before a grate while but if I was in his place and had ban hit so many times as he was I wood never com back unless they gave me a nice place the Col for if there is a man in this army that is wonting of it is Col Cross but I don't know what we should do with out him for to look out for ous." One Fifth sergeant who countered Sanborn wrote, "Cross was anything but a lovable man except to those who liked things hot."[14]

Even Captain Larkin, who commanded half of the regiment through some of the winter, missed the colonel. While they had argued and fought over pay and came into conflict prior to the battle, Fredericksburg had solidified the bond between the two men. Cross respected Larkin's ability to handle the remnant of the Fifth in action, while the captain looked up to the colonel as a proven combat leader without whom the regiment seemed to break down. Larkin wrote, "The Col. stands higher with the regiment now than he ever did before he was cool and brave." With Cross recovering in Concord, Larkin received word that Cross had visited Larkin's wife, Jenny, and their two children. The captain wanted to receive the coveted position of recruiting officer for the regiment, allowing him to be at home with his family. Cross promised Jenny Larkin her husband would receive the assignment, but the captain knew better: "I hope you know enough of him not to have believed it. You can't place any more confidence in his word than in the wind. He always has some fine story for every one and that is the last of it."[15]

Lieutenant August Sanborn, like many in the regiment, worried about the effect Cross' long absences had on the Fifth (U.S. Army Military History Institute).

Cross' continued absence from the Fifth gave rise to a serious rumor in the Fifth's camp. Knowing that the colonel had spent considerable time before the war in Arizona and that the area was finally granted separate territorial status from New Mexico, some soldiers began to speculate that Cross and the

Fifth would receive a transfer out of the Army of the Potomac to garrison the frontier. The very thought of it raised some spirits in the hopes that Colonel Cross would once again contribute to the welfare of his men. Corporal Peabody wrote, "Very likely we shall go with him and spend the rest of our time there. I had rather do that than to remain here for we shall not have so much fighting to do there. And I think we have done our share of that." Unfortunately for Peabody, and the regiment, the light duty never came.[16]

With Burnside defeated at Fredericksburg, Lincoln again took action in January 1862, replacing him with Joseph Hooker, a "fighting" general who had done well as a division commander on the Peninsula and was wounded as a corps commander at Antietam. Hooker immediately took command and tried to raise his men's sagging morale. Sixty-five-year-old General Bull Sumner retired as commander of the Second Corps, replaced by the very capable and competent General Darius Couch. Throughout the army, the men welcomed the changes, hoping it would bring victory in the spring campaign. General Hancock retained command of the division, while Caldwell, who still struggled with the rumors that he had been absent at Antietam, retained the brigade.[17]

At Falmouth, with only 150 men able to bear arms, many of them hoped that Hapgood and Major Cross would be able to secure a furlough for the Fifth's return to New Hampshire to recruit its ranks. This would have been welcome news to those who hoped to return home after so much bloodshed. But instead of forwarding men to the unit, the state continued to raise new regiments rather than fill up the veteran regiments. Many of the regiments, like the Fifth, were well below half strength. Although Governor Berry, serving out his last few months in office promised the men he would bring them home, the truth was different. The Second New Hampshire, Marston's Republican regiment went home earlier that winter to recruit, while the Fifth, a solidly Democratic regiment under a Democratic colonel, did not go home to regain its strength. Instead, the few recruits from New Hampshire went to those units that proved loyal to the Republican Party.[18]

As the ground began to thaw and spring arrived in Virginia, to those who had survived the drudgery of the Falmouth camp it was apparent that they would once more be under the command of the man who had led them into action before. However, it was now apparent that Edward Cross would continue to wear the eagles of a colonel rather than the stars of a brigadier general.

CHAPTER ELEVEN

Hooker's Campaign

Hooker has not the amount of brains necessary to manage a vast army. — COL. E.E. CROSS, MAY 1863

Two weeks after meeting with Lincoln, Cross was back in camp at Falmouth, still suffering from his wounds but ready to rejoin the army. With the realization that the eagles on his shoulders would not give way to stars, despite Lincoln's promise, Colonel Cross knew he was bound to return to command his regiment instead of a brigade. For all his zeal and dedication shown to the Union cause, sustaining wounds in every battle he had been in, he now realized that despite all the letters of recommendation from generals and politicians, and meeting with two of the men he hated the most, he would not be receiving anything from the government. Sergeant Gove noticed: "He looks poor but is as gritty as ever. He ought to be a Brig Gen." While most men would resign their commission in the face of such wounds and daunting odds, Cross decided to soldier on and remain with the Fifth. His firmly held belief in the idea of union, that the United States had to endure as a nation no matter what the cost, combined with the fact that he had already given so much of himself to the cause meant that he would stay in the service.[1]

The fact that a promotion was not coming severely upset Cross; Lincoln was a man of his word, and had broken a promise to the colonel. In another ranting letter to former President Pierce in Concord, Cross wrote that he had received notification of the promotion and orders to report to Arizona. A few days later, the War Department countermanded them. Cross believed the reason was the death of General Edwin Sumner, one of his greatest supporters and a man of some influence with the Lincoln administration. The colonel wrote, "This hope kept me in the service, together with the natural reluctance which a commander feels to leave the tried, true, & brave men of his command, who have so nobly acquitted themselves in this war." Adding fuel to Cross' fire was the fact that several of Lincoln's nominations included colonels

Cross had accused of rape, drunkenness, and incompetence. Cross felt they were promoted simply because they "cover their deficiencies with the cloak of Abolitionism." He firmly believed there were spies in the service whose sole purpose was to report on him and others who opposed the administration to those in power. These men went on to higher command because of their support of the administration, while Cross retained command of his regiment. He was not the only superb regimental commander to find promotions elusive. Other excellent colonels, such as H. Boyd McKeen and Zenas R. Bliss, remained colonels as well. Cross was one of many who were slighted by the administration or had their record overlooked.

Perhaps most infuriating to Colonel Cross at the time besides not gaining promotion was a rumored order that would require the mustering out of all surplus officers in regiments mustering under 500 men, which would include most of those in the Fifth, thus consolidating it with another New Hampshire unit. He felt this order would destroy the morale of the army, calling it "one of the most *insane* & foolish ideas that could be entertained at this time. We should have another lot of armed *mobs* for the next year to secure defeat & disgrace." Much as he had during the previous year, Cross continued to press the adjutant general to forward recruits to the Fifth and the other veteran regiments in the field rather than create new commands. President Pierce listened attentively to Cross' ranting comments but could do little to influence the situation, as many in the North saw Pierce as a southern sympathizer. In many of his private writings, Cross asked the recipient to keep the letter private, but on occasion the content became public.[2]

Without the responsibility of higher command, the colonel continued to work hard, trying to improve the conditions in camp, drilling what few recruits came to the regiment, and supervising a new crop of officers promoted to replace the

Dr. William Child respected Cross as an officer and stood by, helpless to act, as he died (U.S. Army Military History Institute).

eight lost at Fredericksburg and others through resignation that winter. Unlike the year before, when he cast those he felt incompetent from the regiment and suffering severely for it, this time the promotions came without problem to young sergeants and corporals who had proved themselves in the 1862 campaigns and now became commissioned officers. Many of these men viewed their colonel as a larger than life figure who was the heart of their regiment. Although somewhat ill, Lieutenant Charles Trask wrote "the Col. is all right," despite walking on occasion with a cane. Captain Larkin was pleased to see the colonel back in camp, especially since he seemed to forget the trouble between the two of them prior to Fredericksburg, as he brought the regiment back into line. "Col. Cross seemed glad to see me he has been as nice as a pin since he got back."[3]

While the Fifth slacked somewhat under Hapgood, Cross' presence in camp had an immediate effect upon the officers and men. "He displayed his authority in a striking way, which showed how strict his ideas of discipline were." The colonel insured noncommissioned officers knew their duties; close order drill and the manual of arms became perfected. The commissioned officers of the Fifth New Hampshire, who had survived over a year under Cross' command, decided that winter to show their appreciation for Colonel Cross by taking up a collection for an ornate dress sword, watch, spurs, and belt for the colonel. Manufactured by Tiffany, the watch arrived at Falmouth as Cross returned to the regiment. The sword, which featured an eagle on the pommel, Cross' own motto of "Steady and Fire Low," and the battles he led his men through, was on back order and never arrived. The gifts were not designed to gain favor from the colonel, rather they served as a testament to the respect the surviving officers had for Cross. Despite the harshness he sometimes exhibited towards them, they viewed the thirty-one-year-old Cross as the father of their regiment.[4]

After a demoralizing, disease-filled winter at Falmouth, the Fifth New Hampshire was a small but veteran regiment of 200 men. The reduced numbers worried the colonel, who pleaded with Governor Berry to let him come home and raise men for the Fifth: "We have hard service, more so than any Rg't from the state. We are worn down — we feel entitled to a little rest." Despite the calls for support, no reinforcements were coming to the regiment. Cross had again instituted schools for the many new officers, sergeants, and corporals, who would be leading men into combat for the first time, paying particular attention to the basics of close-order drill and loading. With new officers, and a renewed spirit with their colonel finally back in camp, many of the men hoped this time the Federals would prevail.[5]

In the last days of April 1863, General Joseph Hooker began his long awaited campaign, each man carrying over thirty pounds of equipment. The bulk of the Army of the Potomac, including Cross' men, marched west, while a smaller force decoyed the Rebels in front of Fredericksburg. The Federals hoped to catch Lee off guard by marching up the Rappahannock River and then crossing the river. Deploying in the open, they would use their superior numbers to outmaneuver and destroy Lee's army. The plan worked until May 1, when Hooker suddenly stopped.[6]

For this campaign, General Hancock appointed Cross to command a Fifth Brigade in the First Division. Hancock allowed the colonel to select the regiments he wanted to lead. Cross picked the Fifth New Hampshire, Eighty-First Pennsylvania, and Eighty-Eighth New York, which although an Irish Brigade unit was a crack outfit. The vital task given to these men was to move in advance of the rest of the army, securing hamlets and crossroads to prevent Lee from knowing the Federals were advancing. It was a mission normally relegated to cavalry, but Hooker sent his troopers on a raid to the south.

Leaving at 9:00 on the morning of April 28, the regiments went into camp near the U.S. Ford on the Rappahannock. Captain Alexander Moore of Hooker's staff personally escorted Cross' men, posting them at every house, crossroad, and business along the route to insure that none of the southerners informed the Confederates that the Federals were advancing. The soldiers of the Fifth promptly went to work picketing the area, and helping to lay a corduroy road to assist the artillery in gaining access to the ford. No Rebels were encountered, but the colonel kept his men alert, preparing for the unknown as the rest of the Army of the Potomac crossed further upstream at Kelly's Ford, trying to outflank Lee.[7]

Cross promoted Charles Hapgood to lieutenant colonel following Fredericksburg, and Hapgood led the Fifth at Chancellorsville and Gettysburg (U.S. Army Military History Institute).

After marching up the Rappahannock, the Army of the Potomac arrived and dug in around a small hamlet called Chancellorsville, some ten miles west of Fredericksburg.

Hooker received reports that Lee had left the city and was rapidly approaching his forces. On the morning of May 1, Hancock called Cross' Fifth Brigade up from the U.S. Ford and ordered them to deploy to a reserve position to support the rest of the First Division. Although always one to want to fight on open ground, face to face with the enemy, Cross heeded his commander's advice and ordered the brigade to dig in. The Wilderness, a large tangle of undergrowth, was the primary feature of the Chancellorsville battlefield, with occasional large meadows interrupting the landscape, making it difficult for the Federals to gain the advantage with their superior numbers. With the initiative lost, Robert E. Lee was ready to risk the largest gamble of his military career by dividing his forces in three parts and sending the bulk of the Army of Northern Virginia on a wide flanking move to the west to strike the Eleventh Corps on the exposed Federal left. Lee planned for an attack on the afternoon of May 2, 1863.[8]

The Confederates hit the Union flank, sending thousands of Federal soldiers fleeing for their lives. The Eleventh Corps and then the Third Corps buckled and ran under extreme pressure, leading to over 300 casualties in the Twelfth New Hampshire alone as small pockets tried in vain to slow the Rebel advance. Thousands of scared Union soldiers ran towards the Second Corps position near Chancellorsville as Hancock did the best he could to rally the line and prevent the escape. As Jackson's men pushed from the left, Lee took command of the forces in front of the Army of the Potomac, moving artillery and two divisions into place as part of the coordinated attack to destroy the Army of the Potomac. Hancock spotted the fresh men of Cross' Brigade and instructed them to "put backbone into the Eleventh Corps" and fix bayonets in an attempt to stop the flight, but the panicked men continued to run. Ever quick to distinguish among ethnicities, Cross wrote, "The cowardice of the German troops was ludicrous. They hid in the woods—forced their way into our rifle pits. In fact, they seemed half scared to death." Several companies of the Fifth went forward on the skirmish line and engaged in a long-range firefight with the Rebels before being called back to the entrenchments by Cross. Both sides halted late in the evening of May 2, preparing for the fighting to come the next morning.[9]

By the morning of May 3, Confederate forces gained the advantage, pushing the Union forces into a tight ring around Chancellorsville. As the fighting intensified, Hancock called upon Cross' Brigade to act as the division reserve, as it was brought into combat near the Chancellor house. The Confederates managed to capture the high ground at Hazel Grove, moving artillery batteries into position that began shelling the panic-stricken Union soldiers, who tried to dig in as best as they could. Dr. Child, who was nearby Cross attending to the wounded, recalled, "The bullets rattled like hail in the oak trees. I assure you it was not very pleasant being there." Caldwell, still in command of the old First Brigade, struggled as the Confederates pressed the line, losing scores of his men as prisoners of war. Seeing additional reinforcements coming from the Confederate line, Hancock called on Cross to deploy his small brigade on the left of the Second Corps line, directly across from the Chancellor House, and tie into the already hard-pressed Twelfth Corps. For the men who survived the shelling at Fredericksburg, many considered this the worst fire they experienced in the war; they struggled to use shovels, cups, and hands to protect themselves from the incessant shelling coming from three directions. To show inspiration to his men, Cross calmly strode the length of the line as the shells crashed in, giving words of encouragement to the men.[10]

As the bombardment continued, Hooker was stunned by a shell fragment and rendered insensible; he decided to fall back instead of fight. A Second Corps officer recalled, "The Chancellorsville plateau was now a hell of fire — shot screaming over it from every division but the northeast; the house itself in flames; yet Hancock's Division alone stood." Hancock's First Division had the most dangerous task on the line; they were the rear guard of the Army of the Potomac. "Colonel Cross' brigade was given the arduous and desperate duty of holding the enemy in check at Chancellorsville," noted Captain Livermore. The artillery duel from Hazel Grove continued unabated, with the occasional shell striking a member of the Fifth. Cross called it "a terrible storm of shot and shell." The hope of victory against the Rebels died in the woods near Chancellorsville. Disgusted by Hooker's timid generalship in not attacking earlier against superior numbers, Cross wrote in a private letter, "Hooker has not the amount of brains necessary to manage a vast army." He finally decided that the battle was lost for the Union. Taking a cracker board for a desk, he sat down near the Fifth as the shells exploded and wrote his battle report under fire, taking note of the events of the past few days. Cross praised his men, being careful not to voice his opinions of incompetence to the high command in an official document.[11]

Because the men of the Fifth followed their officer's orders, they remained in position as the rest of the line collapsed. As others fell back, the Fifth continued to engage the Rebels, but it was a losing fight. Hancock sent a messenger to Cross and asked why the Fifth was running, mistaking other men for Cross' regiment. Outraged at the accusation, Cross sent a Fifth officer back to the general, with orders to "tell General Hancock, by God, sir, my regiment never runs." General Couch, the Second Corps commander, hurried along the line, bringing up batteries and tightening the position around Chancellorsville. As he brought up another battery, Couch noticed the men of Cross' Brigade and wrote, "The gallant Colonel Cross, of the Fifth New Hampshire, and his command claim my admiration." By 10:00 on the morning of

Eleven: Hooker's Campaign 143

May 3, 1863, the situation was desperate for Hancock's Division, the last large body of Federals still holding onto their position. Assaulted from three sides, the men grudgingly began to lose ground as the enemy advanced even closer.

With the Rebels only 200 yards away, Cross' men continued to engage, quickly going through the 120 rounds each man brought into the fray. "For about 40 minutes my command was under the heaviest fire it ever experienced," recalled the colonel. Captain Livermore became dejected and said to his commander, "I wish we were out of the business." Cross corrected his young subordinate, telling him not to express such opinions, as they would eventually defeat the enemy. Livermore later recalled, "It did me good then and I think it did afterwards, and it was the same spirit that he infused into the regiment." To inspire his men, Cross wrapped his red handkerchief around his head and fired a Parrott rifle at the advancing Rebels, sending a shell into their ranks. Dr. Child watched: "The Col. amid a perfect storm of shell went alone loaded and fired one of the guns. He is perfectly cool in battle, though he will 'dodge' a shell as well as myself." As he was about to order men to operate the battery, Hancock ordered Cross' Brigade, the last Union troops still on the Chancellorsville plateau, to fall back. Major Richard Cross went down with a severe wound to the chest, granting him a brief furlough home. Nearly surrounded, low on ammunition, and with the enemy close by, Edward Cross reluctantly obeyed Hancock's order to fall back to the ford. Leaving a scattering force of skirmishers to cover the retreat, the colonel, outraged by the defeat, began the sprinting run north to avoid being captured.[12]

With fewer men, the Army of Northern Virginia had flanked an entire Union army, blocked a corps coming to the Army of the Potomac's rescue, and cleared the Federals off the Chancellorsville plateau. Now Lee risked it all by sending

James Larkin wrote home passionately about the respect and hatred he experienced from Colonel Cross. In the end they became good friends (U.S. Army Military History Institute).

massed attacks against the Federals, who withdrew into a tight semicircle against the U.S. Ford. After pulling back from Chancellorsville, the men of the Fifth and Cross' Brigade ran towards the ford, becoming somewhat strung out and soldiers disappearing as they were hit by artillery rounds or became lost in the forest. It was the first time that the Fifth broke apart under fire, but the officers quickly regrouped the shell-shocked men, as they again began to hastily dig in near the ford, waiting to attack or be attacked. Cross saw General Thomas Meagher, who "lay among the enlisted men of Company G — evidently badly scared. As soon as the firing ceased, he ran as fast as possible to the left rear where he had a private fortification constructed." For the next three days, Cross' Brigade and the Fifth remained dug in with their backs to the U.S. Ford and their front to the enemy. Lee continued to probe the line, with firefights erupting all hours of the day and night. But the men remained secure behind their fortifications, until orders finally came to retreat on May 6. It was the second major loss for the Army of the Potomac in six months, this time costing nearly 18,000 men.[13]

For the first time, Lieutenant Colonel Hapgood commanded the Fifth under fire. Although the regiment fought without Cross during the Seven Days, this time he was present but attending to a brigade. Hapgood proved to be a competent commander to many in the regiment, but he was not Cross and did not inspire the amount of fiery devotion that the colonel did. Lieutenant Sumner Hurd wrote, "Lt. Col. Hapgood does very well." Sergeant George Gove added Hapgood was "cool, calm, and brave as a lion." In selecting a second in command for his regiment, Cross had picked a good candidate. While the lieutenant colonel performed well under fire, Cross had, as with his other battlefield performances, handled his brigade with the approbation of his superiors, his men having performed the desperate duty of being the rear guard of the entire army. As usual, General Hancock wrote that the colonel "performed distinguished services."[14]

Chancellorsville was the fourth major battle of Cross' career, and after this battle, he again became the subject of renown around the nation. *Frank Leslie's,* a major national news magazine, was in the process of preparing a biographical sketch of Cross (which he wanted 500 copies of for his men). The sketch was taking longer than Cross expected, leading him to write to one correspondent, "They are doubtless waiting, with commendable patience, for me to be killed. However, having received nine wounds in the present war, I am not afraid of rebel bullets." The colonel again survived a terrible engagement, while gaining celebrity around the North for his actions in combat. Cross relished the fame, believing that the regiment earned it and finally the public was taking notice of the hard fighting the Fifth New Hampshire had been enduring since Fair Oaks. While his actions earned the bulk of the praise in the newspapers, in the reports Cross never failed to mention that it was his "brave men" who were responsible for those actions.[15]

As Cross had been wounded so often, many people were surprised that Chancellorsville was the first major battle that Colonel Cross came through unharmed yet his brother took a serious chest wound. The miraculous escape led him to write, "If I am to die on the battlefield, I pray it may be with the cheers of victory in my ears." In all of his engagements, at Fair Oaks, Antietam, and Fredericksburg, he had witnessed incompetent commanders blunder their way into combat, sending their men straight into the enemy's fortifications, unwilling to adopt new tactics. In a seething letter to friend Murat Halstead from his newspaper days, Cross wrote, "My life, my all, is at the service of this county, but let me tell you, it is *hard fighting against stupidity foolishness and treason at home.*" Captain Livermore, who was inspired to continue with the losing struggle at Chancellorsville, fondly recalled of Cross, "If all the colonels in the army had been like him we would never have lost a battle." [16]

Returning to their small huts at Falmouth after the ten-day expedition to Chancellorsville and back, the Army of the Potomac was demoralized, as it was after Fredericksburg, feeling that incompetent generalship on the part of the Federals had again robbed them of the chance of victory. To cheer up his men, Cross passed out a ration of whiskey to the soldiers "and had them fed as well as the circumstances would allow." Throughout the campaign, Cross suffered severely from his Fredericksburg wounds, which still, five months later, had not healed properly, in addition to the other injuries he sustained at Fair Oaks and Antietam. Although the colonel could easily have received a medical discharge and returned home, he decided to again lead by example and stay with his regiment, despite suffering agonizing fevers, leg aches, and stomach pains at times. Dr. William Child was inspired by Cross, writing, "He must be a man of iron to endure what he does."[17]

Back in their Falmouth camp, on May 15, 1863, the Second Corps was in for a major reorganization. Writing that he could no longer serve under Hooker, General Couch was relieved of command and reassigned to the Department of the Susquehanna in Pennsylvania. This opened the command of the corps to Major General Winfield Scott Hancock, who carried the particular nom de guerre of "The Superb." Hancock's First Division passed to principal turned general John Caldwell, who had performed well at Chancellorsville. But many still remembered his absence in the sunken road fight at Antietam. Meanwhile, orders placed Colonel Edward Cross in command of the First Brigade. With the mustering out of several New York regiments, the colonel became the senior colonel in the Army of the Potomac, his commission dating back to August 1861. Despite his seniority over the hundreds of

In battle, Cross always carried his .36 Colt revolver (bottom) and lost it when he was shot in the Wheatfield. He captured the .44 Remington (top) at Fair Oaks (courtesy Lancaster Historical Society).

other regimental commanders in the army, the colonel finally knew no promotion in rank was coming, despite now officially commanding a brigade and after ably handling the three regiments at Chancellorsville.[18]

Cross continued to divide his time between the Fifth New Hampshire and his new command, the First Brigade, First Division, Second Corps. Deserters continued to be pursued with a vengeance; in one case, he personally offered fifty dollars for the capture and arrest of Charles Hutchinson of Lancaster, who had deserted on the eve of Chancellorsville. In addition, Cross wrote several letters of recommendation to officers of the Fifth who distinguished themselves in action, but because of wounds or illness received a discharge and were now seeking to return to the army as members of the newly created Veterans Reserve Corps. In one letter for Captain Thomas Rice, who left the Fifth because of illness contracted on the Peninsula, Cross wrote, "At all time — in field or camp he bore himself with honor to the regiment. I earnestly recommend him." Another Fifth officer nominated was Prussian born Captain Jacob Keller of Claremont, severely wounded at Fredericksburg. One officer Cross did not give an endorsement for was Ira McL. Barton, who desperately needed a letter from his former colonel to get into the corps.[19]

Although now a brigade commander, Cross' attention was still directed at the Fifth New Hampshire. With the recent battle at Chancellorsville taking yet another forty men from the regiment, there were fewer than 200 men fit for duty. Knowing of the slaughter that the Twelfth New Hampshire endured in a desperate stand when the Third Corps line was overwhelmed, he began to contemplate a temporary consolidation of the two regiments, both severely under strength. The officers of the Twelfth rebelled against the idea, not wanting to be part of the Fifth. Cross tried to defend his point, writing, "My letter was written in the kindest spirit + my only intention was to give the two regts. an opportunity to associate + sympathize with each other after the scenes of the recent campaign believing that it would be beneficial to both regts." While he struggled to find reinforcements for the Fifth, the colonel received a ten-day furlough and went to Washington on "business of the utmost importance." This time he met with Secretary of War Edwin Stanton to have the Fifth ordered home on recruiting duty to bring the unit up to strength, but again Stanton refused the colonel, no political favors going to the Democratic regiment, which continued to want for men.[20]

For the next month, the Army of the Potomac remained in their old camps near Falmouth, Virginia, again recovering from the horrors of a losing campaign. Colonel Cross took the time to adopt a pair of tortoises, keeping them tied up near his tent. During this time he wrote recommendations and trained his brigade. When the orders finally came to move in mid–June 1863, it would be Edward Cross' final campaign.

CHAPTER TWELVE

The Wheatfield

Boys, you know what's before you today. Give 'em hell.—COL. E.E. CROSS, JULY 2, 1862

With the freshness of his victory at Chancellorsville, Lee decided on yet another fateful course of action, to draw the Army of the Potomac out into the open where it could destroyed. Using the Shenandoah Valley to cover his movements, the lead elements of the Army of Northern Virginia quietly slipped out of the camps near Fredericksburg and marched north on June 8. Once he knew Lee had moved, Hooker set the Army of the Potomac in motion to find and destroy the Army of Northern Virginia. Cross returned from his brief furlough to Washington, while Major Cross returned from a five-day visit to Lancaster. On June 1, the men of the First Brigade had a reunion with General Howard, still suffering from the turmoil of his corps' defeat at Chancellorsville, in commemoration of the first anniversary of Fair Oaks. A few days later, Cross commanded a reconnaissance in force across the river to ascertain the location of the Rebels. The Army of the Potomac left their camps around Falmouth on June 15, after discovering the Confederates were marching north; the Second Corps acted as the rear guard of the army.[1]

The march north was tiresome for both officers and men. Colonel Cross knew what was ahead and pushed his men hard. As an officer who always followed orders, he obeyed Hancock's command to push the column forward, without stopping for rest or water. By June 25, the First Brigade passed Thoroughfare Gap on its way into Maryland. On this day, Cross performed an act that was nothing new to the men of the Fifth New Hampshire but severely upset the soldiers of the One Hundredth and Forty-Eighth Pennsylvania, a regiment assigned to the First Brigade shortly before Chancellorsville, where they performed commendable service in the rearguard action. The colonel felt the Pennsylvanians did not comprehend the seriousness of the situation to move as fast as possible; in crossing a stream, Cross struck one member with the flat of his sword, sending him into the stream, which soon caused the regiment to become outraged against their brigade commander, who would always be remembered as a "tyrant." While the action was unjustified, as regulations forbid officers from striking enlisted men, Cross again was not reported to his superiors or disciplined. He always felt that swift and unmerciful punishment was a necessity to show others the penalty for breaking the regulations he so closely believed in; he had nearly worn out his copy of the *Army Regulations*.[2]

Cross having survived a thigh wound at Fair Oaks, a head wound at Antietam, and multiple serious injuries at Fredericksburg, to many in the Fifth their colonel seamed indestructible. For some particular reason, as he approached Pennsylvania, Cross again developed a sense of fatalism in the coming battle, even stronger than the one experienced before Fredericksburg. Charles Hale, who had always been impressed by Cross' actions on the field and was now a lieutenant serving on the First Brigade staff, was deeply upset by the colonel's comments, writing, "He had at times seemed in a sort of abstracted mood that was not usual with him." Several times over the next few days, Cross inventoried his personal effects, specifically asking his aide to watch the contents of his camp chest, which contained his personal papers; he wanted them returned to his family if something happened. Hale was familiar with the colonel but felt his attitude was uncalled for and uttered "something about the foolishness of entertaining such ideas" to the colonel. Cross took great offense at Hale's comments and did not speak to him until the next day. The colonel had been through enough in his battles to believe on the eve of every engagement that his number might be up. On the march to Pennsylvania, it was not a premonition so much as a battered man unable to resist the thought that his luck was going to run out one day, and he and others should be prepared for it.[3]

On the morning of July 1, 1863, the Army of the Potomac and the Army of Northern Virginia met at the crossroads town of Gettysburg, Pennsylvania. Through the morning and early afternoon the Federals held their ground to the west and north of town, fighting savagely to gain time for the rest of the Army of the Potomac to arrive. By that afternoon, Confederate reinforcements arrived, driving the First and Eleventh Corps back from their positions, until they rallied on the high ground on Cemetery Hill, Cemetery Ridge, and Culp's Hill. Throughout the night of July 1 and into the second, Union reinforcements began to arrive and as the Federal line began to take the shape of a fishhook, anchored on Culp's Hill and extending down Cemetery Ridge. By this point Hale had thought Cross had forgotten the comments of the past few days, but late that night "he said to me in a grave, firm, way, 'Mr. Hale: attend to that box of mine at the first opportunity;' that was all, but it convinced me that he was in dead earnest and had firm conviction of impending fate." The comments of impending death continued to upset the young subordinate, who, like many in the Fifth, idolized his colonel as something larger than life.

At 6:00 on the morning of Thursday, July 2, 1863, after an exhausting march of thirty-two miles, the soldiers of the First Division, Second Corps, finally began to arrive at Taneytown, just south of the Pennsylvania border. On the road, a wagon passed carrying the body of Major General John F. Reynolds, killed fighting west of Gettysburg the previous morning. Pushing forward, Cross' men passed Little Round Top as they filed into a vacant portion in the line on Cemetery Ridge, forming the left of the Second Corps, while the Third Corps rested on the far left. Caldwell massed the First Division in "closed column of regiments," not line of battle, thus being able to move quickly if called upon.

Arriving on the field, Cross' entire attitude and demeanor changed dramatically. The fatalistic, nervous, depressed man of a few days before who argued with Lieutenant Hale became the colonel that Hale knew: "His grave manner of the previous day had entirely disappeared; he was now full of fire, showing the sharp impulsive manner that had always possessed him on former battlefields. His eyes flashed as he said to us, 'Gentlemen: it looks as though the whole of Lee's rebel army is right here in Pennsylvania; there will be a great battle fought to-day.'" The colonel spotted Captain Livermore, who had been promoted to ambulance duty over Cross' objections, and jokingly said, "We shan't want any of your dead carts here today!" Cross mounted his horse Jack, the same

Promoted from the ranks, Charles Hale served on Cross' brigade staff and was haunted by the last glance he saw of the colonel walking into Rose's Woods (U.S. Army Military History Institute).

mount that had carried him into action since Fair Oaks, and went alone to survey the field, taking note of General Howard's position to the north and the Second New Hampshire to the left.[4]

During the late morning hours, Hancock sent orders for Cross to detach a regiment for guard duty near the Taneytown Road. The colonel pulled Hapgood and the Fifth out of line, and sent the regiment away, thus arranging the brigade with the Sixty-First New York in front, followed by the Eighty-First and One Hundredth and Forty-Eighth Pennsylvania. While the men from Pennsylvania still fumed over Cross' striking one of their number with his saber, the other soldiers in the brigade were recipients of the colonel's enthusiasm that morning. He strode among the squads and platoons resting, cooking, and playing games, speaking to the men. "Boys you know what's before you. Give 'em hell." The men eagerly replied, "We will, Colonel!" The colonel met with his remaining regimental commanders, planning the action of the day and assigning his staff to various duties. Some of the staff continued to be distressed about the comments their commander had made on the way to the battlefield, especially when he said that his second in command, Colonel H. Boyd McKeen of the Eighty-First Pennsylvania, would most likely command the brigade by nightfall. The same feelings he experienced before Fredericksburg continued to assert themselves, but this time, instead of simply writing it in his journal, Cross shared his comments with his fellow officers. In the ranks, the men waited anxiously in the hot July sun. Cross was "little concerned" that this might be his last day; instead he waited impatiently to go into action, pacing the ground restlessly, checking on his men, waiting for Caldwell's orders to go in.

On the left, General Daniel Sickles, who commanded the Third Corps, began to move his men out of position on low-lying Cemetery Ridge to what he perceived was higher ground a half mile to the front. This unordered movement opened a huge gap in the Union line as the Third Corps advanced and rested its flanks on a peach orchard to the right and a clump of boulders called the Devil's Den to the left. In the center of the line stood the Second and the Twelfth New Hampshire, deployed on the Emmittsburg Road. Cross watched intently as the Third Corps advanced in a mile-long line of battle, but, like many on Cemetery Ridge, he knew they would soon be "tumbling back."[5]

By 3:00, the artillery had opened up, as two Confederate divisions formed on the Army of the Potomac's left flank. Soon after the crashing sounds of musketry erupted, Cross knew that the time for action had come. For some time he had been pacing back and forth among the men in his brigade, surveying the line, with his hands clasped tightly behind his back. Always at his side, Lieutenant Hale watched as Cross removed his hat and wrapped a black silk handkerchief around his head. Cross asked Hale to tie it tight several times. As the men began to assemble in formation, General Hancock rode up to speak with Cross. Rather than discussing the battle or what was about to occur, Hancock stated, "Colonel Cross, this day will bring you a star." Cross looked up at Hancock, shook his head, and in a calm voice replied, "No General, this is my last battle." Hancock said nothing in reply and rode on to the next brigade.[6]

For the last 150 years, historians have given a literal interpretation of his words, based on Hale's comments that Cross believed he was about to die. It must be remembered that Hale wrote his account of Cross' last days years after they happened, with the hindsight of what he may have been implying. Like many soldiers of the time, Cross always had a sense of fatalism before an engagement. The interpretation of "this is my last battle," has been that Cross was telling Hancock he was going to die in the coming fight. However, there is a much deeper meaning to his words. Hancock had been Cross' champion in the army, doing what other officers would not do, writing impassioned letters of recommendation for his promotion to brigadier general. He wrote yet another letter on July 1, which General George Meade, the new commander of the Army of the Potomac, endorsed as well. But it was simply forwarded to the War Department and was added to Cross' already bulging file of recommendations. Hancock could do only so much for Cross, who lacked the necessary political connections to obtain a star. What Cross implied to General Hancock was, in his own dramatic way, that when the battle was over he would give him an answer as to his future in the Army of the Potomac. The colonel had three options before him, to remain in the service with the same rank, facing no real future, resign his commission and return home, or, the third, he was going to die that afternoon.

Even though he was the senior infantry colonel in the Army of the Potomac, Cross knew that he had a slim chance in obtaining a promotion. When others of lesser seniority received promotions, Cross still commanded a brigade, but without the rank that went with it. While he believed deeply in the Union, he was continually frustrated in his failure to receive promotion, giving him a reason to leave the service. Wounded in three battles, he had devoted himself to the Union cause. It was apparent that there was no return for that sacrifice, outside of the praise of his commanders and scant newspaper coverage in far off New Hampshire.

Since the first letters he wrote to Henry Kent in the 1850s, he had wanted to be a soldier, to have a war to call his own. Now an officer in the United States Army, Cross realized that he was at a crossroads in his life; he was unsure what the next step in the adventure would be. With his regiment finally ridden of shirkers and cowards, the small crop that remained behind loved their commander as a father. He would not abandon his men on the eve of a fight; instead he would see them through at least one more time. Slowed down by his old wounds, with no opportunity for advancement, Cross had a tough decision to make after this engagement, if he survived. While he told the members of his inner circle that he was going to die in his next battle, he had expressed the same thoughts before Fair Oaks and Fredericksburg and had survived, if barely, those engagements.

While Cross' wearing of a black bandanna seemed fatalistic to some, it was part of the dramatic acts that made up his life. Since Antietam, he had given up the habit of wearing a hat in action and instead took to wearing a handkerchief as a bandanna.

Colonel H. Boyd McKeen assisted Cross in the defense of the line at Antietam and took over the First Brigade after Cross fell (U.S. Army Military History Institute).

In his own mind, Cross' life was one dramatic act after another. He took immense pleasure in reading of his actions on the battlefield and reveled in the columns that reporters wrote about him. He was living the life he had always dreamed about, and his actions at Fair Oaks and the repelling of Hill's assault at Antietam added to his ego. By wearing a black, rather than a red, bandanna at Gettysburg, he was creating part of the Cross persona, a dramatic flourish, that in time has grown to disproportional standards based largely on Hale's writings. Cross wore black as an indicator of a future he was unsure of. It might be his last battle, through death or resignation, but either way he would leave in a dramatic fashion. He feared, like many soldiers that afternoon, he might die, but Cross told Hancock in his own way that he would make a major decision about what his future in the Army of the Potomac would be after this engagement was over.

At 5:00, as the fighting raged on the Army of the Potomac's left flank, Caldwell's Division went into action to assist the faltering Third Corps. With Cross' brigade in front, the men quickly formed their long familiar column of fours, and prepared to go into action. Hale was at Cross' side and remembered "how well Cross rode; I can see him yet; tall in the saddle, straight as an arrow, lithe like an Indian, with a head on his shoulders and everything in the range of vision." As he moved out, the colonel witnessed Father William Corby giving absolution to the Irish Brigade, an organization that he felt never belonged in the same division as his men. Cross caught a glimpse of Dr. William Child, and he turned his horse to meet him. Cross handed Child, a noncombatant, his gold Masonic ring, several letters, and his pocketbook for safekeeping, much as any officer would do who was going into battle. Cross told the doctor, "It will be an awful day, good bye." The First Brigade was one of the smallest in the army, mustering barely 800 muskets in addition to officers, smaller than the regiment Cross mustered at Concord in 1861. As the brigade moved its position off Cemetery Ridge, Hapgood double quicked the Fifth back into line, filing in the rear of the One Hundredth and Forty-Eighth Pennsylvania. The colonel positioned himself at the head of the small column as they pressed forward to help save the crumbling left flank.[7]

After a short ride and walk for the men through a series of woodlots, the brigade passed the Wheatfield Road as two staff officers from the Fifth Corps galloped up to Cross, announcing, "The enemy is breaking directly on your right. Strike him quick!" The Third Corps line was on the verge of breaking, pressed by two Confederate divisions on both flanks and the center. The colonel instantly ordered his men into action, deploying them by the right flank along a small crossroads. With the brigade in line of battle, Cross ordered them to left face, bringing the men to face the open field to their front. While the unorthodox maneuver was not in the tactics manual, it quickly placed them in position. The officers filed to the rear, placing the rear rank in front, with the shorter men in back.

Cross' Brigade was deployed with the right of the Sixty-First New York on the Wheatfield Road and the left with the Fifth New Hampshire in Rose's Woods, a thick, tangled lot that separated the Wheatfield from the Devil's Den along Houck's Ridge. To their front was a twenty-acre field of wheat ready for harvesting. For many, the noise to the right was deafening, as the Confederates directly in the woods to their front, five regiments of Georgians under G.T. Anderson, held their fire for the moment. The small brigade instantly deployed into the wheat and "was advancing steadily into the Wheatfield as though on parade." Cross dismounted from his horse Jack, taking his Colt .36 revolver out of his pommel holster. He then sent Hale to round up some Confederate prisoners as he passed among the men in the ranks, yelling words of encouragement at them. For a moment, there was silence in the Wheatfield as the Georgians held their fire and the First Brigade entered the fray.[8]

The Sixty-First New York, Eighty-First Pennsylvania, and seven companies of the One Hundredth and Forty-Eighth Pennsylvania deployed in the open. In Rose's Woods, the other three Pennsylvania companies and Hapgood's Fifth New Hampshire leaped over a stone wall and immediately began a desperate engagement with the oncoming Confederates. A member of Caldwell's staff recalled, "Cross opened a tremendous fire in return, and the old 1st brigade stood firm as usual, though placed at a terrible disadvantage." The four regiments pushed forward into the storm of lead, unleashing a torrent of musketry at the Rebels to their front. In the woods, much as it was at Fair Oaks, the Fifth's fight against Anderson's Georgians was an up close, deadly affair, the New Hampshiremen giving it their all to hold back the enemy. Company K of the Fifth went in with thirteen men under Sergeant George Gove and came out with four men. Major M.J. Bass of the Fifty-Ninth Georgia wrote of the fight against the Fifth New Hampshire: "The enemy stood their ground, defending themselves gallantly, and we were repulsed. We charged them a second time and were repulsed again. Musket balls fell in a shower like hail around us. I could hear bones crash like glass in a hailstorm." Even without their colonel present, the men stood firm, taking heavy casualties while quickly going through much of their ammunition.[9]

At 6:00, after only ten minutes of fighting, Colonel Cross knew that the situation was desperate, as the color of the ground started to change from the golden yellow of wheat ready for harvesting to the blue and red of dead and wounded Union soldiers. The men of the Sixty-First New York and Eighty-First Pennsylvania fired their muskets into the enemy in the woods on the other side of the field. The smoke of hundreds of muskets going off hung low over the wheat, veiling the Union and Confederate positions. But occasionally the wind would clear the field, as the two sides slugged it out at distances of under fifty yards. Captain George Hillyer and the men of the Ninth Georgia were confronting Cross' right flank. Hillyer wrote, "It seemed that not a bullet went above their heads or below their feet. They fell right and left. This line thinned rapidly. In a few minutes, the fire from the enemy slackened, and there was not one of the enemy left standing in our front. There was a long blue line on the ground, so close together that anyone could have walked over them as far as their front extended without touching the earth."

With severe casualties on the right, the over abundance of officers in some regiments led them to take up muskets and join in the firing line. From his position on the right of the line, Cross knew that his small brigade could not hold on for long. The needed support from General Samuel Zook's Brigade, which he expected to hook into his right flank, never materialized, as Zook decided to rush his men into action farther to the right to support the hard-pressed Third Corps. The Irish Brigade, which should have been in the rear of Cross' men, had not arrived yet. Alone and unsupported, Cross had to make a decision, as his men were being shot down in the open. A ball hit his hand, slightly injuring him, and wrapped it with his red handkerchief. Never one to retreat from a fight, the colonel decided to take his men forward in a charge and drive the Confederates back from their protected position at Stony Hill. Unknown to Cross, Anderson's Georgians were not the only Confederates in the vicinity, as a large force, including Kershaw's Brigade of South Carolinians and another Georgia brigade under Paul Semmes, was working its way into the fight after destroying the New Hampshire, New Jersey, and Pennsylvania regiments in their front.[10]

Meanwhile, on Cross' left, two regiments of the Texas Brigade, which had just cleared Devil's Den, were connecting with Anderson's right flank and beginning to push back the remnants of the Twentieth Indiana, and the rest of John H.H. Ward's Brigade that was fighting to the left of the Fifth New Hampshire. The situation was critical for the small brigade, facing a division-sized force of Rebel infantry. With his customary bravado, the colonel was ready to launch the assault against the enemy. His hand bleeding, Cross passed along the line, heading toward his left flank, yelling, "Boys, instruct the commanders to be ready to charge when the order is given; wait here for the command, or, if you hear the bugles of the Fifth New Hampshire on the left, move forward on the run." As the First Brigade prepared to advance, Cross became the lion he was known for in combat, being keenly aware of the situation, giving words of encouragement to his men, and keeping them aware of what was about to happen. With the right of the brigade being decimated in the ripe wheat, Hale, in a woodlot with his prisoners, "looked after him sort of regretfully as he vanished among the trees" as the colonel moved towards his old regiment. The last glimpse Hale caught of Cross haunted him for the rest of his life, as he was helpless to prevent what was about to happen next.[11]

As the right of the brigade prepared to advance, Cross, his hand bandaged, brandishing his revolver, calmly strode alone into Rose's Woods to notify Hapgood and the Fifth of the planned charge. Heavily engaged, the Fifth "was tearing things all to pieces," taking fire in its right from the Fifteenth Georgia, in front from the Fifty-Ninth Georgia, and in the left flank from the First Texas, losing severely, but holding their ground. Directly to the Fifth's front, some forty yards away, was a large boulder that was of some concern to the officers of the regiment, as a sharpshooter was specifically aiming at the Fifth's officers. Unaware of the situation, Cross finally approached the Fifth to initiate the assault. Hapgood saw Cross coming to his side, but at the same time he noticed, "a flash of a piece from that rock and the colonel fell." At six feet, two inches tall, wearing the full uniform of a Union infantry colonel, and with his head swathed in black, Cross made an easy target for southern riflemen. A minie ball fired from the Rebel behind the rock hit Cross in the navel, ripped through his intestines and exited his back. The colonel instantly dropped his pistol and fell to the ground in the middle of the Fifth's line. Immediately Hapgood ordered some men from the Fifth to bring the fatally wounded Cross to a waiting ambulance by the Wheatfield Road. Sergeant Charles Phelps of Amherst was ordered to kill the Rebel behind the rock. Cross would never get the opportunity to tell General Hancock what he meant by the words "this will be my last battle."[12]

While the mortally wounded Cross was being taken to the rear, his life ebbing away, the other three brigades of the Second Corps' First Division entered the fray. The Wheatfield became a whirlwind

Sergeant George Gove of Company K wrote home frequently about the actions of Colonel Cross (U.S. Army Military History Institute).

of confusion, as attack and counterattack ensued, leaving thousands dead and wounded in the wheat. Colonel John Brooke and his Fourth Brigade, together with the remnants of Zook's and Cross' commands pushed the Rebels back to Stony Hill, Cross' original objective, but they themselves were finally pushed back by additional Rebel reinforcements as the sun began to set. After fighting for hours, the First Division, for the first time, turned, broke, and retreated out of the Wheatfield. The same men who fought so valiantly at Fair Oaks, Antietam, Fredericksburg, and Chancellorsville would never be the same again. As the rest of the division fell back, the Fifth held firm in the woodlot, "until every round of cartridge in this portion of the brigade was expended and even then held their position," as they took rounds from the boxes of the dead and dying, fighting the Texans in their front to a standstill. Finally, the Fifth turned and ran back towards Cemetery Ridge, a disorganized force that emerged from the fighting with barely 100 men.

Lieutenant Hale searched in vain for the brigade staff after the First Brigade fell back at 9:00 that evening. Three hours later, Hapgood returned with what was left of the Fifth New Hampshire, which held the exposed flank once again. Colonel H. Boyd McKeen, who took over for the mortally wounded Cross, and others dissuaded Hale from searching for Cross, insisting they had work to do with the brigade. The lieutenant finally collapsed in exhaustion after being told the colonel was mortally wounded. Hale felt "hope was dead." The men knew the day ended with their blocking the Confederate effort, but the cost was frightful. Nearly half the men in the First Brigade were dead or wounded in the Wheatfield and Rose's Woods.[13]

The ambulance that carried Cross also transported Captain Rodney Crowley of the Sixty-Fourth New York, who had admired the colonel since his days at Camp California, to the First Division, Second Corps, hospital on the William Patterson farm, a few hundred yards behind the main Second Corps line on Cemetery Ridge. Along the way, in the ambulance without springs, the mortally wounded colonel screamed out in agony, pleading for someone to end his misery and unable to find his revolver to do the deed himself. To look after their leader, Lieutenant Colonel Hapgood dispatched the Fifth's surgeons, Drs. John Bucknam and William Child, along with younger brother Major Richard Cross, as the shattered remnants of the regiment struggled to regroup.

The sun set late on July 2 as Dr. Bucknam, who had grown up with Cross, examined the stomach wound and determined there was nothing he, or any surgeon of the day, could do. Although both doctors had graduated from Dartmouth and were skilled in their profession, Cross was beyond saving. All they could do was make him comfortable as he waited for the end; Dr. Bucknam knew it would not be long. Dr. Child stood nearby, helpless to do anything. He recalled, "The gloom of a deep darkness covered all. Some campfires crackled and glimmered, flashed and cast weird shadows around the group of friends and attendants. All faces were sad, all hearts were sorrowful."

As Cross lay dying, he managed to gain enough strength to make a final request: burial at sunset in the family plot on a small hill overlooking the village of Lancaster. Despite having traveled the country, his heart always remained in the granite hills of northern New England. Although he had engaged in severe arguments with most of the commissioned officers of the Fifth at some point in their careers, Cross called for them; but few could make it, as the regiment was still scattered. To the northeast, on Culp's Hill, was half brother Colonel Nelson Cross and the Sixty-Seventh New York, but the "other Colonel Cross" never made it to his brother's side. Instead, Richard Cross would be the bearer of Edward Cross' unknown messages to mother and family at home in Lancaster.[14]

When told the Union had won the day, Cross managed to smile, even as the pain and delirium intensified. Captain Crowley, who lay by his side with his own wounds, continued to hear the colonel "speaking as though all his thoughts had turned back to the days of his early campaigning" as he continued to scream out battle commands and call for friends and comrades from happier days in Arizona. Child recalled, "He constantly murmured, 'my brave men.'" Cross' screaming kept many of the wounded awake in the makeshift hospital. It was not a glorious death with his face to the enemy, but rather, a long and extremely painful, gruesome experience.

Finally, at 12:30 A.M. on July 3, 1863, and some six hours after receiving his wound in Rose's Woods, Colonel Edward Ephraim Cross died at the age of thirty-one years, two months, and ten days, his dark eyes looking up at the night sky and his long chestnut beard resting on his chest. Dr. Bucknam closed the colonel's eyes as several Fifth New Hampshire officers gathered around to have one last look at the man who had been both a father figure and a terror in their lives but had done so much for them and the regiment. The last audible words they heard Cross utter, in a gross understatement to an epic life, were, "I think the boys will miss me."[15]

With the regiment back in position on Cemetery Ridge, several Fifth officers the colonel had been calling for were finally able to reach the hospital. To their deep regret, Cross was already dead. Captain Livermore finally managed to get relief from bringing in the wounded and arrived at the Patterson farm, seeking Cross. One of the Fifth's doctors calmly pointed to a blanket, which covered the body. Livermore recalled, "The starlight enabled me to see his features distinctly. They were placid and exceedingly lifelike, and it was hard to persuade myself that the flush of life had gone from them. His lofty forehead was smooth, his long, silky beard lay upon his breast undisheveled, and he looked more as he would if he slept than seemed possible." Major Cross cut a lock of his brother's hair as he prepared to send the remains home.[16]

As in all of his battles, Cross gained laurels, this time posthumously, for his actions at Gettysburg. In a battle that produced many deeds of valor, his again stood out. Cross' men assisted in stopping the massive Confederate assault on the end of the Union line and ultimately helped win the battle by their stubborn fight, which prevented the enemy from gaining the high ground. Major General Winfield Scott Hancock, Cross' most vocal supporter, wrote, "This officer has borne a reputation in this corps for the most intrepid bravery on nearly every battlefield on which this army has fought. His regiment, under his discipline was excelled by none." John Caldwell, the man who commanded the Fifth's brigade at Antietam and Fredericksburg and now commanded the First Division, was also moved by Cross' death, as his style of leadership required dependable subordinates Now two of his brigade commanders, Cross and Zook, were dead. Of them, Caldwell wrote, "They were both old and tried soldier, and the country can illy spare there services. They both fell in the front of battle while driving back the invader and they lived long enough to know that their blood had not been shed in vain." In his final action, Cross again lived up to the same high standards he had set for himself and those under his command.[17]

While Colonel Cross' battlefield exploits at Fair Oaks, Antietam, Fredericksburg, and Chancellorsville were bold and gallant inspirations to lead his men into action, Cross made perhaps his first and final mistake on the battlefield on the afternoon of July 2, 1863. While his rapid deployment of the First Brigade into the Wheatfield blunted the Confederate push to gain the high ground and bought enough time for the rest of the division to enter the fight, it was Cross' actions after entering the Wheatfield that proved to be in error. Exposed in the open, Cross knew the brigade had to advance to Stony Hill to gain the high ground. While he was right in ordering an attack against the forces in the Wheatfield, the colonel selected the worst possible position from which to lead the charge. In the thick woods where the Fifth and three companies of the One Hundredth and Forty-Eighth Pennsylvania fought, it was impossible to control or observe the rest of the brigade in the assault. Cross' proper place was in the open, where he could direct the bulk of his men. After months of lobbying for brigade command, the colonel was finally in command of a force larger than his old regiment, that required his overall attention rather than the individual regiment.

Aides and couriers such as Lieutenant Hale were available to ride to the left of the line and notify Hapgood, who could not see the fighting in the open, to advance with the rest of the brigade or to charge by the bugle as the Fifth trained to do in the din of battle. Instead, Cross felt compelled, as he always did in combat, to be with the Fifth New Hampshire, leading the regiment instead of the brigade. Not pushing the bulk of his brigade forward allowed the New York and Pennsylvania regiments in the open to bleed their strength away instead of rushing for Stony Hill. Although the enemy greatly outnumbered the First Brigade, such a movement would have temporarily stunned the Confederates, much as the charge of the First Minnesota did, allowing the rest of Caldwell's Division to press the advantage gained by the First Brigade. Cross was also negligent in not telling his second in command, Colonel Boyd McKeen, of his plan to charge the Rebel lines. McKeen, not realizing Cross was shot in the woods, remained in the open waiting for orders as the brigade ran out of ammunition and was eventually forced to retreat. In the end, Colonel Cross' mistake cost many unnecessary lives, including his own.

While the news of his death was quick to circulate among the New Hampshiremen at Gettysburg, most of whom expressed universal regret at the loss, Cross' death also inspired joy from the men of the One Hundredth and Forty-Eighth Pennsylvania, who felt they had been slighted by the colonel for marching slower than he had expected and for striking a member of the command with his saber. Among the Confederate prisoners captured in the fierce fighting on July 2 was Colonel Robert M. Powell, whose men fought in the Devil's Den not far from the Wheatfield. Brought to a prisoner collection point near the Second Corps line, Powell met Major Cross. When Powell found out that men of the Texas Brigade fought Cross' New Hampshiremen in the woodlot, Powell expressed regret, because he knew the colonel from his days in Texas.[18]

The Fifth under Major Cross pushed on in pursuit of Lee's retreating army on July 5. Although they survived the defining battle of the war, many of the soldiers were too exhausted to write home to count what the battle meant or cost their regiment. Sergeant Rodney Ramsey of Company G wrote home to his father about the two-month Pennsylvania Campaign: "Our regiment lost heavy, Col. Cross was killed. I think this Rebellion is played out." Ramsey was correct in his statement. The Civil War finally and fully turned in favor of the Union, but the cost to the Fifth New Hampshire was more than the regiment could fathom. Thirty-four more New Hampshiremen died in the fierce fighting in Rose's Woods. As in all the Fifth's battles, the larger percentage were commissioned and noncommissioned officers, indicating that those who wore straps and stripes led their men from the front. New recruits could replace the loss of men in the battle such as Private Joseph Craig of Claremont, Sergeant Samuel Dolbear of Milford, or Private Nathan Osmer of Newport. As the Fifth marched away from Gettysburg, Pennsylvania, those in the ranks knew their regiment would never be the same again; there would be no one to replace Colonel Cross. Musician Charles T. Moody of Claremont summed up the feelings of many when he wrote, "The Regt. will never be the old 5th again." To add to the sense of loss, Sergeant George Gove, severely wounded in the Wheatfield fight, wrote, "It is the greatest blow the old 5th ever got."[19]

CHAPTER THIRTEEN

"The boys will miss me"

Sometimes I think I shall return to dwell under the shadow of our ancient mountains. — E.E. CROSS, MARCH 1, 1857

With Lieutenant Colonel Hapgood ill following the battle, Major Richard Cross, the highest ranking Fifth officer still on duty, was unavailable to take his brother's remains home. In the meantime, Lieutenant Hale took care of Cross' personal effects, giving his camp chest to Major Cross. The young lieutenant who believed Cross to be a lion who stood ten feet tall in battle felt the sounds of battle were an appropriate farewell to Cross. "The mighty thunder of the guns along the rock-bound ridges at Gettysburg, was a fitting requiem for the gallant soldier whose body was being borne to his far-away home among the Northern hills."

Captain Welcome Crafts, a native of Coos County, performed the honorable and difficult task of bringing Colonel Cross back to Lancaster. Through "great and rapid effort," Crafts was able to get the body in a wagon to Westminster, Maryland, and then on a train to Baltimore. Here it was prepared, dressed in the uniform, and the casket covered with a flag as Cross began his final journey home. Captain Crafts took a train from Baltimore to Concord, arriving on July 6, and reaching in Lancaster the following day. No member of the governor's staff, the adjutant general's office, or any other state officer followed the body on its journey to Lancaster, Captain Crafts continuing alone. Many were still bitter about the actions Cross took in his lifetime against them and did not want to celebrate the fallen leader in death. Former corporal John M. Davis, wounded at Antietam and discharged from the Fifth, was in Concord when Cross' remains passed through. He wrote to another former soldier in the regiment who despised the colonel, Ira McL. Barton, and considered his death "good news."[1]

The news of Cross' death arrived in Lancaster on July 4, a stormy, rainy day in the mountains. Richard P. Kent, Henry's father, who supplied Abigail

Cross with groceries, wrote, "Intell. recd. of the death of Col. Edw. E. Cross killed in battle at Gettysburg, Pa." The news fell hardest at first on Henry O. Kent: "It was with the emotions of the deepest grief that I heard of his death, for he was the friend of my boyhood, sharing fully, many of the warmest feelings of my heart." Kent had returned home after his failed stint at leading the Seventeenth New Hampshire and was once again serving on the adjutant general's staff and as a representative to the general court. The Cross family placed him in charge of planning the services. One townsperson wrote, "The news of the death of Col. Cross was received and threw the whole town into mourning, for the people had come to recognize in him one of the bravest officers."

The fallen leader's remains arrived at the family homestead on Main Street on July 7. The casket was draped with an American flag, while his worn cap and the saber that had been such a terror to those who did not follow his command rested on top. As he had requested, the funeral took place at 6:00 on the evening of July 9, on his family's porch. Rather than a military funeral, his brothers in the North Star Lodge buried Colonel Cross with Masonic honors. Henry Kent wrote, "The national flags drooped at half-mast, the band played solemn dirges, the fraternity, in large numbers, assisted in the solemn ceremonies, and amid a throng of friends who had known him from boyhood, the brave solder, the impulsive and honorable man, was borne to his final resting place in the valley he loved so well."[2]

For eighteen months the people of New Hampshire had read and heard of Cross' battlefield heroics through their local newspapers, as well as glowing descriptions of his antics both on and off the field through letters received from his subordinates. In that short time, the colonel had become the military hero of the Granite State, with many comparing him to John Stark, the hero of Bennington. Whether Republican or Democrat, he had been someone who had inspired many. His Fifth Regiment became the state's favorite and most famous Civil War unit. Even for those who did not know him personally, the colonel's death was hard to bear, as he was a sort of celebrity, one who had given his life for the Union. More than a few New Hampshire diarists simply stated, "Col. Cross is dead."[3]

While Cross' death was felt hardest in New Hampshire, newspapers around the nation carried word of his passing. His actions in combat at Fair Oaks and Antietam were well known, and his death in command of a brigade was also widely circulated. Many of the accounts tried to make sense of what had contributed to Cross' being a superb combat officer. Where other men of equal rank and experience faltered under fire, Cross could comprehend the situation and lead his men through it. In a front-page obituary in the *Boston Journal,* a reporter wrote, "Firm resolution, indomitable energy, superior bravery under all circumstances, and a quickness of apprehension which enabled him in the heat of battle to take every advantage of the enemy — all conducted to elevate him to a position of eminent superiority."

The *Cincinnati Times* also covered Cross' death in detail, as he still had many acquaintances living in the West. In a headlining obituary on July 4, the paper wrote, "He died unpromoted, a lasting disgrace to the Washington people who slighted him after his valor on the battlefields in Virginia and Maryland. But the faded eagles on his shoulders will shine with greater luster in the history of that mighty conflict, then though he had borne the insignia of his merited rank, the stars of a major general." The Boston and Cincinnati accounts were widely published, allowing many Americans to read what he had accomplished in his short life.[4]

In New Hampshire, the subjects of Cross' death and how he should be remembered were as controversial as his life had been. Senator John Hale, the same man who escorted Cross to see President Lincoln, when told of his death said, "He was a damned Copperhead and I am glad he's dead." Even though the two never got along, Hale's comment, to many in the state, was pure slander, spoken against a man who gave his life for the Union cause and was a popular hero throughout New Hampshire despite his views. In August 1863, Hale again gained scorn from Cross supporters in an address to Fifth New Hampshire veterans in Concord, recently returned from the front. Hale urged the crowd not to give any money to the monument fund that was being set up to finance a memorial to Cross. The veterans were indignant that their senator would publicly slander the memory of their colonel, and they hissed and jeered at Hale.

A few days later, the *Granite State Free Press* in Lebanon wrote, "Surely no one here at home in New Hampshire, can stand by his grave, and not feel a compunction throb, that he should have ever treated unkindly, the brave spirit that once tenanted the body that now lies there moldering beneath his feet." As in life, Edward Cross remained a controversial figure in the Granite State and the nation, with Democrats and Republicans being unable to decide how to best honor his memory.[5]

The news of Edward Cross' death hit Colonel Henry O. Kent the hardest after Cross' mother. Lifelong friends and companions, the two men drifted apart in both travels and viewpoints throughout the 1850s and the Civil War years. While Cross gained famed traveling and reporting, Kent decided to stay home, serving in equally important roles in the militia, as a surveyor, journalist, store owner, father, politician, and editor. As Cross performed excellent service on the battlefield, Kent did an equally important job working for the adjutant general in Concord, recruiting New Hampshiremen to fight in the war. In politics, the two men were equally different, Cross a hardened Democrat who was always willing to voice his opinion of the opposition and Kent a Republican and supporter of Lincoln. Despite their vast differences, the two men remained lifelong friends, a bond broken only by death. In the July 14, 1863, edition of the *Coos County Republican,* Kent had the hard task of writing the obituary of his friend. He did an admirable job in summing up the main points of Cross' colorful life, following his adventures both before and during the war. He closed with words of a poetical nature that fully summed up the feelings of grief and pride the people of Lancaster showed for Colonel Edward Cross: "Life's troubled warfare o'er, he sleeps near the home of his youth, among his friends of his boyhood and noble manhood. A life crowned with active, honorable labors, has ended in a warriors death. That his memory will flourish ever verdant among the people for whom he gave his life, is the last tribute that a sorrowing community can offer to his virtues."[6]

Cross' death pained President Pierce. The former president wrote to the *New Hampshire Statesman*: "He was as high in his moral tone, as in

Every summer the veterans of the New Hampshire gathered at the Weirs, and in 1889 they dedicated the weekly encampment to Colonel Cross' memory (courtesy Lancaster Historical Society).

his dauntless courage. He inherited and exhibited the qualities which so signally illustrated his family." Pierce began to agitate immediately for a monument to the fallen leader, a hero to the Democratic Party in New Hampshire. When others were unwilling to speak out against the administration, it was Cross who did, and his actions cost him dearly. According to one New Hampshire Democrat, "I wish he could have worn the silver stars he wanted so much and had earned so well, though they could have added no splendor to his kind and gentle life and his glorious death." He fought for the cause of preserving the Union, but in the end he died to free the slave as well. In addition, the president and others also began to collect Cross writings, which, when published, were to support his mother. M.S. Perley of Concord, who "loved and valued him very much," wrote Pierce two weeks after Cross' death: "His talk was wonderfully pleasant and his wild adventures as related by himself if they could be written down in the same words, would be as charming almost, as Robinson Crusoe." Unfortunately, the project failed, denying Abigail Cross a source of income and future historians a valuable work.[7]

In death, Cross continued to garner both respect and scorn. Items that he owned and letters he wrote became valued relics of the slain commander. Richard Cross managed to bring his brother's saddle, journal, belt, sword, and revolver home to Lancaster, while the contents of Cross' personal chest were divided among the officers of the Fifth. Cross' papers became widely scattered across the nation, many being destroyed as the years went on. The beautifully engraved sword ordered for Cross by members of the regiment arrived later that summer and was given to the Cross family, who then gave the sword and watch to Henry Kent, who shortly before his own death presented them to the State of New Hampshire. The flag that George Nettleton captured at Antietam was returned to the Cross family after the colonel's death and took an honored position in the family parlor. In 1898, in the midst of the national period of reunion, Persis Cross Chase sent the flag back to North Carolina, where it still resides. Between Fredericksburg and Gettysburg, Cross maintained a sporadic correspondence with historian Benson Lossing, who wrote, "I have two or three letters from him + also his photograph, which I highly prize as mementoes of one of the bravest saviors of the Republic"[8]

The officers of the Fifth who survived Cross' purges, temper, and the war elected, in public at least, to forget the harshness their commander exhibited towards them during the war. Many chose to remember him as a peculiar, excellent combat officer who made the Fifth what it was, rather than as a hard, vain man with a drinking problem. Although he commanded the Fifth New Hampshire from Chancellorsville to Cold Harbor, Colonel Charles Hapgood always referred to it as Cross' regiment: "Col. Cross made it what it was, and to him belongs all the honor which it has achieved." Dr. William Child knew that "this Regt. will never be what it has been" after the colonel's death. Charles Hale, haunted by the last image of Cross walking into Rose's Woods, recalled, "I never see a lion stalking up and down but what I think of Cross. I can see him now, as I used to see him, stalking up and down in his restless way, stroking that tawny beard and looking seventeen different ways out of his eyes for Sunday."

Mather Cleveland, a New Hampshire historian and veteran of both World Wars, wrote of the tumultuous relationship between the colonel and his line officers: "Colonel Cross was a commander who never spared himself and expected and required the same sort of effort from his company commanders. Some measure of his high standards or perhaps a difficult personality is indicated by the fact that of his ten original company commanders, one was discharged, and five others resigned." The purges that Cross conducted on contributed to the Fifth's becoming a superb outfit, filling vacancies with men from the ranks who, like their colonel, knew the business of war. One Fifth officer vividly remembered in his memoirs "that anything that stood in front of the 5th when Cross saw his first chance to get a whack at the Johnnies was more than likely to get hurt." The public memory of these officers precluded the harshness he exhibited towards his subordinates and contributed to his popular memory as a fearless combat leader.[9]

The adjutant general of New Hampshire, despite the frequent complaints and requests Cross sent the department, wrote, "Colonel Cross was a man remarkable for his activity, courage, and fertility of resources in all emergencies. He had led a life almost romantic in its adventures and perils." Although he often proved a burden on the Republican administration in New Hampshire, Cross' command of the Fifth Regiment proved admirable and a credit to the state Second Corps commander. General Winfield Scott Hancock considered Cross "a magnificent fighter" and remembered him throughout his life. A member of Hancock's staff recalled, "If Colonel Cross ever knew fear, no one ever discovered it."[10]

Immediately after his death, a collection was started in the state to erect a monument in memory of Colonel Cross, to be placed over his then unmarked grave in the Wilder Cemetery in Lancaster. The *Cincinnati Times,* Cross' employer in the 1850s, also canvassed the West for funds, writing, "The object is a laudable one, and should be persisted until a structure shall mark the grave of the valiant officer, indicative of the appreciation in which he was held by those who knew him well." Residents of Lancaster and veterans of the Fifth gathered money to pay for it. Among those contributing the most was William Heywood, whose son was among the first to die when the Fifth took the field. Some hoped the monument would be greater than that erected in honor of Revolutionary War general John Stark. Instead, the money gathered barely paid for a large, five-foot tall block of granite. The monument was finally ready in late 1866 and was placed over his grave. Again, it passed to Henry Kent to write a fitting record in memory of his friend. The tall monument included the Masonic square and compass, and this inscription:[11]

> Col. Edward Cross
> 5th N.H. Infantry Vols.
> Born April 22nd, 1832. Mortally Wounded
> July 2, 1863, while leading his command,
> The 1st Brigade, 1st Division, 2nd Army Corps
> at the Battle of Gettysburg, Penn.
> The Fighting Fifth
> Raised and Disciplined by Col. Cross
> performed distinguished service through
> the War and was led by him in the Battles
> of Rappahannock, Fair Oaks, Yorktown,
> Savage's Station, Peach Orchard, White Oak
> Swamp, Malvern Hill, Charles City, Antietam,
> Fredericksburg, and Gettysburg.
> This Monument
> is Erected in Memory of
> The Accomplished Journalist, Brave Pioneer,
> Chivalric Soldier, Affectionate Son,
> True Friend and Faithful Craftsman
> Who after a life of adventure at the
> Commercial and Political centers and in
> the distant Territories of the Republic.
> Died for its Honor and Integrity.
> Gentle, Courteous, and Brave. The story of
> His Life closes with the fitting record
> Died on the Field of Honor.

Still standing over Colonel Cross' final resting place, the monument is a daily reminder to those who climb the steep hill in Lancaster of the service, life, and death of Edward Cross.

After the death of their son, Abigail and Ephraim Cross continued to live in the old family house on Main Street in Lancaster, living off their son's pension, granted in May 1864, at the rate of thirty dollars a month. His estate of some 10,000 dollars, earned from the Arizona silver mines, was enough to pay off his father's debts, but many in Lancaster worried that Ephraim Cross would continue to sell off Cross family property as he struggled to make a living growing vegetables. After supporting his mother for years, the funds came as little solace to Abigail, who, destroyed by the news of her son's death, became a recluse, barely leaving the family home and refusing to meet with visitors who came to discuss her son. She worked closely with Henry Kent, in his only action as an attorney, to petition for and receive an additional monthly amount, but again the politicians held firm and denied the advancement, believing the family to be financially sound after the colonel's estate settled. Colonel Ephraim Cross died in 1876, still using the title he earned in the militia many years earlier, and Abigail died in July 1883. The *Coos County Democrat* remembered her as "a woman of strong mind, great memory, a keen observer," all traits she passed to her eldest son, Edward.[12]

In a state that produced few nationally known Civil War soldiers, Colonel Cross became a symbol of the Granite State, representing men who could cope with the hardships of campaigning and always seemed to stand like "men of granite." Stories of Cross' actions in combat, especially at Antietam blocking D.H. Hill's flanking movement by screaming like an Apache warrior, became part of the campfire stories retold by veterans at reunions and Grand Army of the Republic meetings. In 1879, at the dedication of the Civil War monument in Manchester, the Rev. J.J. Hall gave a passionate discourse to thousands about the men from New Hampshire who served in the war. Of the Fifth, Hall said, "The picture of Col. Cross at Antietam is the picture of bravery not often surpassed. Though struck in the head by a piece of a shell early in the day, yet with his head bound around with a handkerchief, and face crimsoned and eyes darkened by blood, he led his men until the darkness of night closed the conflict. And on the field of Gettysburg he showed the world how the sons of New Hampshire can hold the foe back."

This large granite monument, with a long inscription, marks Cross' final resting place in Lancaster (author's collection).

Beginning in 1875, the Civil War veterans of New Hampshire began holding reunions at the Weirs, on Lake Winnipesaukee, a lake once visited by a young Cross. The Fifth was there as well, building a large "cabin" to hold their annual reunions in, where stories of their colonel and his battles were a constant memory. On the wall of the veterans' gathering place hung a painting of Colonel Cross; in 1889, the New Hampshire Veterans Association dedicated their weeklong reunion to his memory, naming the Weirs encampment Camp E.E. Cross.[13]

In 1886, the veterans of the Fifth returned to Gettysburg to dedicate a monument to the regiment. Composed of granite boulders recovered nearby and an upright granite block with bronze plaques carved and cast in New Hampshire, the monument, a single feature on the battlefield, gave the illusion of General Richardson's order at Fair Oaks to stand like the stone walls of New Hampshire. Efforts to erect a statue to Cross' memory in Concord failed, instead the state paid, in 1871, to have a lifelike portrait of him placed in the state house, along with other fallen officers from the state. As much as the Gettysburg monument was for the other men of the Fifth who died in the war, it was truly a memorial to the colonel. Indeed, one of the plaques stated, "On this spot fell mortally wounded Edward E. Cross, Col. 5th N.H. Vols. Comndg. 1st Brigade, 1st Division, Second Corps. July 2nd 1863." Often visited by the veterans of the Fifth, the monument was, and remains, an enduring reminder of the regiment's service at Gettysburg. Many veterans of the regiment, especially the original volunteers from 1861, were proud to state, they were "with Cross and the Fifth New Hampshire at Gettysburg."[14]

While Edward Cross died a hero's death at Gettysburg, his brother Dick ended his Civil War career in disgrace. He became the Fifth's lieutenant colonel based on seniority, but he was never respected in any capacity by his fellow officers. Without the protection of his brother, Cross could not function in the army. After spending the winter of 1864 guarding Confederate prisoners near Point Lookout, Maryland, he was charged with absence without leave, conduct unbecoming an officer, disobedience of orders, and drunkenness on duty. After a lengthy court martial, with many Fifth officers testifying against Cross on his habits, vices, and leniency with suspected southern sympathizers, he was cashiered and dismissed from the service. With his military service over, Cross returned to Lancaster and, like his older brother, suffered from the wounds he received at Fair Oaks and Chancellorsville. He held a variety of positions after the war throughout the country, including working as a "magnetic healer" and working in Ontario, for a railroad, where he married a Canadian woman.

By the late 1880s Dick Cross was again serving, this time as a police officer at the Treasury Building in Washington. As he aged, his Chancellorsville wound continued to plague him, and as he coughed up blood and phlegm constantly. His widow wrote, "He was obliged to sleep in his chair. Many times when exhausted by a long attack of coughing, he would fall asleep." On occasion, as the attacks increased, Cross went days without sleep, fearing he would choke to death. Fellow officers in the Fifth rallied to his side, writing affidavits to the Pension Bureau about the nature of his wounds. Former lieutenant Everett S. Fitch wrote of the Chancellorsville injury and stated, "I know him to be a person worthy to be believed." The coughing spells soon gave way to heart problems, with a heart attack finally doing what Confederate bullets did not, in September 1894 when he was fifty-nine. His body was returned to Lancaster and buried near his brother, while the stone was simply inscribed, "Lieut. Col. 5. Regt. N.H.V." The third Cross brother, Frank, returned to Lancaster after his service on the Peninsula, and then, like his older brother, went west to Kansas City, Missouri. He died there in 1884. Colonel Nelson Cross survived the war, and, unlike his half brother, became a brevet brigadier general for "gallant and meritorious services." He resumed the practice of law and moved to Boston after the war.[15]

While his war service was not as spectacular as that of his friend, Henry Oakes Kent served the Union effort as well, recruiting and forwarding his neighbors to the front. After the war, Kent remained in Lancaster, where he helped organize the Edward E. Cross Post 16, Grand Army of the Republic, honoring his friend and neighbors who died in the war each Decoration Day, and serving as the post and state commander. He became a popular speaker and was active in Norwich University alumni affairs his entire life. Always a businessman, Kent sold the *Coos Republican,* and the paper, which remains in print today, again became the *Coos Democrat.* He also ran a paper mill and a bank. He aligned himself with his old friend's party in 1872, three times being a candidate for Congress. He raised two children and continued to be active in Lancaster affairs until his death in March 1909 at age seventy-five. With his passing went the man who had known Edward Cross the best.[16]

Since Cross' death at Gettysburg, there has been a strong effort to have Cross posthumously promoted to brigadier general. Indeed, two other men killed in the vicinity of Cross on the afternoon of July 2, 1863, Colonel Strong Vincent and Brigadier General Samuel K. Zook, were both promoted after their deaths to the next higher rank. Surprisingly enough, the Lincoln administration on March 13, 1865, awarded hundreds of brevet promotions to many in the army who worked in supply, administration, and other rear echelon areas instead of on the front line; again Cross did not even earn a brevet promotion to brigadier general.

While a myriad of reasons could have prevented the Cross promotion —

such as vigorously pursuing deserters, swift justice, striking men with a sword, threatening subordinates with violence, and a host of other causes— one thing stands out above all others. From the time he received his commission, Cross battled the Republican administration, both in Washington and Concord. As a Democrat, Cross believed that those in power were doing little to pursue a policy that would reunite the nation. He preferred restoring the Union and leaving slavery intact, believing that the Constitution, at the time, protected the institution. As his actions in combat earned him national acclaim and the attention of those who could promote and further his quest for a star, he became even more outspoken in his disdain for the Lincoln administration. This, combined with actions such as prosecuting Orastus Verry even after receiving orders to the contrary, the contents of his private letters leaking out, and throwing out well-connected Republicans such as Captain Richard Welch, doomed his case.

At the beginning of the war, Lincoln needed a strong Democrat base to support the war effort, and promoted politically successful but militarily incompetent men such as Benjamin Butler and others to high rank. As the Emancipation Proclamation went into effect and the war turned in favor of the Union, the president no longer needed the support of men such as Butler and Cross and could get away with not promoting men like them to higher grades. William English, a New York based reporter, stated plainly why Cross never received a promotion: "The Colonel was not right with his own State authorities politically, and also in addition to his Democratic views was not slow to give vent to his likes and dislikes; talked too plainly perhaps." To this Henry Kent added, "Col. Cross was ardent, impetuous and unreserved in his acts and feelings. He was wont on all occasions to canvass freely the policy or motives involved in the struggle." In the end, Edward Cross was his own worst enemy and denied the promotion himself.[17]

The root cause of Cross' behavior off the battlefield has also been the subject of some speculation, with some belief that Cross had a mental condition that contributed to his erratic behavior. While some mental condition might have been present, the colonel himself, a lifelong alcoholic, documents the cause of this behavior. By his own admission, Cross made no excuse for heavy drinking in his prewar days, even going so far as to describe the amounts he drank and the actions that it led to, such as breaking bar stools over German immigrants' heads and fighting the Cincinnati police. Cross loved sherry, eggnog, and whiskey and was constantly searching for his next drink. Many in the Fifth never saw their colonel drink in public, but the bottle was always present in the background. James Larkin, who ended the war as the Fifth's lieutenant colonel, referred to Cross as "a whiskey spiritualist," and said he had "seen its effect (drinking) on many occasions." In the customs of the time, it was common for army officers to drink with their fellow officers at night, but Cross found the bottle too tempting and drank to excess, thus leading to much of his rough behavior in camp. Unlike many others, however, Cross knew when duty called and was always sober in combat.[18]

As the 1900s began, and with the deaths of many Fifth veterans, the story of Cross and his actions off and on the battlefield began to fade from memory, despite many speeches on the colonel ending with "New Hampshire should never forget such men." Instead, William Child in his regimental history and Thomas Livermore through his colorful narrative *Days and Events* told the story of Cross and the Fifth. In Concord, Cross was a constant presence, as a well-placed portrait of him and Major Edward Sturtevant looked down upon visitors and politicians alike, as a memorial to two of New Hampshire's sons who never came home.

It was not until the late 1980s that a major push got underway again to have the United States Army award Cross his star. Spurred on by a group of Civil War buffs, a part-time sanitation worker, and a local police chief, the movement ebbed and flowed over the years, the Senate refusing to take action and the Army denying the case as "there is a policy against promoting people after they died." While the push to promote Cross is a noble one, trying to correct a historical wrong, the colonel himself would not think so. He earned it while he lived and it was denied to him because of his anti-

In 1886, the veterans of the Fifth gathered to dedicate a monument on the spot where Colonel Cross fell (Gettysburg National Military Park).

Republican politics. Cross did not compromise with the Lincoln administration and it cost him the star. Even if he had survived Gettysburg and the war, Cross never would have received a promotion.

On April 22, 2004, following a renewed surge of interest in Colonel Cross, Governor Craig Benson promoted Cross to brevet brigadier general in the unorganized New Hampshire State Militia, a rank and award that held no real weight and is perhaps an insult to the man. The same month, the politicians in Concord sent a proclamation to the United States House of Representatives asking for Cross' promotion, stating, "The New Hampshire General Court finds that Colonel Cross's record of conduct, performance, and devotion to duty reflect his allegiance to the highest standards of the military profession, and that, if not for his untimely death at Gettysburg, Colonel Cross would have received a promotion of brigadier general." The House never took up the resolution, and the motion died. A promotion, whether awarded in 1863 or 2013, would do nothing to change the man and his views. Perhaps the most interesting facet of Cross' life involves his long sought after promotion and its continued denial, despite his earning it many times over. Colonel Cross died as a colonel and needs to be remembered as such today.[19]

The Fifth New Hampshire ended the Civil War with a reputation that few other regiments, North or South, were able to garner. The Fifth returned from the Army of the Potomac in August 1863 to refill its vacant ranks, unfortunately with substitutes and deserters who broke the fine tradition of excellence that Cross established. The regiment returned to the front lines in June 1864, fighting at Cold Harbor and Petersburg before finally ending the war with severe losses in the pursuit to Appomattox. When it was over, 2,496 men had served in the Fifth New Hampshire, and 295 of its officers and men died in combat operations. The fact that more men from the regiment died in action than any other infantry regiment in the Union army made it unique, while the reputation of standing firm under fire and never retreating while Cross was in command contributed to the well-earned reputation. A veteran of the Fifth remembered it was his colonel's "character, intrepid spirit, and power" which helped mold the Fifth New Hampshire into an excellent combat unit. After the regiment had been filled with recruits, substitutes, and malcontents who deserted by the score, George Gove, promoted to lieutenant for his heroism in the Wheatfield, wrote, "The glory of this regt departed when Col. Cross was killed." [20]

In the many published histories of the Civil War, Colonel Cross has always been a prominent and controversial figure. For most historians, three widely available sources have represented the most referenced sources on Cross for the last century. The first published source that brought Cross to light was Otis Waite's 1870 *New Hampshire in the Great Rebellion*. Using published newspaper accounts and official battle reports, Waite produced a 600-page tome that documented the complete story of the Granite State in the Civil War. Using available resources, Waite was able to produce a short biographical sketch of the colonel and followed his life through the battles. Waite's task was to write a heroic sketch of the colonel, focusing only on his battlefield antics, and not discussing his actions off the battlefield that alienated him from the high command.[21]

In 1893, Dr. William Child, who ended the war as the Fifth's regimental surgeon, wrote the official history of the regiment in *A History of the Fifth Regiment New Hampshire Volunteers in the American Civil War*. Following the standard practices set by other New Hampshire veterans beginning in the 1880s, the book is a colorful potpourri of veteran's remembrances, letters, diaries, pictures, rosters, and battle descriptions. Child, who did not join the regiment until after the Peninsula Campaign was over, heavily relied on Cross' wartime diary and papers to write his history, which was paid for by subscriptions raised by Fifth New Hampshire veterans. Throughout the book, Colonel Cross is a prominent figure Child on more than one occasion gave Cross credit for making the Fifth what it was, one of the finest infantry regiments in the Union army. In describing Cross' character, he wrote this:

> Colonel Edward E. Cross was an ideal leader for a volunteer regiment. Dignified in bearing, well proportioned, tall, erect, features handsome, beard brown and flowing, earnest, eager expression of face, manner nervous, perhaps restless, and having eyes that were mild when quiet, but which blazed in moments of excitement, riding like a Mexican, and having the nervous stride and free swing of a frontiersman, he impressed the imagination of his men with his presence as well as with his impetuous spirit, and the reputation of his previous romantic career. In battle his proud courage, his fervor of attack, his intrepid bearing in defense, his quiet perception of all the chances of the conflict, made his men the willing instrument of his will. And, unconsciously, the greater the danger and doubt, the more they recognized him as their leader.[22]

While Child easily praised Cross' actions both on and off the battlefield, describing how he cared for his men, the doctor also was quick to point out the actions he took against those he felt were not up to his standards as a soldier. Child wrote of his faults—hitting men, arguing with officers, and other trespasses—but did not delve into detail about his politics or battles with Republicans and abolitionists. Child's colonel is a man with some troubles who was a highly competent officer in combat, and was both loved and feared by his men. Child's *History of the Fifth New Hampshire* has, since 1893, remained the standard source for firsthand material on the regiment, being extremely rare as an original, and popular as a reprint.

Captain Thomas Livermore, who ended the war as a colonel, owed much to Colonel Cross for his own rapid rise in rank. Livermore was typical of many young Fifth officers, such as Charles O. Ballou, Charles Hale, William Adams Moore, and Frank Butler, who rose to prominence under Cross, showing him the respect the colonel expected, and knowing how to behave around him to avoid problems. While Livermore was only nineteen when the colonel died, he was able to be an effective observer of the events that transpired in the Fifth's history. Cross' mentoring and leadership were a continuing inspiration to him long after the war. After the war, Livermore began writing a book about his experiences in the Civil War called *Days and Events,* which provides one of the best views into Cross' wartime experiences. He was also one of the few Fifth veterans who gave an impartial look at Cross:

> He was a very brave man, and clear-headed in a fight; he took the most excellent care of his men in a sanitary way, and was a good disciplinarian. He had his faults which injured him more than any one else; such as jumping at conclusions, and criticizing and condemning men and measures without stint. It was his too free animadversions in political matters at home which prevented his promotion, which he had long deserved before he died, and it is or ought to be a reproach against those politicians who were instrumental in retarding his promotion that they allowed his words to weigh against his deeds; for I am informed that it was his criticisms of the administration and Republican politicians that convinced them that he was a Copperhead, when no man was more earnest for success in the field. If all the colonels in the army had been like him we should never have lost a battle.[23]

Livermore was the only Fifth New Hampshire veteran who wrote objectively about the colonel and fully knew the reason why his promotion failed. Because of Livermore's close association with Cross, *Days and Events,* which was published after Livermore's death, has remained the most cited volume for those researching Cross. Livermore did not maintain a diary during the war and wrote the memoir afterwards from memory. While excellent in its details about Cross, Livermore was often confused about actual dates and withheld names of those he felt would be offended, making some details confusing. Despite some problems, *Days and Events* remains the single best source on Cross' wartime service with the Fifth New Hampshire.

With the passing of the last Fifth New Hampshire veterans in the 1930s, the living memory of Colonel Cross and his deeds faded from memory. Antiquarian bookshops stocked expensive copies of *Days and Events,* while Child's regimental history was in most village libraries throughout New Hampshire. It was not until the 1950s that a resurgence of interest in the Civil War, spurred on by the upcoming centennial, that an interest in the actions of Cross began to resurface. Casting a wide net, Bruce Catton conducted extensive research and produced a three-volume series in the 1950s about the Army of the Potomac. His described the colonel as "a tall, lean, rangy man with reddish whiskers, and a balding pate. A man of rough and jocose energy who had made his regiment one of the best combat units in the army and was obviously in line for promotion."

The only mistake Catton made, like many over writers the years, is stating that Cross served in the Mexican War rather than in the Reform War of 1860. Unlike Livermore and Child, who wrote of Cross' faults off the battlefield but tried to make them a part of the Cross persona, Catton chose not to write of Cross' transgressions, instead simply praising what he did on the battlefield. Catton introduced a new generation of readers to the Civil War, while giving more attention than usual to Colonel Cross and the Fifth New Hampshire than to other regiments in the narrative. Perhaps Catton's greatest comment on the Fifth was that "he had never been able to determine which of two regiments was the most courageous combat units in the Union Army — the Black Hats of Michigan, or the Fifth New Hampshire Volunteers." In a 1973 *Historical New Hampshire* article on the Fifth New Hampshire, Donald H. Richards wrote, "Colonel Edward E. Cross was probably the greatest determinant in the welding together of this fighting unit."[24]

Even in later life, Henry Kent always remembered his best friend (courtesy Lancaster Historical Society).

While Cross became a popular literary character through Catton's writings, it was surprising that the attention did not garner additional scholarship from Civil War historians. In a well-written 1975 B.A. thesis, Janet R. Youngholm, a Lancaster native and undergraduate student at Princeton University, wrote a biography of Cross' life, focusing primarily on his Civil War years. Using Cross' long-lost journal for the first time, she was able to tell the story of Cross' life as he experienced it, but she did little in the way of analysis or interpretation. Being a thesis, the work was not widely circulated but was consulted from time to time by historians. In 1993, the subject of Cross as an academic work arose again when chose by United States Navy commander

J.P. Wilkins for his master's thesis at the Army War College, Carlisle Barracks, Pennsylvania. Using the collections of the neighboring United States Army Military History Institute, Wilkins gave a glancing overview into Cross' actions in the battles of Fair Oaks, Antietam, Fredericksburg, Chancellorsville, and Gettysburg. Using his knowledge of military tactics, Wilkins tied Cross' individual actions in his five battles into the overall picture of the war, concluding that "Cross was a complex man, a symbiosis of virtue and vice, rigidity and compassion, iron resolution and human weakness." Much like Youngholm's work, Wilkins' thesis sat on the dusty library shelves, forgotten and unused.[25]

In published Civil War books, Cross again occasionally became a subject of discussion by historians, but more often than not by National Park Rangers at Richmond and Antietam National battlefields, and Gettysburg and Fredericksburg/Spotsylvania National Military parks. Here, the rangers, in leading battlefield tours that covered the fields the Fifth fought on, would tell of his actions both on and off the battlefield, often simply quoting Child and Livermore. This introduced new generations to the colonel from New Hampshire, but did not generate widespread interest. Still, every summer when the Lancaster Historical Society opened its Wilder House Museum, the occasional visitor who had heard of Cross would travel to the remote town to visit his gravesite and perhaps see a small case containing photographs of the colonel, along with his revolver, sword, and saddle.

It was not until 2001, however, that Colonel Cross became widely known outside of New Hampshire and the Civil War community. With the publication of their book, *My Brave Boys: To War with Colonel Cross and the Fighting Fifth,* Mike Pride and Mark Travis were able to update the Fifth's story and bring it to a wider audience. The editors of the *Concord Monitor,* Pride and Travis were able to gather sufficient materials from newspapers, letters, diaries, and pension records to tell the story of the Fifth New Hampshire outside of simply paraphrasing Livermore and Child. In their book, Cross is the central figure in the molding of 1,000 New Hampshiremen into a unit that fit his idea of what a soldier should be. Richly balanced between camp life and the battlefield, *My Brave Boys* proved to be a successful social history of the Fifth that brought Cross and his regiment back from the point of obscurity. The authors were able to break from the traditions of Waite and others to portray the colonel for what he truly was, a lion in battle and a political extremist away from it. Despite their treatment of Cross, *My Brave Boys* is primarily a history of the Fifth New Hampshire and not a biography of Cross.

In 2003, the publishing of "*Stand Firm and Fire Low*": *The Civil War Writings of Colonel Edward E. Cross* expanded the bibliography of Cross works. Combining unpublished Cross journals, reports, letters, and poetry, Walter

Holden and the special collections staff at the University of New Hampshire were able to produce an edited and annotated compilation of Cross' known war time writings in print, affording scholars and buffs across the nation a ready source of his powerful writings in print form.[26]

Since Cross' death, "innumerable" people have traveled to Lancaster, New Hampshire, with the idea of writing a biography of Colonel Cross, only to end the project before it began. Among them was MacKinlay Kantor, a well-published author, whose work included the acclaimed *Andersonville*. In his 1952 book, *Gettysburg,* Kantor wrote that Cross was a tyrant who "was a cruel man who issued unnecessary orders merely because he had the power to do so." Kantor himself considered writing a biography of Cross but found Cross' involvement with the American Party a disgrace and decided against it. Still others have made the attempt, pursuing the project for years, only to die before completing it, or being unable to find the mother lode of material that resides in repositories around the nation.

In 2005, shortly before her own death, Faith Kent, Henry Kent's grand-

A century and a half after his death, Cross remains one of the most revered soldiers in the Granite State; his grave is frequently visited by modern-day members of his regiment (courtesy Lancaster Historical Society).

daughter, gave an everlasting treasure to the people of New Hampshire by donating the seventy-five letters that Cross wrote to her grandfather from 1850 to 1863 to the New Hampshire Historical Society. This gift, in addition to Walter Holden's 2003 donation of Colonel Cross' journal and other personal papers to the University of New Hampshire in Durham, has finally opened up the door to further research the life of Cross. Advancements in technology to search for newspaper articles written by and about Cross and long forgotten published and unpublished sources from Cross' contemporaries such as Edward E. Sturtevant, Charles O. Ballou, George Gove, and newspaper correspondents have added much new material about his life and service, finally making a biography possible.[27]

In 1936, Helen Cross Denison, Colonel Cross' last surviving sibling, died at age eighty-six, and, like the rest of the family, was laid to rest in the family plot in the "ancient cemetery." She willed the old Cross homestead on Main Street to the Town of Lancaster, hoping it would serve as a memorial for her family, who gave so much to the Union cause. In addition, she donated 3,000 dollars to build a proper memorial to her fallen brother in the town center. The Lancaster town council voted to raze the old structure that Richard Everett had built and erect the monument and park in its place. The memorial was in the form of a blue granite obelisk characteristic of the granite hills that had produced the fighting colonel from New Hampshire. The monument was inscribed with the same words that Cross' best friend, Henry O. Kent, wrote in 1866. Added to it, however, was a line from Milton's *Samson Agonistes*, a testament to the way Colonel Edward Ephraim Cross had lived and died, as a magnificent fighter: "Nothing is here for tears, Nothing to wail or knock the breast; No weakness, no contempt, dispraise or blame, Nothing but well and fair, And what may quiet us into a death so noble."[28]

Appendix

"The Young Volunteers"

Using the pen name of Richard Everett, Edward Cross wrote many fictional stories during the antebellum era that were widely reprinted all over the nation. Of all the stories that he wrote at this time, perhaps none gained more acclaim than "The Young Volunteers." The story is a fictional look at a group of men from Grafton County, New Hampshire, who fought in the Ninth United States Infantry during the Mexican War. Although fictional, it is heavily based on Cross' interactions with these men growing up in Lancaster. He based the specifics of the story on the lives of three Concord printers who died in the Mexican War fighting in the Ninth. Written in 1854, this was a story from his youth, not a prediction of the future but a work of fiction based in fact. Despite the eerie similarities in "The Young Volunteers" that eventually occurred when Cross was in command of the Fifth New Hampshire, it must be remembered that this story is not a prediction of events to come in the Civil War.

This is the first time "The Young Volunteers" has been reprinted in its entirety since the story first appeared in the November 19, 1854, edition of the Cincinnati Dollar Weekly Times. Here, for the first time in 160 years, is the story as Edward Cross wrote it.

The Young Volunteers
An Incident of the Mexican War
By Richard Everett

There is no class of men who have more passion for venture, the love for excitement, so largely developed, as printers. They are continually wandering from city to city, from land to land restless, unsettled; and ready to engage in any enterprise that promises honor and profit, or affords them an opportunity to "see the world." Being always intelligent, well-informed men, (their business makes them so,) they generally fall into leading rank but ventures, by a common consent. There are few *old* printers; the business is followed awhile and then left for something more productive of that great necessity to human enjoyment—cash. It is an excellent business to rise from; it furnishes many of our most talented and popular men-authors, editors, speakers, lawyers, physicians, and even clergymen. A printer is well versed in human nature—there is no place like a printing office to sharpen a man's ideals, and give him a knowledge of the *real* motives, intents, and actions of humanity. Thus a printer grows wise, as it were, has an inexhaustible store of miscellaneous information, and no one can say that they would not do their part towards moving on the world. They are great lovers of the drama — many of them become actors, and good ones, too. We know half a dozen at the present time, who have left well "the art preservative of arts," to "hold the mirror up to Nature," on the stage. Printers are peculiar men; they have attended melancholy near natures, a sort of deep conviction that this world is a monstrous humbug—they have found it out—there's no sincerity, no confidence in it. We have noticed this characteristic often, in prevails thrall the whole craft.

The Mexican war illustrated the ease with which our country could raise a volunteer army at short notice. The merchant left his counting room, the lawyer his office, the farmer his plough and scythe—and hurried to the battlefield. But more printers volunteered in proportion to their numbers, than any other class of our citizens. And they were splendid soldiers. Many a disciple of Faust, Gutenberg, Stanhope, Caxton, Franklin, and a host of other illustrious men who have honored the noble craft—"sleep their last sleep"— "where the rolls of the yellow Rio Grande," or beneath the clods at Aztec soil. And so it was in Cuban expedition, and later in Col. Walker's mad crusade to lower California; the little army with one third printers. They are adventurous beings.

The role of the drum had scarcely echoed among the New England hills, calling our citizens to arms, one was proposed to raise a volunteer company in one of the districts of New Hampshire. He was soon accomplished, and enrolled in the ninth Regiment, commanded by Colonel Ransom. This Regiment was composed of one company from each of the New England States, in its commander was a soldier by profession, being, at the time of his appointment, president of a well-known military academy. A few weeks were spent in drilling and making ready, and one pleasant morning the battalion left for it Newport, Rhode Island, and marched on board the transport ships "Lapland" and "Reindeer," which would speed their way directly to Vera Cruz. The piers were thronged with people, friends, and relatives of the volunteers, waiting to say one parting word, and take their last messages to the dear ones at home. Soon, a cheer proclaimed the soldiers were coming, and with a quick martial step the approach toward the wharf. Their colors were unfurled, their arms shone brightly, and the drums and fifes peeled off that sweet old tune to a soldier loved so well "The

Girl I Left Behind Me!" A brief period was spent in leave taking; many hands were there clasped for the last time on earth, and manly voices humbled as they said "goodbye!" It was a time to the holy emotions of the human heart to be aroused in gush forth. It was not a compensatory movement on the part of these soldiers to engage in foreign war. They had not been torn from their homes to fight battles! No they were simply entering their countries call—freely joyfully for her, for her cause was her cause! They were all *volunteers!* It was a noble, patriotic spectacle!—Fathers parting with their sons—brothers with brothers—with a feeling of patriotism and pride that swell far over their sorrow.

The Regiment filed on board the ships, the cables were loosened—white sails shaken out the breeze, and then, amid cheers and martial music the vessels quieted out to see carrying nearly 1000 men. 18 months passed away, and one day a lone vessel the same harbor, came to her moorings at the pier, and from her deck *one hundred and fifty men*, ragged, sick, mutilated, marched silently and entered the fort. They were the shattered remnants of the "Bloody Ninth!"—War, pestilence, and death in many forms had claimed the residue. Their bones are scattered from the sands of Vera Cruz to the green valley of the capital of Mexico. The neglected graves about Jalapa, Perote, and Puebla, tell where scores and scores are buried while on the fields of Contreras, Churubusco, Chapultepec lie their bleached remains. Noble Regiment! Well did it earn and bear its terrible appellation! When did it waver in the charge? When did it fail to meet the shock of battle and hurl in furiously back? Brave men and true! Boldly did you sustain the war like reputation of your fathers Stark, and, Preston, Putnam, Green, those men of well proved valor. Honor to the glorious dead!—"O, it is sweet for our country to die where ranks are contending! Bright is the wreath of our fame, glory awaits us for aye—Glory that never is dim shining on with the light never-ending—Glory that shall never fade—never, O never! Away!"

In the second platoon of "Company H," the New Hampshire corps, were two young printers—"Tom," a sergeant, and "Harry," a corporal. Bold, ambitious, and of martial bearing, they were among the foremost to enroll themselves as volunteers; and from the hour they were "mustered in," until each found a soldier's grave, braver men never marched to battle.

The Ninth landed at Vera Cruz, and joining the brigade commanded by General Pierce, for the main army, which under Scott was waiting at Puebla. It was toilsome work, marching over the hot, yielding sand under the blistering sun and carrying heavy musket with the usual accoutrements of a soldier but the men bore it cheerfully. Water was scarce, and when procured miserable stuff, warm and brackish—very unlike the cold, pure element that gushed from the native hills of our two friends. Many young men were in the ranks, and it was cheering to see the patience with which they bore every hardship, and how proficient they soon became competent in company and battalion drill and in the manual of arms, for Col. Ransom was a strict tactician. He was proud of his regiment, proud of the intelligence, bravery, and good behavior of his men. And they in turn, loved their Col., and respected him as a skillful, kind and, and gallant officer. Such was the mutual feeling of regard between officers and men, that existed all through the volunteer portion of our army; and it was one great element of their efficiency. It is the right feeling, and renders an army almost invincible.—Among the "regulars" it was different. There was a wide gulf between those who commanded and those who obeyed. The men looked on their superiors as petty tyrants, whom they obeyed from compulsion, and not from choice. For to their shame be it said, a majority of the regular officers treated their men like dogs—continually banking upon them spleen and ill humor; and at the same time, totally regardless of their comfort and privileges. It was not so with the volunteers, and anyone who served in the Mexican war so testify.

The train approached the "National Bridge," and here the Mexicans were arrayed to check its progress. As the head of that long column came within cannon range—suddenly a volume of white smoke poured forth from the heights above the bridge, and simultaneously there was a loud, startling hiss in the air a few feet above the heads of our men—it was the whizzing of 18 pound shot—not very sweet music to the raw soldier's ear. Our men could not help "ducking" their heads, every time the storm of iron hurtled over them—it was a natural movement, still not calculated to ensure safety; for one does not hear the whiz of a bullet until it has passed by him. The brave Captain Bodfish, who commanded the Grenadier company from Maine—all great stalwart men—saw this "ducking;" he did not like it at all; so turning to his company, he called out—"Boys! I don't want you to dodge—it looks bad, it's unsoldierly you've got to stand fire!" Here a piercing hiss directly over his head caused him involuntarily to dodge in the very style he was condemning, to the great amusement of the "boys" who shouted with merriment. Quick as a thought, the Captain straightened up, the color deepening on his sunburnt face and continued—"it's cowardly, and I'll be damned if *we'll* do it again!" Nor was it done, although the iron darts of war sang their song nearer and nearer.

As our two boys (for neither was 21 years old,) marched along, they whispered to each other a few hasty directions, in case of death, for the order "no loud talking"—had passed down the line. It was the first time they had been under fire, in the opening lesson is always a severe one, especially when given by artillery. Soon, the Mexican guns found their true range, and the balls came lower, tearing up the earth, and now and then making a long bloody lane through the ranks. However, by marching in "open order" much carnage was avoided, and few men were killed. Our volunteers behaved splendidly, obeying their orders with feverish precision and often sending the enemy loud cheers of defiance. And when the American guns open their fire so fierce and rapid was it, that foe soon retreated, and the train passed over in safety. Next came the bridge of Plan del Rio, which the Mexicans had rendered impassable by blowing up. The river's banks were steep and rocky; and the engineers reported that the army could not cross. "All damned nonsense," said giant Captain Bodfish — "give me 500 men and the tools, and I'll build a road there any one day." — The men and tools were furnished, and the road was built in good time. The Captain had built roads before that day, in the lumber swamps of Maine. You couldn't learn him how to cross a river. He "guessed" the Kennebec and Penobscot were pretty considerable streams and he'd bridged them. He wanted to show those "West Pint" fellows that they had some things to learn yet. And so he did.

The country through which our army now marched, was beautiful; for climate fine, and provisions were plenty. But sickness broke out among men, and every day the hastily made graves by the roadside received their victims. The guerrillas, also, were a constant annoyance by their sudden attacks, and cowardly modes of warfare. Woe to the poor straggler that fell into their hands; he met a barbarous and cruel death; they gave no quarter. Company H. did not suffer much at that time, from sickness or guerrillas. The men were temperate, ate little fruit, and never lagged behind. While at Jalapa, our friends Tom and Harry, had an adventure worth recording. By permission of their captain they had walked out of the city a short distance, and as the sun was hot they turned into a cool grove for shelter. — Here they filled their canteens from a bubbling spring, and talked of their hopes and prospects and the various fortunes of war to which they were exposed. Suddenly, Harry espied three melted guerrillas riding slowly towards the grove, with the evident key design of cutting off the Americans from the city. "Come, come, let's leave," urged Harry. "Hold on," was the cool reply "I'm going to have a shot at that chap with a red jacket!" By this time the Lancers were within easy musket range, and just unslinging their escopets. Stepping out of the grove, Tom slowly brought up his musket, poised it a moment — fired, and the "chap a red jacket" tumbled heavily from his horse. — "Good shot," said Harry, "ram down a cartridge — quick! — they're coming." "Fire, then shoot the forward one!" shouted Tom, jerking out his bayonet and fixing it. The Lancers flourishing their weapons, and yelling defiance put their horses to a gallop, and charged toward the grove. The fire lept out of Harry's gun, and the foremost rider, dropping out his uplifted lance swayed back upon his saddle — grasping frantically at vacancy — the blood spouted from his throat, and he too pitched from his seat, a dead man. The survivor, frightened and dreading a dose of lead, reined up his steed — wheeled, and galloped off. Our friends then made a short cut for the city, rejoicing at their good luck, and fully content to remain in camp until excursions to the outskirts could be made with less risk. About 2 o'clock on the 6th day of August, General Pierce's command entered the city of Puebla, and joined the war worn forces of the commander-in-chief. Two days after, the van of the whole army, under Gen. Twiggs, started for the Aztec capital. Gen. Pillow's division, in which marched the Ninth, formed the rear guard. For a time no enemy appeared. The strong pass of the Rio Frio mountains and the frowning hill of El Penon, were alike deserted. Only a few troops of guerrillas, under their notorious chief Padre Jarauta were seen, and they were easily scattered by a few rounds of grape. But on the morning of the 18th, General Worth's division discovered the Mexican army strongly entrenched in and about the village of San Antonio. Then came the first skirmish of Contreras, which lasted until evening without any decisive results. All that night, in a cold, heavy rain, our troops stood to their arms. Some few found shelter in the church of San Geronio, but the main body laid down on the soaked earth without fires, tents, or any shelter, and passed the dismal night. In the Mexican camp could be heard rioting and rejoicing; for their general was so confident of victory that he had sent several couriers to Santa Ana with word that "the barbarians of the North, were completely destroyed!" Those dispatches were next day contradicted by Gen. Valencia in person, for he was one of the first to make tracks from these same "barbarians." Our army rested until about 4 o'clock in the morning, and then set itself in motion. The wet charges were drawn from the guns, dry powder obtained, and then the troops silently formed into columns of attack. Just as day was breaking, Smith's division fell upon the enemy's entrenchments their charging cheer sounding fiercely across the misty field, and in a short time the battle was won.

Tom and Harry faced death like veterans. As they were marching to the assault over some rough ground, a grape shot struck Tom's musket near the lock, in such a direction as to pitch its owner head over heels into a little ravine nearby. Harry's first impulse was to stop and see if his friend was dead, but the stern command *"forward"* that instant came along from the front, and with a deadly feeling of sorrow he took his friend's place and hurried on. A few moment's passed when somebody shouted in Harry's ear — "All right! — tie this handkerchief around my head!" Harry wheeled and there stood Tom, covered with dust and dirt, with the blood streaming from a gash in his forehead, cut by his fall upon the rocks. "It stunned me a moment, that's all. Now if I can pick up a gun, I'm ready!" He was not long in finding a musket, for men were dropping all around him; and half an hour after he used it in the final charge.

"What are those fellows cheering about?" inquired Harry of a comrade, pointing to a group of artillerists who were making the air ring with their cheers over two small cannon. "Why those are O'Brien's guns he lost at Buena Vista," was the answer. "His men have retaken them." Yes they were the same six-pounders and the men were wild with joy at their recovery. Some even hugged and embraced those begrimed pieces like old, long-lost friends. The news spread over the field, and soon Harry saw the tall form of the commander-in-chief in the throng, and saw him waiving his hat and joining in the cheers.

Our two volunteers passed unharmed through the battle of Churubusco. The Ninth did its duty nobly that day, facing the hottest fires without flinching one foot. A brief armistice followed this action, and our tired and ragged troops were recruited and clothed anew. Tom and Harry improved this short interval in writing letters to their friends, and in filling up their journals. We have a letter from one of them, written a few days before the terrible battle of Molino del Ray, in which he says, among other gossip:

"We are getting along pretty well now, since our soldier-life is becoming so exciting. But there are not a few drawback to our comfort; I had a clean shirt yesterday, the first for three weeks. We are promised new shoes, but the Lord knows where our commissary will find them. My volume of Campbell's poems is carefully preserved; I read it moonlight evenings and by the light of our picket fires. It is the only book except Bibles in our company; almost all of our boys have either a Bible or Testament. Some great movement is on foot; we have been making ladders, fascines and fascines for two or three days. We shall have dreadful fighting before we revel in the famous "Halls of the Montezumas." Tom says the aforesaid halls are humbugs. He is well, and today is away on forage duty; you know he is a capital hand at that."

Like brothers these two young soldiers lived; sharing each other's duties and little comforts, and rendering mutual help in the hour of need. They were full of hope, and now that they had seen enough of bloodshed, were anxious for news of peace. They looked forward to the happy hour of meeting with those they had left at home in the "Old Granite State." To their comrades they were much endeared. Officers and men respected and esteemed them as honorable men and good soldiers.

The armistice was broken up, Molino del Rey taken, after one of the most sanguinary battles ever fought on the American Continent. Here, a sad and fearful duty was assigned to the Ninth Regiment; a duty of all others, demanding immediate attention at the hands of humane and careful men. This duty was—*to bury the dead and bring off the wounded.* All that night the regiment pursued its melancholy labor, and—"By the sturdy moonbeam's misty light, And the lanterns dimly burning." They consigned friend and foe to the grave in that trampled and blood-dampened earth. Great trenches were dug in some places, and in others the excavations made by bursting shells were used as graves. Thousands of men had fallen, and the dead lay scattered singly or in great heaps, over an extent of many acres. From the hundreds of wounded there arose a wail of agony fearful to hear. Villainous looking lepers, priests, and prowling camp-followers wandered like ghouls over the field, plundering the dead and dying. The ground was strewed with mangled limbs, and all the slippery with human gore. Fragments of broken wagons, dismounted cannons, muskets, and all the paraphernalia of war, were mingled with the fallen. It was a sickening ghastly sight! Ambulances, wagons, and rude biers were used to convey the wounded to the tents and hospitals, which were soon crowded to overflowing. Many of our men were hurt by the copper shot thrown by the enemy, and in such cases death was sure to follow for the wound instantly gangrened and spread poison into every vein.

On that field was strewn the representatives of many nations and States. There were Aztecs, Germans, Hungarians, French, English, Irish, Americans. There were men from every state of our Union, from Maine, New York, Missouri, Georgia, Texas, who a few hours before had battled with common hopes and glory, side by side beneath a common flag. They had come from their distant homes, strangers to each other, to fight the battles of their country, and together found a common grave in a hostile soil. It was a mournful duty for our volunteers; they would sooner face a storm of fire and death than to gather up and bury the slain, and toil among such scenes of horror. It was too much of the reality war. In Harry's journal, which was kindly sent us by one of his comrades, we find this passage:

"Nearly all last night our regiment was engaged in burying the dead, and in removing to the hospitals such of the wounded as had any chances of life. We took care of all alike, that the enemy may learn humanity if possible; for they often kill our wounded men. It was such dreadful work, that I am absolutely sickened of war. I saw one awful sight, more sad, if possible than any other. In a little hollow, into which a great deal of blood had drained, lay a young and very beautiful Mexican woman. A stray bullet had passed through her head, and killed her instantly. Lying across her breast was an infant moaning wretchedly as it endeavored to draw nourishment from the lifeless bosom of its mother. The little innocent was all dabbed with blood and was the most pitiful sight I ever beheld. We found a Mexican priest, and conducting him to the spot requested him to take care of the child and we would bury the mother. But the brutal wretch, without answering one word stealthily drew a long knife, and plunged it into the babe's throat. Then, muttering that the child would trouble us no longer, he was about to sneak away. We were astonished at such an awful deed, for a moment, but he was soon seized by our indignant men and bayoneted on the spot. Even that was too good for him. We expect another battle soon."

That battle came; it was the storming of Chapultepec. The hill was steep and rocky; it was mined, a deep ditch surrounded the strong fort, which was garrisoned by the flower of the Mexican army. A "forlorn hope" was made up; axes, ladders, picks, fascines, etc. prepared and at 8 o'clock in the morning, the storming parties began to move. They were covered by the heavy battery of Captain Drum, which sent a storm of shells over their heads into the enemy's fortress. Directly after the "forlorn hope" and the voltigeurs, came the Ninth, in columns of companies, open order. Up the hill they pressed, amid the bursting mines, the thick smoke, and the shot that came in torrents. Men fell by scores, every moment. As they neared the fort, a grape shot killed the brave Col Ransom—"Forward the Ninth!" shouted Lieut. Colonel Seymour, as he took command. There was a sudden rush— the ditch was passed—ladders reared against the wall—a fierce hand to hand struggle commenced. Several times were our men repulsed, but the old Puritan blood was up and nothing ever did or ever will stand before it. As our troops gained a foot-hold they used the bayonet and soon cleared the walls. Then, with a chorus of wild cheers, the Mexican flag was hauled down by Seymour, and our stars and stripes run up the tall staff to float victorious over the fortress of Chapultepec. The Ninth lost many men that day. Company H was nearly destroyed, half its members being either killed or wounded. Tom and Harry were each slightly injured.

It was while this assault was going on, that *thirty Irish deserters*, who were captured at Molino del Rey, were summarily hung for their treachery. They had been taken with arms in their hand, and formed a part of "Saint Patrick's Legion," which was made up of Irish deserters and commanded by the infamous Riley. As the colors which they had deserted were seen through the smoke to mount the fort, they were launched off the scaffold and met with a well merited fate. "Thus perish all traitors!"

Harry's journal says:

"We have gained another victory. I cannot call it a 'glorious victory.' It has been bought so dearly. Our brave Colonel is dead, and many other excellent officers. Company H is nearly broken up; only twelve men are left unhurt in my platoon. I write this in great haste, while the boys are filling their cartridge boxes, for we move on the city at once. I hope to write my next in the 'Halls of the Montezumas.'"

He never wrote another line. The troops fell in, and commenced their attack on the outworks of the capital. All the forenoon a sharp fire was kept up on both sides; heavy shot and shells were continually falling under the arches of the great aqueduct where a detachment of the Ninth, with some riflemen and the 2d Pennsylvania regiment were posted. Tom and Harry, becoming greatly fatigued sat down for a moment to rest and eat a few morsels from their haversacks. Although the situation was exposed, they heeded it not, until a six-pound ball, striking the earth within ten feet of them, scattered sand and rubbish in their faces. "This is close work, Tom," remarked Harry. "hadn't we better move?" "Yes, let's—" It was too late. Down came a huge shell, right between them, bursting as it touched the earth. The smoke cleared away, and the men ran eagerly to the place to look for their comrades. What a sight met their eyes! Only a part of Harry's burned and mangled body was there! His head, both arms, had been blown to fragments. Tom, covered with blood and blinded by sand, was lifted from the pit. He was dreadfully wounded. His left arm hung in tatters from its socket, his right foot was torn away, while the left side of his face was burned to a crisp. As his friends carefully laid him upon a blanket, he faintly whispered—"Is Harry killed?" "Yes," was the sad answer—"Then," he returned, "don't move me, I can't live; bury us together where the shell burst." But he was taken to the hospital tent; and although there was no hope of his recovery, he was tenderly cared for. In the meantime the city of Mexico had surrendered, and thus after an immense sacrifice of human life, Mexico was humbled, and our conquering banners mounted the palace of the Aztec kings.

"General Pierce, Sergeant Thomas S. of Company H, Ninth Infantry is but just alive and he wishes to see you," said an orderly to the commanding officer of the brigade, three days after. Tom was almost gone. He had suffered two amputations of his wounded leg, and a third was now necessary. He felt that he should die under the operation. One by one, his few uninjured comrades had been admitted, and bade him an eternal farewell. For many long months had he cheered them on in every hardship. And now they gathered in little groups, and spoke sorrowfully of his sad fate—to die now that the war was ended, and danger past. The Captain and Lieutenant of his company stood beside the amputating board on which the poor boy was stretched. The surgeon and his assistants were ready with upturned sleeves; they only waited for the General, whom Tom wished to see once more. A strong delirium had been working on his brain all morning, but he was now quite calm. The folds of the tent parted, and General P. entered. With a smile, the death stricken youth took his commander's hand, and said— "General, it's all over with me. Doctor B. says I shall certainly die under this amputation but I want it performed. I haven't much to live for. God knows I've tried to do my duty—have I not, Captain Bowers?" "Always, always, Tom, there never was a better soldier," answered the captain. "You hear that General; tell father and mother what the captain says will you?" "I will; I know you have done well," said General P., pressing the trembling hand he held. "And Harry Pike—can't you say the same of him?" "Yes," was the simultaneous reply from the little group. "And now," continued Tom, "I've one thing to ask; will you bury me in the pit that shell made—it's my last request?" 'Any place you wish my poor lad," was the mournful and choking answer. "Well, then, God bless you all, farewell. Captain, let me take your hand. General, when you get back to the old Granite State, tell my friends I died like a soldier. Doctor I'm ready—be quick!" and closing his eyes he sank back upon the board.

Doctor B bared the swollen limb, seized his knife, and with a rapid movement passed the keen, thin instrument into and around the quivering flesh. Then followed a few rapid passes from a saw, and the third amputation was over. For a few seconds the sufferer lay motionless, a deadly pallor on his face and a close compression of the hands he clasped, alone showing the mortal agony that thrilled in every nerve. They bathed his hot forehead with vinegar, which revived him. His eyes opened, but their unnatural glare told that the light of Reason had been overpowered by wild Delirium. His brain was filled with visions of his distant home. Raising up, and gazing earnestly at vacancy, he said in a quivering voice: "It is mother! but she does not know me! Sisters! Brother Will! Have you *all* forgotten me! I have got home again — the war is ended. Ah! how sweet the green elms are waiving — how the sunbeams dance up on the meadows. I am home once mo—" and he fainted in the surgeon's arms. "Oh! God!" whispered the captain, "this is dreadful!" "How can he live an instant!" But again Tom revived, and snatching away the hand his captain held he waved it wildly above his head while he shouted in harrowing tones—"Captain! The lancers are coming — I see their horses through the smoke. Steady boys! They can't break our square! Now fire! That's the way the Ninth does it!" Then, changing his voice to tones of encouragement, he went on. "Come on boys; Harry, let's keep together. Our guns will open soon. There comes the General and his staff — the artillery are cheering them, let's join in — hurrah! Hurrah"— He fell back, a dead man.

That afternoon the muffled drums beat the "Dead March" for Sergeant Thomas S.— as his comrades carried his mortal remains to be buried in the excavation made by that fatal projectile which caused his death. Harry was already interred there, and Mexican soil rests upon few better or braver men than those two boyish volunteers.

Throughout the whole Mexican war our soldiers acquainted themselves with honor. Terrible in battle, humane in victory; bearing danger and hardship without complaint, and always true to their colors. How beautifully did General Scott speak of "the dead, the wounded, and the few unscathed," who had participated in the bloody conflicts, and borne their country's standard through every danger to an honorable peace.

Chapter Notes

The following abbreviations designate the sources for manuscript material:

AAA — American Antiquarian Society, Worcester, Massachusetts.
ANB — Antietam National Battlefield, Sharpsburg, Maryland.
CCCH — Coos County Court House, Lancaster, New Hampshire.
DCL — Rauner Special Collections Library, Dartmouth College, Hanover, New Hampshire.
FRSP — Fredericksburg and Spotsylvania National Military Park, Fredericksburg, Virginia.
GNMP — Gettysburg National Military Park, Gettysburg, Pennsylvania.
LHS — Lancaster Historical Society, Lancaster, New Hampshire.
LOC — Library of Congress, Washington, DC.
NA — National Archives and Records Administration, Washington, DC.
NHA — New Hampshire Department of State Archives and Records Management, Concord, New Hampshire.
NHHS — New Hampshire Historical Society, Concord, New Hampshire.
UNH — University of New Hampshire, Milne Archives and Special Collections, Durham, New Hampshire.
USAMHI — United States Army Military History Institute, Carlisle Barracks, Pennsylvania.

Chapter One

1. Grant Powers, *Historical Sketches of the Discovery, Settlement, and Progress of events in the Coos County and Vicinity* (Haverhill, NH: J.F.C. Hayes, 1847); John Wingate Weeks, Lancaster History Scrapbook, NHHS.

2. *The Grafton and Coos Counties Bar Association: Rolls of Membership, Officers, Proceedings, and Miscellaneous Papers*, vol. 3 (Littleton: The Association, 1899), 441–445; *Massachusetts Soldiers and Sailors of the Revolutionary War*, vol. 5 (Boston: Wright & Potter, 1899), 427.

3. A.N. Somers, *History of Lancaster, New Hampshire* (Concord: Rumford Press, 1899), 88–90.

4. *Grafton and Coos Bar*, 446–450; Faith Kent, "Richard Clair Everett," *Lancaster Historical Society Sketch Book* 7, no.1 (Spring, 1989).

5. *Grafton and Coos Bar*, vol. 3, 451–456; Kent, "Richard Clair Everett."

6. Somers, *History of Lancaster*, 48–51; *Grafton and Coos Bar*, 457–466; Kent, "Richard Clair Everett."

7. *Grafton and Coos Bar*, 563–565; Cross Family Genealogy, LHS; information inscribed on Cross family headstone, Old

Cemetery, Lancaster, NH; Somers, *History of Lancaster*, 192.

8. Lancaster Birth, Marriage, and Death Records, Lancaster Town Hall; Cross Genealogy. Many writers over the years have mistakenly given Edward Ephraim Cross' middle name as Everett. All official records, and Cross himself, indicate that his middle name was the same as that of his father, Ephraim. Richard Cross carried the Everett name as his middle name after his maternal grandfather. Adding to the confusion, Edward went by the name of "Richard Everett" in his antebellum writings.

9. Somers, *History of Lancaster*, 348–349, 392–393, 515; *Grafton and Coos Bar*, 564–565; Alonzo Weeks to C.C. Carr, October 26, 1866; Edward E. Cross, Service File, NA; Faith Kent, "The Lancaster House," *Lancaster Historical Society Sketchbook* 9, no. 1 (Spring/Summer 1995).

10. Donald B. Cole, *Jacksonian Democracy in New Hampshire, 1800–1851* (Cambridge: Harvard University Press, 1970), 141–158; Lex Renda, *Running on the Record: Civil War Era Politics in New Hampshire* (Charlottesville: University Press of Virginia, 1997), 1–15; Somers, *History of Lancaster*, 523–527.

11. *Report of the Adjutant General of the State of New Hampshire*, vol.1, *Military History of New Hampshire* (Manchester: John B. Clarke, 1866), 305; Jack Noon, *Muster Days at Musterfield Farm: New Hampshire's Muster Day Tradition, 1787–1850* (Portsmouth, NH: Peter E. Randall, 2000), 11–26; Somers, *History of Lancaster*, 543–544.

12. Somers, *History of Lancaster*, 228; *Journal of the Honorable Senate of the State of New Hampshire* (Concord: Carroll and Baker, 1846), 53–55, 94, 139; *Journal of the Honorable Senate of the State of New Hampshire* (Concord: Butterfield and Hill, 1849), 599–603; *Grafton and Coos Bar*, 565.

13. *Grafton and Coos Bar*, 563.

14. *Grafton and Coos Bar*, 562, 566–568; Edward E. Cross to Henry O. Kent, June 1, 1850, NHHS; Don Carlos Seitz, *Artemus Ward: A Biography and Bibliography* (New York: Harper, 1912), 7.

15. Edward E. Cross to Henry O. Kent, February 17, 1853, NHHS; *Military History of New Hampshire*, 335–336; *Cincinnati Dollar Times*, November 11, 1854.

16. Somers, *History of Lancaster*, 544; Richard Peabody Kent, "Early Lancaster," 1881, Lancaster Historical Society; *Lancaster (NH) Coos Republican*, September 13, 1859; Edward E. Cross to Henry O. Kent, July 3, 1856, NHHS.

17. Noon, *Muster Days*, 83–95; *Military History of New Hampshire*, 356–366.

18. *Proceedings of the Editors, Publishers, and Printers' Association of the State of New Hampshire* (Manchester: C.F. Livingston, 1872), 47–48; Cole, *Jacksonian Democracy*, 168–170; *Grafton and Coos Bar*, 300–310.

19. *Cincinnati Dollar Weekly Times*, November 19, 1854; George P. Rowell, *Forty Years an Advertising Agent, 1865–1905* (New York: Printers Ink, 1906), 15–16.

20. Edward E. Cross to Henry O. Kent, April 17, 1856, NHHS; Cole, *Jacksonian Democracy*, 216–218.

21. Mary R.P. Hatch, "Lancaster, New Hampshire," *Granite Monthly* 51 (1919), 591–594; Edward E. Cross to Henry O. Kent, May 15, 1852, NHHS; Seitz, *Artemus Ward*, 7–8.

22. Seitz, *Artemus Ward*, 7–8; *Denver (CO) Rocky Mountain News*, September 10, 1859.

23. *Proceedings of the Editors*, 49; Rowell, *Forty Years*, 15–16; *Rocky Mountain News*, September 10, 1859; Edward E. Cross to Henry O. Kent, April 14, 1851; Seitz, *Artemus Ward*, 8–9; *Coos Republican*, August 23, 1859.

24. *Rocky Mountain News*, September 10, 1859; *Coos Republican*, August 23, 1859; *Proceedings of the Editors*, 49; Seitz, *Artemus Ward*, 9–11; Rowell, *Forty Years*, 15–16.

25. *Proceeding of the Editors*, 48.

Chapter Two

1. Edward E. Cross to Henry O. Kent, May 15, 1852, NHHS; Weeks to Carr, October 26, 1866; Undated *Boston Transcript* clipping, 1863, Edward E. Cross Papers, UNH.

2. Cross to Kent, June 1, 1850; *Salt Lake (UT) Deseret News*, January 25, 1855.

3. Cross to Kent, June 1, 1850; Anderson C. Quiesenberry, *Lopez's Expeditions to Cuba, 1850 and 1851* (Louisville: John P. Morton, 1906), 30–37.

4. Cross to Kent, June 1, 1850.

5. *Grafton and Coos Bar*, 568–570; Nelson Cross to John W. Weeks, March 20, 1847,

NHHS; 1850 U.S. Census, County of Coos, New Hampshire, Town of Lancaster, NA; Cross to Kent, June 1, 1850.

6. *Cincinnati Dollar Weekly Times,* headline; Edward E. Cross to Henry O. Kent, April 14, 1851, NHHS; Cross Pension File.

7. Cross to Kent, April 14, 1851.

8. Cross to Kent, April 14, 1851; William A. Ellis, *Norwich University: Her History, Her Graduates, Her Roll of Honor* (Concord: Rumford Press, 1898), 1–35.

9. Edward E. Cross to Henry O. Kent, November 11, 1851, NHHS.

10. Edward E. Cross Passport, UNH; Thomas L. Livermore, *Days and Events* (Boston: Houghton Mifflin, 1920), 25–26.

11. Cross to Kent, May 15, 1852; Edward E. Cross to Henry O. Kent, November 7, 1852 and April 19, 1853, NHHS.

12. Edward E. Cross to Henry O. Kent, August 14, 1852 and October 28, 1852, NHHS.

13. Tyler Anbinder, *Nativism and Slavery: The Northern Know-Nothings and the Politics of the 1850s* (New York: Oxford University Press, 1992), 10–47.

14. Cross to Kent, October 28, 1852, November 7, 1852 and January 15, 1853, NHHS.

15. Edward E. Cross to Henry O. Kent, December 9, 1852, NHHS.

16. Edward E. Cross to Henry O. Kent, February 13, 1853, NHHS; *Cincinnati Times,* February 21, 1853.

17. Edward E. Cross to Henry O. Kent, March 16, 1853 and April 19, 1853, NHHS; Anbinder, *Nativism and Slavery,* 24–25.

18. Edward E. Cross to Henry O. Kent, April 21, 1853, NHHS.

19. Edward E. Cross to Henry O. Kent, April 21, 1853 and July 18, 1853, NHHS.

20. Cross, Pension File. Edward E. Cross to Henry O. Kent, September 23, 1853 and December 4, 1853, NHHS.

Chapter Three

1. Edward E. Cross to Henry O. Kent, December 4, 1853 and December 25, 1853, NHHS.

2. Cross to Kent, December 25, 1853; *Cincinnati Times,* January-February 1854.

3. *Deseret News,* January 25, 1855.

4. Lucy Crawford, *Lucy Crawford's History of the White Mountains* (Hanover: Dartmouth Publications, 1966); *Cincinnati Dollar Weekly Times,* November 16, 1854. This writer can attest to the dangerous weather conditions faced on Mt. Washington, even in the summer.

5. Edward E. Cross to Henry O. Kent, September 14, 1854, NHHS; *Sandusky Register,* August 14, 1854.

6. *Cincinnati Dollar Weekly Times,* November 16, 1854; *Military History of New Hampshire,* 351–353.

7. Edward E. Cross to Henry O. Kent, November 4, 1854 and November 22, 1854, NHHS.

8. Edward E. Cross to Henry O. Kent, December 16, 1854 and December 20, 1854, NHHS; Somers, *History of Lancaster,* 457–458.

9. Edward E. Cross to Henry O. Kent, February 14, 1855 and February 24, 1855, NHHS; Anbinder, *Nativism and Slavery,* 162–179.

10. Edward E. Cross to Henry O. Kent, April 3, 1855 and May 4, 1855, NHHS.

11. Cross to Kent, April 3, 1855.

12. Cross to Kent, May 4, 1855; *Cincinnati Daily Times,* July 5, 1855; *Fayetteville (NC) Observer,* October 15, 1855; *Raymond (MS) Hinds County Gazette,* January 30, 1856; *Newark (NJ) Advocate,* January 21, 1857.

13. Edward E. Cross to Henry O. Kent, March 16, 1856 and January 20, 1856, NHHS; *Cincinnati Times,* February 24, 1856.

14. *Cincinnati Times,* February 20 – March 15, 1856; Murat Halstead, *Trimmers, Trucklers, and Temporizers: Notes of Murat Halstead from the Political Convention of 1856,* ed. William B. Heseltine and Rex G. Fisher (Madison: State Historical Society of Wisconsin), 1–12.

15. Edward E. Cross to Henry O. Kent, March 24, 1856 and April 16, 1856, NHHS; Anbinder, *Nativism and Slavery,* 220–245.

16. *Cincinnati Times,* April-May 1856. This is the same *Merrimac,* named after the large river in New Hampshire, which became the *C.S.S. Virginia.*

17. Edward E. Cross to Henry O. Kent, July 3, 1856 and August 1, 1856, NHHS.

18. Edward E. Cross to Henry O. Kent, August 26, 1856 and December 16, 1856, NHHS; Anbinder, *Nativism and Slavery,* 220–245.

19. Edward E. Cross to Henry O. Kent, March 1, 1857 and March 28, 1857, NHHS; Anbinder, *Nativism and Slavery,* 247–278.

20. Cross to Kent, March 28, 1857 and July 4, 1857, NHHS; Cross Pension File.

21. Edward E. Cross to Henry O. Kent, March 28, 1857 and July 10, 1858, NHHS.

Chapter Four

1. Thomas J. Cram, "Railroads and Mines in Arizona: The Cram Memoir of 1858, ed. Gerald E. Thompson, *Arizona and the West* 10, no. 4 (Winter 1968), 363–368; Kenneth Hufford, "Journalism in Pre-Territorial Arizona," *The Smoke Signal* 14 (Fall 1966), 78–80.

2. Constance Wynn Altshuler, "The Life and Death of the *Weekly Arizonian*," *Arizona and the West* 18, no. 2 (Summer 1976), 265–267; *Cincinnati Times*, July 27, 1858.

3. Edward E. Cross to Henry O. Kent, July 28, 1858, NHHS.

4. *Cincinnati Times*, July 27, 1858. The Washington hand press used by Cross had a storied history in its own right. After Cross used it to print the *Weekly Arizonian*, the Confederate forces occupying Arizona in 1862 briefly used the press. It then moved around the state for the next fifty years, variously to Tucson, Prescott, and Tombstone, until finally being retired in 1913. Today the press is on display at the Tubac Presidio Museum in Tubac, Arizona, and still works, over 150 years after arriving in the territory. See Hayden Files, Arizona Historical Society.

5. *Cincinnati Times*, August 20, 1858 and August 31, 1858.

6. *Cincinnati Times*, September 29, 1858.

7. *Cincinnati Times*, September 30, 1858.

8. *Cincinnati Times*, October 14, 1858 and October 19, 1858; Phocion R. Way, "Overland via 'Jackass Mail' in 1858: The Diary of Phocion R. Way, Part I," ed. William A. Duffen, *Arizona and the West* 2, no. 1 (Spring 1960), 35–42.

9. *Cincinnati Times*, November 9, 1858 and November 22, 1858.

10. *Cincinnati Times*, November 29, 1858 and December 5, 1858.

11. Albert D. Richardson, *Beyond the Mississippi* (Harford: American, 1869), 243–244; *Cincinnati Times*, January 3, 1859.

12. Way, "Overland via 'Jackass Mail' in 1858, Part II," ed. William A. Duffen, *Arizona and the West* 2, no. 2 (Summer 1960), 158–161; *Cincinnati Times*, February 9, 1859.

13. Elizabeth R. Brownell, *They Lived in Tubac* (Tucson: Westernlore, 1986), 1–7; Phocion R. Way, "Overland via 'Jackass Mail' in 1858, Part III," *Arizona and the West* 2, no. 3 (Autumn 1960), 279–283; Cram, "Railroads and Mines in Arizona," 369–375; *Cincinnati Times*, March 17, 1859.

14. *Cincinnati Times*, March 17, 1859; Way, "Overland via 'Jackass Mail' in 1858, Part IV," *Arizona and the West* 2, no. 4 (Winter 1960), 353–370.

15. Hufford, "Journalism in Arizona," 80–82.

16. Hufford, "Journalism in Arizona," 81–84; *Weekly Arizonian*, March 3, 1859. Very few original copies of the *Weekly Arizonian* exist today.

17. *Weekly Arizonian*, March 10, 1859, March 17, 1859, March 24, 1859 and March 31, 1859. There is a large gap in the Cross-Kent correspondence at the New Hampshire Historical Society between March and the fall of 1859. While several sources state that Cross wrote to the *St. Louis Missouri Republican* and the *New York Herald*, a careful digital and microfilm search through the holdings of the papers held at the American Antiquarian Society in Worcester, Massachusetts, does not reveal any writings by Cross to their papers under his known pen-names of "Gila" or "Richard Everett"; furthermore, none of the few letters published from the West read in the style that Cross was known for. The only logical thought is that Cross was so occupied with his own work with the *Arizonian* that he had little time for other correspondence.

18. Edward E. Cross to Henry O. Kent, March 13, 1859, NHHS.

19. *Weekly Arizonian*, April 14, 1859.

20. *Weekly Arizonian*, April 7, 1859, April 14, 1859, April 21, 1859, April 28, 1859, May 5, 1859, May 12, 1859, May 19, 1859 and May 26, 1859; Hufford, "Journalism in Arizona," 82–85. This is same Richard Ewell who would later gain fame as commander of the Second Corps, Army of Northern Virginia.

21. B. Sacks, "Sylvester Mowry: Artilleryman, Libertine, Entrepreneur" *American West* 1, no. 3 (Summer 1964), 14–24; Lynn R. Bailey, "Lt. Sylvester Mowry's Report on His March from Salt Lake City to Fort

Tejon," *Arizona and the West* 7, no. 4 (Winter 1965), 329–346; Sylvester Mowry, "Arizona and Sonora," *Journal of the American Geographical and Statistical Society* 1, no. 3 (March 1859), 66–75.

22. *The States*, February 26, 1859; Hufford, "Journalism in Arizona," 85–86.

23. *The States*, March 1, 1859.

24. Ibid., May 24, 1859.

25. *The States*, July 23, 1859; *New York Times*, July 23, 1859; Hufford, "Journalism in Arizona," 85–86.

26. Jo Ann Schmitt, *Fighting Editors: The Story of Editors Who Faced Six-Shooters with Pens and Won* (San Antonio: Naylor, 1958), 17–18; (Prescott) *Arizona Enterprise*, March 3, 1892; *The States*, August 4, 1859.

27. *The States*, August 4, 1859. The location of the duel is now the parking lot of the Tubac Presidio Museum in Tubac, Arizona. The event is one of the most celebrated in early Arizona history, and is reenacted on occasion by locals.

28. Albert D. Richardson, *The Secret Service, the Field, the Dungeon, and the Escape* (Hartford: American, 1866), 276–278; Hufford, "Journalism," 86–87; Edward E. Cross to Henry O. Kent, August 25, 1859, NHHS; *Tuscon Arizona Daily Star*, November 29, 1879; *The States*, August 4, 1859; *New Hampshire Patriot*, August 8, 1859.

29. *Weekly Arizonian*, July 7, 1859 and July 14, 1859; Schmitt, *Fighting Editors*, 18–20.

30. The following papers all provided coverage of the Cross-Mowry duel: *Charleston Mercury*, August 5, 1859; *The States*, August 4, 1859; *Baltimore Sun*, August 3, 1859; *San Antonio Ledger*, July 27, 1859; *Wooster Republican*, August 4, 1859; *New Hampshire Patriot*, August 8, 1859; *New York Herald*, August 5, 1859; *New York Times*, August 5, 1859; *Rocky Mountain News*, September 10, 1859; *Coos Republican*, August 16, 1859; *New Hampshire Patriot*, August 15, 1859 (Zenas R. Bliss, *The Reminiscences of Zenas R. Bliss: 1854–1876*, ed. Thomas T. Smith, Jerry D. Thompson, Robert Wooster, and Ben E. Pingenot (Austin: Texas State Historical Association, 2007), 206).

31. *Rocky Mountain News*, September 10, 1859; *New York Times*, August 18, 1859; Edward E. Cross to Henry O. Kent, September 14, 1859; *Coos Republican*, August 23, 1859.

32. *Weekly Arizonian*, July 14, 1859 and July 21, 1859; *Arizona Daily Star*, November 29, 1879; Altshuler, "Life and Death of the *Arizonian*," 265–266; Hufford, "Journalism in Arizona," 87–89.

33. *The Weekly Arizonian*, July 21, 1859 and August 4, 1859; Cross to Kent, August 25, 1859.

Chapter Five

1. Edward E. Cross to Henry O. Kent, September 14, 1859 and October 15, 1859, NHHS; *New York Herald*, October 5, 1859.

2. *The Weekly Arizonian*, July 21, 1859; *Daily Evening Bulletin*, December 10, 1859.

3. Edward E. Cross to M.A. Otero, December 29, 1859, RG 94, Records of the Adjutant General's Office, Old Army Papers, 014 1860, NA.

4. Information on Cross' participation in the North Star Lodge has been kindly provided by the members of North Star Lodge Number 8, Lancaster, New Hampshire.

5. Information about Cross' finances, his role in supporting his mother, and his accounts are all drawn from the Edward E. Cross Pension File, NA. Unfortunately, there is no record of what Abigail Cross purchased in Richard P. Kent's records at the NHHS.

6. Edward E. Cross to Henry O. Kent, December 14, 1859 and December 30, 1859, NHHS. On the 1860 election and New Hampshire, refer to Elwin L. Page and Mike Pride, *Abraham Lincoln in New Hampshire* (Concord: Monitor, 2009). It is interesting to note that in all of Cross' surviving writings he never gave his personal feelings towards Abraham Lincoln.

7. Edward E. Cross to Henry O. Kent, February 4, 1860, NHHS.

8. *New York Herald*, August 20, 1860; Thompson M. Turner, *Latest from Arizona!: The Hesperian Letters, 1859–1861*, ed. Constance Wynn Altshuler (Tucson: Arizona Pioneers' Historical Society, 1969), 39–48, 55; 1860 U.S. Census, Territory of New Mexico and Arizona, NA.

9. William D. Child, *A History of the Fifth Regiment New Hampshire Volunteers in the American Civil War, 1861–1865.* (Bristol, NH: R.W. Musgrove, 1893), 311–312; Turner, *Latest from Arizona*, 102–112; Richard S.

Ewell, *The Making of a Soldier: Letters of General R.S. Ewell*, ed. Percy Gatling Hamlin (Richmond: Whittet & Shepperson, 1935), 92–94.

10. Ewell, *Making of a Soldier*, 95–98; Donald C. Pfanz, *Richard S. Ewell: A Soldier's Life* (Chapel Hill: University of North Carolina Press, 1998), 100–121; Richard S. Ewell to Dabney H. Maury, July 24, 1860, RG 393, Letters Received, Department of New Mexico, Letter 822 1860, NA; Edward E. Cross to J.B. Floyd, April 20, 1860, RG 94, Letters Received, Adjutant General's Department, Old Army Letters, C117 1860, NA.

11. Edward E. Cross to Henry O. Kent, July 3, 1861, NHHS; Child, *Fifth New Hampshire*, 312; Otis F.R. Waite, *New Hampshire in the Great Rebellion* (Claremont: Tracey, Chase, 1870), 323–324.

12. Burton Kirkwood, *History of Mexico*. (Westport, CT: Greenwood, 2000), 103–160; *New York Herald*, January 14, 1861.

13. *New York Times*, March 1, 1861. Cross' saddle is now at the Lancaster Historical Society (Livermore, *Days and Events*, 26).

14. Edward E. Cross to Nathaniel Berry, July 3, 1861, NHA; Cross to Kent, July 3, 1861; Charles N. Kent, *History of the Seventeenth Regiment, New Hampshire Volunteer Infantry* (Concord: Rumford, 1898), 41–45. Readers of Cross' original letters will notice he had an interesting habit of writing on whatever paper was available and sometimes ripped a page from his regimental books to write a hasty note to officials in Concord.

Chapter Six

1. Edward E. Cross, *Stand Firm and Fire Low: The Civil War Writings of Colonel Edward E. Cross,* ed. Walter Holden, William E. Ross, and Elizabeth Slomba (Hanover, NH: University Press of New England, 2003), 7–8. Although this author has read and taken extensive notes of the original Cross journal at the University of New Hampshire, information here is from the published version of the journal in *Stand Firm and Fire Low* to better direct the reader to the source of the quotation.

2. *Military History of New Hampshire*, 333–334; Waite, *New Hampshire in the Rebellion*, 345–348: 469–471; Kent, *Seventeenth New Hampshire*, 41–46.

3. Cross to Berry, July 3, 1861; New Hampshire Executive Council Minutes, August 14, 1861, NHA. For a discussion of Democrat-Republican politics in New Hampshire refer to Renda, *Running on the Record*, 64–92.

4. Cross, *Stand Firm*, 7–8. The only wartime images of Cross date to late 1861 and show him wearing this uniform. It is unknown if he changed to the looser, informal "sack coat" once he entered the field; as he was a stickler for regulations he insisted on uniformity among his officers and men.

5. *Farmer's Cabinet,* September 27, 1861; Edward E. Cross to Nathaniel Berry, August 31, 1861, NHA; Maurice D. Clarke, *Manchester: A Brief Record of Its Past and a Picture of Its Present* (Manchester: John B. Clarke, 1875), 347–354; Edward E. Cross to Joseph Foster, September 27, 1861, UNH.

6. *Coos Republican,* August 27, 1861; Henry O. Kent to Nathaniel Berry, August 9, 1861, NHA.

7. Edward E. Cross to Henry O. Kent, September 15, 1861; Child, *Fifth New Hampshire,* 7–9; Waite, *New Hampshire in the Rebellion,* 252–261;William A. Moore, Letters, NHHS.

8. Cross to Kent, September 15, 1861; Edward E. Cross to Nathaniel Berry, August 30, 1861, NHA; Waite, *New Hampshire in the Rebellion,* 252–254; Luther M. Knight to Nathaniel Berry, August 26, 1861, NHA.

9. Cross, *Stand Firm,* 8; Colt Manufacturing Company to Terry Thomann, private collection.

10. Cross, *Stand Firm,* 8; Livermore, *Days and Events,* 24–26; *National Eagle* (Claremont, NH), November 14, 1861.

11. Winfield Scott to Nathaniel Berry, October 21, 1861 and October 24, 1861, NHA; Child, *Fifth New Hampshire,* 10–18; Livermore, *Days and Events,* 26–27.

12. Livermore, *Days and Events,* 27–28; William Marvel, *New Hampshire's Hall of Flags: Preserving a Legacy* (Concord: State of NH, 1993); *Report of the Adjutant General of the State of New Hampshire,* vol. 2 (Manchester: John B. Clarke, 1866), 539 (hereinafter *1866 N.H. A.G. Report*).

13. Child, *Fifth New Hampshire,* 6–8; Cross, *Stand Firm,* 8–9.

14. Cross, *Stand Firm,* 9–10; Theodore L. Flood, *The Chautauquan* (Meadville, PA:

T.L. Flood, 1895), 201; Oliver O. Howard, *Autobiography of Oliver Otis Howard*, vol. 1 (New York: Trow, 1907), 166–170; Edward E. Cross to Nathaniel Berry, November 11, 1861, NHA; *War of the Rebellion: A Compilation of the Official Records of the Union and Confederate Armies* (Washington, DC: Government Printing Office) 5: 385–387 (hereinafter cited as *O.R.*).

15. Cross, *Stand Firm*, 11; Cross to Berry, November 11, 1861; Livermore, *Days and Events*, 39–40; Paddy Griffith, *Battle Tactics of the Civil War* (New Haven: Yale University Press, 1989), 137–151.

16. *New Hampshire Patriot*, February 12, 1862; Cross, *Stand Firm*, 11–13; Charles O. Ballou to Sister, May 19, 1862, AAA; William A. Moore to Adams Moore, January 2, 1862, NHHS; Edward E. Cross to Henry O. Kent, November 14, 1861 and December 17, 1861, NHHS.

17. Howard, *Autobiography*, 188–189; Edward E. Cross to Henry O. Kent, December 17, 1861, NHHS; Edward E. Cross to Amelia Richards, December 23, 1861, RG 153, NA; Edward E. Cross to Henry O. Kent, December 27, 1861, NHHS.

18. *Report of the Eighth Annual Reunion of the 64th N.Y. Regimental Assn.* (Randolph, NY: Enterprise Press, 1896), 34–36; Child, *Fifth New Hampshire*, 36–39; Cross to Kent, December 17, 1861; Francis A. Walker, *History of the Second Army Corps in the Army of the Potomac* (New York: Charles Scribner's Sons, 1887), 1–13, 102; Howard, *Autobiography*, 184–188.

19. Child, *Fifth New Hampshire*, 26–32; Miles Peabody to Parents, January 26, 1862, USAMHI; Cross to Kent, December 27, 1861; Livermore, *Days and Events*, 38–39; Edward E. Cross to Henry O. Kent, January 20, 1862, NHHS.

20. George S. Gove to Parents, February 16, 1862, UNH.

21. Frank Cross, Service File, NA; James E. Larkin to Jenny Larkin, January 5, 1862, NHHS; Mike Pride and Mark Travis, *My Brave Boys: To War with Colonel Cross and the Fighting Fifth* (Hanover, NH: University Press of New England, 2001), 57; Duane E. Shaffer, *Men of Granite: New Hampshire's Soldiers in the Civil War* (Columbia: University of South Carolina Press, 2008), 53–54.

22. *New Hampshire Patriot*, February 5, 1862; Child, *Complete Roster*, 187. The second part of Child's regimental history of the Fifth is a "Complete Roster," which, although part of the book, is paginated separately.

23. *New Hampshire Patriot*, February 5, 1862.

24. Lorenzo Thomas to Edward E. Cross February 28, 1862, Cross Service File, NA; *Keene Sentinel*, March 6, 1862; *New Hampshire Patriot*, November 19, 1862.

25. Ira McL. Barton to Edward E. Cross and Edward E. Cross to Ira McL. Barton, February 20, 1862, DCL; Cross, *Stand Firm*, 14–16.

26. Edward E. Cross to Henry O. Kent, January 29, 1862, NHHS; Waite, *New Hampshire in the Rebellion*, 255–261.

27. Livermore, *Days and Events*, 34–40; George S. Gove to Parents, February 9, 1862, UNH; Charles O. Ballou to Sister, February 27, 1862, AAA; Richard Welch and James B. David to Nathaniel Berry, March 10, 1862, NHA.

28. Gove to Parents, February 9, 1862; Edmund Brown to Nathaniel Berry, May 26, 1862, NHA; Welch and David to Berry, March 10, 1862; John P. Hale to Nathaniel Berry, March 24, 1862, NHA; Edward E. Cross to Allen Tenney, March 30, 1862, NHA.

29. Child, *Fifth New Hampshire*, 21–23.

30. Ibid., 22–23.

Chapter Seven

1. Howard, *Autobiography*, 192–198; William A. Moore to Adams Moore, March 8, 1862, NHHS; Cross, *Stand Firm*, 16–18.

2. Howard, *Autobiography*, 197–198; Cross, *Stand Firm*, 19–20; Child, *Fifth New Hampshire*, 49–51; Livermore, *Days and Events*, 46–47. *O.R.* 12, 411–414; *Farmer's Cabinet*, April 17, 1862.

3. Edward E. Cross to Henry O. Kent, April 6, 1862, NHHS; Edward E. Cross to Allen Tenney, March 30, 1862, NHA.

4. Edward E. Cross to Henry O. Kent, May 3, 1862, NHHS; Cross, *Stand Firm*, 22–24; Child, *Fifth New Hampshire*, 55–56. *Salt Lake Semi-Weekly Tribune*, August 12, 1898.

5. Edward E. Sturtevant to John Kimball, May 25, 1862, NHA.

6. Cross to Kent, May 3, 1862; Cross,

Stand Firm, 24; Edward E. Cross to Ephraim Cross, May 26, 1862, private collection; Waite, *New Hampshire in the Rebellion,* 276.

7. Edward D. Neill, *Incidents of the Battles of Fair Oaks and Malvern Hill* (New York: D.D. Merrill, 1893), 454–547; Cross, *Stand Firm,* 24–25; *National Tribune,* February 19, 1920; Waite, *New Hampshire in the Rebellion,* 276.

8. *New Hampshire Statesman,* June 14, 1862; Child, *Fifth New Hampshire,* 66–68; *New York Times,* June 16, 1862.

9. Cross, *Stand Firm,* 25–26.

10. Cross, *Stand Firm,* 27–29; Howard, *Autobiography,* 237–238; Walker, *Second Corps,* 28–29; James E. Larkin to Jenny Larkin, June 5, 1862, NHHS; Child, *Fifth New Hampshire,* 78–83.

11. Cross, *Stand Firm,* 31–32; Edward E. Cross, "Battle of Fair Oaks," UNH; Howard, *Autobiography,* 242–243; Walker, *Second Corps,* 48–49; Charles A. Fuller, *Personal Recollections of the War of 1861* (Sherburne, NY: News Job Printing, 1906), 16–17; *1866 N.H. A.G. Report,* 542; *New Hampshire Statesman,* June 14, 1862; *People's Journal,* June 20, 1862.

12. Cross, *Stand Firm,* 33–34; Cross, "Fair Oaks"; Fuller, *Personal Recollections,* 17–18; *Eighth Annual Reunion,* 31–37; *Report of the Ninth Annual Reunion of the 64th N.Y. Regimental Association* (Randolph, NY: Enterprise, 1897), 26–28; Waite, *New Hampshire in the Rebellion,* 277.

13. *People's Journal,* June 20, 1862; Edward E. Cross to Bernard J.D; Irwin, July 14, 1862, Irwin Papers, LOC; Frank Moore, *The Rebellion Record: A Diary of American Events,* vol. 5 (New York: G.P. Putnam, 1863), 96–98.

14. Edward E. Cross to Henry O. Kent, June 3, 1862, NHHS; Moore, *Rebellion Record,* 96–98; LaSalle Corbell Pickett, *Pickett and His Men* (Philadelphia: J.B. Lippincott, 1913), 74–82; William H. Spencer, "How I Felt in Battle and in Prison," *War Papers Read Before the Maine Commandery of the Military Order of the Loyal Legion of the United States,* vol. 2 (Portland: Lefavnour-Tower, 1902), 130–131.

15. Cross to Kent, June 3, 1862; George E. Shannon to Father, June 5, 1862, RNB; Cross to Irwin, July 14, 1862.

16. Walker, *Second Corps,* 51. *O.R. 11,* 769–770; *New Hampshire Statesman,* June 14, 1862; *Keene Sentinel,* June 19, 1862; Larkin to Larkin, June 5, 1862; Moore, *Rebellion Record,* vol. 5, 96–98.

17. *New Hampshire Statesman,* June 14, 1862; *Farmer's Cabinet,* July 31, 1862; George S. Gove to Julia Parsons, June 15, 1862, UNH; Cross to Irwin, July 14, 1862.

18. Francis A. Donaldson, *Inside the Army of the Potomac: The Civil War Experiences of Captain Francis Adams Donaldson,* ed. J. Gregory Acken (Mechanicsburg: Stackpole, 1998), 95–96; Harriet Douglas Whetten, "A Volunteer Nurse in the Civil War: The Letters of Harriet Douglas Whetten," ed. Paul H. Hass, *Wisconsin Magazine of History* 48, no. 2 (Winter 1964–1965), 143–144; Laura L. Behling, *Hospital Transports: A Memoir of the Embarkation of the Sick and Wounded from the Peninsula of Virginia in the Summer of 1862* (Albany: State University of New York Press, 2005), 104–111.

19. *New York Sunday Mercury,* June 15, 1862; Cross, *Stand Firm,* 34–35; Thomas T. Ellis, *Leaves from the Diary of an Army Surgeon* (New York: John Bradburn, 1863), 82–84; Edward E. Cross to Lorenzo Thomas, circa June 1862, Cross Service File, NA.

20. Cross, *Stand Firm,* 34–35.

21. Charles O. Ballou to his sister, July 10, 1862, AAA; Edward E. Sturtevant to Anthony Colby, July 14, 1862, NHA; Charles T. Moody to his father, August 5, 1862, USAMHI; Samuel Langley to Lorenzo Thomas, July 22, 1862, Langley Service File, NA.

22. Undated scrapbook clipping, Henry O. Kent Fishing Trip, LHS; *Coos Republican,* July 8, 1862.

23. Edward E. Cross to Lorenzo Thomas, July 25, 1862, Cross Service File, NA; Edward E. Cross to Henry O. Kent, August 12, 1862, NHHS; Cross to Irwin, July 14, 1862.

24. Child, *Fifth New Hampshire,* 98–99; Cross, *Stand Firm,* 36–38; William D. Child, *Letters from a Civil War Surgeon,* ed. Merrill C. Sawyer (Solon, ME: Polar Bear, 2001), 19.

Chapter Eight

1. Charles T. Moody to his father, August 24, 1862, USAMHI; Josiah M. Favill, *Diary of a Young Army Officer* (Chicago: R.R. Donnelly, 1909), 251–252; Walker, *Second Corps,* 55–56.

2. Edward E. Cross to Nathaniel S. Berry, July 9, 1862, NHA; Edward E. Cross to Nathaniel S. Berry, August 13, 1862, NHA; William Marvel, *Race of the Soil: The Ninth New Hampshire in the Civil War* (Wilmington: Broadfoot, 1988), 2–6.

3. Frank Cross, Service File, NA.

4. Walker, *Second Corps*, 97–98; Cross, *Stand Firm*, 38–40; Edward E. Cross to Henry O. Kent, September 5, 1862, NHHS; Child, *Fifth New Hampshire*, 105–110; Livermore, *Days and Events*, 113–114.

5. *O.R. 19*, 287–288; Ezra A. Carman, *The Maryland Campaign of September 1862*, vol. 1, *South Mountain*, ed. Thomas G. Clemens (El Dorado Hills, CA: Savas Beatie, 2010), 398–404; Favill, *Diary*, 184–185; Walker, *Second Corps*, 95–96; Cross, *Stand Firm*, 43–44.

6. Cross, *Stand Firm*, 43–44; Carman, *South Mountain*, 402–404; Livermore, *Days and Events*, 122–123; Richardson, *Secret Service*, 278.

7. Ezra Carman, "Antietam," ANB; Fuller, *Personal Recollections*, 57–58; Walker, *Second Corps*, 102–105; Livermore, *Days and Events*, 128–131; Cross, *Stand Firm*, 44–46. This author has an undated, unpaginated typescript of the Antietam battle section of Carman's report from Antietam National Battlefield in his possession.

8. Cross, *Stand Firm*, 47; George S. Gove to Julia Parsons, October 2, 1862, UNH; Carman, "Antietam"; Walker, *Second Corps*, 112–113. Many believed that Caldwell and his staff hid behind a haystack, but Livermore and Gove are the only sources for that story.

9. Child, *Fifth New Hampshire*, 120–122; Cross, *Stand Firm*, 47–48; Gove to Parsons, October 2, 1862.

10. Livermore, *Days and Events*, 132–134; *1866 N.H. A.G. Report*, 554; Carman, "Antietam"; Fuller, *Personal Recollections*, 58–59.

11. *1866 N.H. A.G. Report*, 555; Carman, "Antietam"; Favill, *Diary*, 186–187; William H. Osborne, *The History of the Twenty-Ninth Regiment of Massachusetts Volunteer Infantry* (Boston: Albert J. Wright, 1877), 186–189; Fuller, *Personal Recollections*, 59–60; Charles Hale, "The Story of My Personal Experience at the Battle of Antietam," ANB. The only source for the report of the Fifth's breaking by companies to relieve the Irish is from Thomas Livermore's *Days and Events*. While the book is the best and most accurate source for information on Edward Cross in the Civil War, it does have some major problems, such as Livermore's forgetting of dates, people, and events that transpired around him. Josiah Favill, a lieutenant in the neighboring Fifty-Seventh New York, supports Ezra Carman, writing, "As we approached the Irish Brigade, it opened files, and we passed through." Ezra Carman based his work on years of study into the 1862 Maryland Campaign, and he is widely regarded by scholars as the best source of material on the Maryland Campaign.

12. Cross, *Stand Firm*, 48–49; Hale, "My Personal Experience"; Child, *Fifth New Hampshire*, 123–125; Carman, "Antietam"; George S. Gove to Julia Parsons, October 2, 1862, UNH; Walker, *Second Corps*, 114–115; Livermore, *Days and Events*, 136–138.

13. Edward E. Cross to Henry O. Kent, September 20, 1862, NHHS; Cross, *Stand Firm*, 48; Walker, *Second Corps*, 114–115; Hale, "My Personal Experiences"; Livermore, *Days and Events*, 138–140; Carman, "Antietam"; Waite, *New Hampshire in the Rebellion*, 279–280; Richardson, *Secret Service*, 238–239. It will give some idea of how difficult a maneuver this was and how the Fifth accomplished it to know that all 250 men in the regiment had to move as one, as the regiment swept like a gate upon its hinge all the while, even as they were swept by a raking fire from front and flank. The Ninth New Hampshire attempted to perform a similar movement on May 12, 1864, at Spotsylvania Court House in the pouring rain. Filled with draftees and substitutes, the Ninth disintegrated in the face of the enemy, and it spelled disaster for the rest of the brigade (Marvel, *Race of the Soil*, 211–214).

14. Gove to Parsons, October 2, 1862; Hale, "My Personal Experience"; *O.R. 19*, 59; Cross to Kent, September 20, 1862; Henry Woodhead, ed., *Antietam* (Alexandria: Time Life Books, 1996), 112–113; Child, *Fifth New Hampshire*, 223.

15. Waite, *New Hampshire in the Rebellion*, 266.

16. Hale, "My Personal Experience"; Cross, *Stand Firm*, 49; Livermore, *Days and Events*, 138–142.

17. Gove to Parsons, October 2, 1862.

18. Hale, "My Personal Experience"; Cross,

Stand Firm, 49; Gove to Parsons, October 2, 1862; Livermore, *Days and Events,* 138–142.

19. Carman, "Antietam"; Cross, *Stand Firm,* 49.

20. Edward E. Cross to Anthony Colby, September 20, 1862, NHA; Cross to Kent, September 20, 1862; W.J. Chaplin, *The Michigan Freemason* (Kalamazoo: Chaplin & Ihling, 1872), 42–43; Undated *Confederate Veteran* article, Masonic Incident, Fifth N.H. vertical file, ANB; Child, *Letters,* 33–34; Cross, *Stand Firm,* 49–50; Livermore, *Days and Events,* 148–149.

21. George B. McClellan, *Report on the Organization and Campaigns of the Army of the Potomac* (New York: Sheldon, 1864), 382–384; *O.R.* 19, 276: 278–279: 284–288.

22. Cross to Kent, September 20, 1862; Edward E. Cross to Anthony Colby, September 20, 1862, NHA; Francis W. Palfrey, *The Antietam and Fredericksburg* (New York: Charles Scribner's Sons, 1906), 100; James Longstreet, *From Manassas to Appomattox* (Philadelphia: J.B. Lippincott, 1896), 266; Cross, *Stand Firm,* 50–51.

23. Hale, "My Personal Experience"; *1866 N.H. A.G. Report,* 558.

24. Cross to Parsons, October 2, 1862; Edward E. Cross to John C. Caldwell, September 27, 1862, GNMP; Caldwell Court of Inquiry Findings, October 23, 1862, GNMP.

25. Edward E. Cross to Henry O. Kent, October 2, 1862, October 14, 1862 and October 24, 1862, NHHS; *New Hampshire Statesman,* October 4, 1862.

26. Cross, *Stand Firm,* 51; Child, *Fifth New Hampshire,* 223; William A. Moore to Edwin Moore, August 3, 1862, NHHS; Charles O. Ballou to his sister, November 20, 1862, AAA; Cross to Colby, September 20, 1862; Edward E. Cross to Anthony Colby, October 2, 1862 and November 20, 1862, NHA.

27. Charles Hapgood to Ira McL. Barton, October 27, 1862, DCL.

28. Child, *Fifth New Hampshire,* 221.

29. Ibid., 148.

Chapter Nine

1. Charles Coffin, *Following the Flag* (Boston: Dana Estes, 1886), 42–43; Livermore, *Days and Events,* 152–154.

2. Child, *Fifth New Hampshire,* 144–145; Cross, *Stand Firm,* 53.

3. James E. Larkin and James Perry, Court-Martial Records, NA.

4. James E. Larkin to Jenny Larkin, November 23, 1863, NHHS; Charges and Specifications against Col. Edward E. Cross, NHHS.

5. James E. Larkin to Jenny Larkin, December 9, 1862, NHHS; Charles Hapgood to Ira McL. Barton, December 3, 1862, DCL.

6. Samuel Langley to Lorenzo Thomas, November 12, 1862, Langley Service File, NA; Sturtevant letters, NHA; Edward E. Cross to Nathaniel Berry, December 5, 1862, NHA; Edward E. Cross to William H. Hackett, November 26, 1862, NHA.

7. William Miller, "A Hot Day on Marye's Heights," *Battles and Leaders of the Civil War* (New York: Century, 1888), 3, 97–99; Cross, *Stand Firm,* 54–55.

8. Child, *Fifth New Hampshire,* 151; Livermore, *Days and Events,* 170–172; Frank Moore, ed., *The Rebellion Record: A Diary of American Events,* vol. 6 (New York: G.P. Putnam, 1863), 94–101.

9. Cross, *Stand Firm,* 55–57.

10. Cross, *Stand Firm,* 57; John A. Duren to "Friend Colony," January 15, 1862, FRSP; Livermore, *Days and Events,* 171–172; *Third Annual Report of the State Historian of the State of New York, 1897* (Albany: Wynkoop, Hallenbeck, and Crawford, 1897), 38–40.

11. George S. Gove to Julia Parsons, December 14, 1862, UNH.

12. Cross, *Stand Firm,* 57–58; *Caledonia Record,* August 1, 1863; James E. Larkin to Jenny Larkin, December 16, 1863, NHHS; *Farmer's Cabinet,* December 18, 1862.

13. Gove to Parsons, December 14, 1862; Child, *Fifth New Hampshire,* 155–157; Cross, *Stand Firm,* 59.

14. Cross, *Stand Firm,* 59–60; *Caledonia Record,* August 1, 1863; Adams, *Inside the Army,* 187–188.

15. Livermore, *Days and Events,* 172–177; Cross, *Stand Firm,* 60; Gove to Parsons, December 14, 1862.

16. Child, *Fifth New Hampshire,* 165; Cross, *Stand Firm,* 60; Gove to Parsons, December 14, 1862. Larkin to Larkin, December 16, 1862; Duren to Colony, January 15, 1863; Child, *Letters,* 71–74.

17. *O.R.* 21, 234–235; Rodney H. Ramsey to Father, December 24, 1862, NHHS; *History of the 118th Pennsylvania Volunteers:*

Corn Exchange Regiment (Philadelphia: J.L. Smith, 1905), 136; Child, *Fifth New Hampshire,* 164–165.
   18. Edward E. Cross to Ephraim Cross, December 21, 1862, UNH; Edward E. Cross to Adams Moore, December 20, 1862, NHHS; Cross, *Stand Firm,* 130–132.
   19. O.R. 21, 229–234; Walker, *Second Corps,* 173–174.

Chapter Ten

   1. Waite, *New Hampshire in the Rebellion,* 116–121; Martin A. Haynes, *A History of Second Regiment New Hampshire Volunteer Infantry in the War of the Rebellion* (Lakeport: Republican Press Association, 1896); George S. Gove to Julia Parsons, February 15, 1863, UNH.
   2. Winfield Scott Hancock to Daniel Clarke, December 29, 1862, UNH.
   3. Winfield Scott Hancock to John P. Hale, December 29, 1862, UNH; E.H. Marston to Edward E. Cross, December 30, 1862, UNH.
   4. Casey et al. to Henry W. Halleck, December 11, 1862, Cross Adjutant General File, NA. D.G. Birmingham and L.W. Bradley to Abraham Lincoln, February 15, 1863, Cross Adjutant General File, NA.
   5. Edward E. Cross to Franklin Pierce, February 19, 1863, NHHS.
   6. *Dover Gazette,* July 24, 1863; *Farmer's Cabinet,* January 8, 1863.
   7. John W. Foney et al. to Abraham Lincoln, February 28, 1863, Cross Adjutant General File, NA; John F. Farnsworth to Abraham Lincoln, February 15, 1863, Cross Adjutant General File, NA; John S. Watts to Abraham Lincoln, March 1, 1863, Cross Adjutant General File, NA; Edward E. Cross to Edwin Stanton, March 1, 1863, Cross Adjutant General File, NA.
   8. James R. Jackson, *History of Littleton, New Hampshire,* vol. 1 (Cambridge: Harvard University Press, 1905), 445–446.
   9. Undated clipping, *Independent Democrat,* circa January 1863, UNH.
   10. Charles Hapgood to Ira McL. Barton, January 9, 1863, DCL; James E. Larkin to Jenny Larkin, January 13, 1863 and February 6, 1863, NHHS; Welcome A. Crafts to David Culver, March 3, 1865, NHA.

   11. Kent, *Seventeenth New Hampshire,* 70–76.
   12. *New York Herald,* February 8, 1863; Edward E. Cross to Henry O. Kent, July 24, 1862 and July 28, 1862, NHHS.
   13. Roy P. Basler, ed., *The Collected Works of Abraham Lincoln,* vol. 6 (New Brunswick: Rutgers University Press, 1953), 133; Edward E. Cross to Franklin Pierce, April 14, 1863, NHHS. Waite, *New Hampshire in the Rebellion,* 118–120. Marston later commanded the prisoner of war camp at Point Lookout, Maryland. Perhaps his greatest accomplishment as a general was using his political pull to have the decimated New Hampshire regiments, the Second, Fifth, and Twelfth, pulled from the Army of the Potomac in 1863 after Gettysburg and assigned to his command where they regained their strength and recuperated from the hard campaigns. Marston later served in the Army of the James.
   14. Miles Peabody to Parents, January 20, 1863, USAMHI; Augustus D. Sanborn to Mother and Brothers, January 1, 1863, courtesy of Terry Thomann; *9th Annual Reunion,* 27–28.
   15. Larkin to Larkin, December 16, 1862; James E. Larkin to Jenny Larkin, January 13, 1862 and January 26, 1863, NHHS.
   16. Miles Peabody to Parents, March 3, 1863, USAMHI.
   17. Favill, *Diary,* 234–235; Walker, *Second Corps,* 200–201.
   18. Charles Hapgood and Richard E. Cross to Nathaniel Berry, March 9, 1863, NHA; Miles Peabody to Parents, April 1, 1863, USAMHI; Renda, *Running on the Record,* 115–119.

Chapter Eleven

   1. Edward E. Cross to John Hatch George, February 25, 1863, NHHS; Cross, *Stand Firm,* 60; George S. Gove to Julia Parsons, March 22, 1863, UNH.
   2. Cross to Pierce, April 14, 1863; Edward E. Cross to Anthony Colby, April 21, 1863, NHA.
   3. Child, *Fifth New Hampshire,* 178–179; Child, *Letters,* 112–113; General Orders, Fifth Regiment, March-April 1863, NA; James E. Larkin to Jenny Larkin, March 22, 1862, NHHS.

4. Livermore, *Days and Events,* 182–183. After being stolen by a state employee in the 1980s and recovered by the FBI, the Cross watch is now in the custody of the New Hampshire State Library in Concord, where special permission must be obtained to view it.

5. Edward E. Cross to Nathaniel Berry, May 16, 1863, NHA.

6. Edward E. Cross, "Hooker's Campaign," UNH.

7. Alexander Moore, Diary, April 28–May 1, 1863, FRSP; Child, *Fifth New Hampshire,* 179–180; Livermore, *Days and Events,* 189–190.

8. Walker, *Second Corps,* 218–220; Moore, Diary May 2–3, 1863.

9. Walker, *Second Corps,* 228–231; Martin Sigman, Diary, May 2–3, 1863, FRSP; Cross, "Hooker's Campaign."

10. Cross, "Hooker's Campaign"; George S. Gove to Julia Parsons, May 10, 1863, UNH; Henry Woodhead, ed., *Chancellorsville* (Alexandria: Time Life, 1996), 119–120; Child, *Letters,* 117; Fuller, *Personal Recollections,* 84–86.

11. Cross, "Hooker's Campaign"; *1866 N.H. A.G. Report,* 562; Walker, *Second Corps,* 243–247; Almira Hancock, *Reminiscences of Winfield Scott Hancock* (New York: Charles L. Webster, 1887), 203–204; *Farmer's Cabinet,* May 21, 1863. The report was reprinted in several New Hampshire papers but never made it into the O.R.

12. Cross, "Hooker's Campaign"; Gove to Parsons, May 10, 1863; Child, *Fifth New Hampshire,* 223; Child, *Letters,* 118; Livermore, *Days and Events,* 199–201: 256–257; *Farmer's Cabinet,* May 21, 1863; *Coos Republican,* May 20, 1863; R.E. Cross, Service File, NA. *O.R. 25,* 307–308.

13. Cross, "Hooker's Campaign"; Livermore, *Days and Events,* 201–205.

14. Sumner F. Hurd to Ira McL. Barton, May 12, 1863, DCL; Gove to Parsons, May 10, 1863; *O.R. 25,* 311–317.

15. Benson Lossing, *Pictorial History of the Civil War in the United States of America,* vol. 3 (Hartford: Thomas Belknap, 1877), 67; Edward E. Cross to John Gilmary Shea, May 28, 1863, Georgetown University. The sketch was not published until after Cross' death.

16. *Caledonia Record,* August 1, 1863; Livermore, *Days and Events,* 256–257.

17. Child, *Letters,* 118.

18. Favill, *Diary,* 235–236; Walker, *Second Corps,* 253–254.

19. Edward E. Cross to *New Hampshire Statesman,* May 7, 1863, Fifth Letter Book, NA; Edward E. Cross to Anonymous, May 18, 1863, Fifth Letter Book, NA; Edward E. Cross to J.B. Fry, April 30, 1863, DCL.

20. Edward E. Cross to John Hancock, May 23, 1863, Fifth Letter Book, NA; Edward E. Cross to John C. Caldwell, May 8, 1863, Cross Service File, NA; James E. Larkin to Jenny Larkin, May 19, 1863, NHHS.

Chapter Twelve

1. Walker, *Second Corps,* 258–260; *Farmer's Cabinet,* June 30, 1863; Child, *Fifth New Hampshire,* 199–201; Livermore, *Days and Events,* 218–221.

2. Walker, *Second Corps,* 261–263; J.W. Muffly, *The Story of Our Regiment: A History of the 148th Pennsylvania Volunteers* (Des Moines: Kenyon, 1904), 532–535; Charles Hale, "With Colonel Cross in the Gettysburg Campaign," GNMP; Child, *Letters,* 135–137.

3. Hale, "With Colonel Cross," 2–3.

4. Walker, *Second Corps,* 269–271; Hale, "With Colonel Cross," 3–4; Livermore, *Days and Events,* 246–247; David L. Ladd, and Audrey J. Ladd, eds., *Gettysburg in Their Own Words: The Batchelder Papers,* vol., 2 (Dayton: Morningside, 1995), 1,193–1,198; Favill, *Diary,* 244–245.

5. Walker, *Second Corps,* 272–274; *Boston Herald,* March 11, 1884; Hale, "With Colonel Cross," 4–5; Fuller, *Personal Recollections,* 92–93; Spencer, "How I Felt," 130–131.

6. Walker, *Second Corps,* 276–277; Hale, "With Colonel Cross," 4–5.

7. Hale, "With Colonel Cross," 5–6; Child, *Fifth New Hampshire,* 217; Fuller, *Personal Recollections,* 93; *O.R. 27,* 381–383; *Boston Herald,* March 11, 1884; Jay Jorgensen, "Anderson Attacks the Wheatfield." *Gettysburg* 14 (January 1996), 64–76.

8. Walker, *Second Corps,* 280–282; Hale, "With Colonel Cross," 6. Cross owned two pistols, carried in pommel holsters on the saddle. The first revolver, a Colt .36, is on display at the Civil War Life Museum in Fredericksburg, Virginia, while the Reming-

ton .44 revolver he captured at Fair Oaks is in the custody of the Lancaster Historical Society in New Hampshire.

9. *Batchelder Papers,* vol. 2: 1,196–1,197, 1,032–1,033; George S. Gove to Julia Parsons, July 9, 1863, UNH; M.J. Bass to Wife, July 8, 1863, GNMP.

10. Child, *Fifth New Hampshire,* 207–208; Favill, *Diary,* 245–248; George Hillyer, *My Gettysburg Battle Experiences,* ed. Gregory Coco (Gettysburg: Thomas, 2005), 19–23; Fuller, *Personal Recollections,* 94–95.

11. Muffly, *148th Pennsylvania,* 536–537; Hale, "With Colonel Cross," 6–7; *Boston Herald,* March 11, 1884; Hale, "With Colonel Cross," 6–7.

12. *Boston Herald,* March 11, 1884.

13. *O.R. 27,* 381–383; Hale, "With Colonel Cross," 7; *Batchelder Papers,* vol. 2: 1,139–1,143; Livermore, *Days and Events,* 253–255.

14. A.W. Bartlett, *History of the Twelfth Regiment New Hampshire Volunteers* (Concord: Ira C. Evans, 1897), 353; Roland Maust, *Grappling With Death: The Union Second Corps Hospital at Gettysburg* (Dayton: Morningside, 2002); Child, *Fifth New Hampshire,* 211–213.

15. Child, *Fifth New Hampshire,* 212–213; *Eighth Annual Reunion,* 34–35; *Coos County Republican,* July 14, 1863; Hale, "With Colonel Cross," 7.

16. Livermore, *Days and Events,* 254–255. This lock of hair was later used as the basis for obtaining the correct hair color for the Cross portrait at the New Hampshire State House, but the lock has since disappeared.

17. *O.R. 29,* pt. 2, 159–160; *O.R. 27,* 380–382.

18. *New York Herald,* July 30, 1863.

19. Rodney H. Ramsey to Father, July 20, 1862, NHHS; John W. Busey, *These Honored Dead: The Union Casualties at Gettysburg* (Hightstown, NJ: Longstreet, 1996), 112–114; Charles T. Moody to George Moody, August 6, 1863, courtesy of Mike Pride; Gove to Parsons, July 9, 1863.

Chapter Thirteen

1. Hale, "With Colonel Cross," 7; Undated clipping, Cross death, circa July 1863, UNH; James M. Crafts and William F. Crafts, *The Crafts Family* (Northampton, MA: Gazette, 1893), 539–541; Hale, "With Colonel Cross," 7–8; John M. Davis to Ira McL. Barton, July 7, 1863, DCL. Ironically, Davis died later that year of the wounds he received at Antietam.

2. *Coos County Republican,* July 14, 1863; Richard P. Kent, diary, July 4–9, 1863, NHHS; Child, *Fifth New Hampshire,* 212–216.

3. Elizabeth A. Livermore, Diary, July 3–7, 1863, NHHS. Literally every paper in New Hampshire covered Cross' death in detail. Most important are the *Coos County Republican, Granite State Free Press, New Hampshire Patriot,* and *New Hampshire Statesman,* all in July 1863.

4. *Frank Leslie's Illustrated,* July 1863; *Boston Journal,* July 16, 1863; *Cincinnati Times,* July 4, 1863; *Ninth Annual Reunion,* 30–31.

5. *New Hampshire Patriot,* August 19, 1863; *New Hampshire Statesman,* July 10, 1863; *Granite State Free Press,* August 15, 1863.

6. *Coos County Republican,* July 14, 1863.

7. *New Hampshire Statesman,* July 10, 1863; *New Hampshire Patriot,* July 8, 1863; M.S. Perley to Franklin Pierce, July 14, 1863, NHHS.

8. Child, *Fifth New Hampshire,* 217; *Farmer's Cabinet,* July 4, 1876; *News and Observer,* February 25, 1898; Benson Lossing to Dexter Chase, December 14, 1871, UNH. The sword, spurs, and pocket watch of Colonel Cross, owned by the New Hampshire State Library, are now on display at the New Hampshire State House. The .44 Remington revolver is in Lancaster. A soldier from Wisconsin picked up the .36 in the Wheatfield and returned home with it, where the gun was later discovered. The regimental flag of the Fourth North Carolina is displayed at the North Carolina History Museum in Raleigh.

9. *Ninth Annual Reunion,* 27–28; *Boston Herald,* March 11, 1884; Child, *Letters,* 273; Cross to Irwin, July 14, 1862; Mather Cleveland, *New Hampshire Fights the Civil War* (New London, NH: NP, 1969), 25.

10. *1866 N.H. A.G. Report,* 536–537; Hancock, *Reminiscences,* 203–204.

11. *Cincinnati Times,* February 6, 1864; *Farmer's Cabinet,* January 10, 1867; Child, *Fifth New Hampshire,* 214–216.

12. Cross, Pension File; John C. Long to Elizabeth C. Spaulding, August 17, 1863, Foster Papers, UNH; *Coos County Democrat,* July 20, 1883.

13. Bartlett, *Twelfth New Hampshire,* 477; *Ceremonies at the Dedication of the Monument Erected by the City of Manchester, N.H., September 11, 1879* (Manchester: Mirror, 1880), 34; Bruce Heald, *New Hampshire in the Civil War* (Charleston: Arcadia, 2001), 79–94. This painting is now at the Lancaster Historical Society.

14. Child, *Fifth New Hampshire,* 225–232.

15. Richard E. Cross, Court-Martial Record, Service File, and Pension File, NA; Child, *Complete Roster,* 45; Somers, *History of Lancaster,* 456.

16. William A. Ellis, *Norwich University, 1819–1911: Her History, Her Graduates, Her Roll of Honor,* vol. 2 (Montpelier: Capital City, 1911), 536–538; Sommers, *History of Lancaster,* 499–501.

17. John W. Forney, *Life and Military Career of Winfield Scott Hancock* (Philadelphia: Hubbard, 1886), 325–326; *Coos Republican,* July 14, 1863.

18. Edward E. Cross and James E. Larkin Letters, NHHS.

19. *Farmer's Cabinet,* April 27, 1872; *Concord Monitor,* June 8, 1997, April 22, 2004, April 23, 2004 and June 10, 2006; *Civil War News,* September 1997; Karen O. Wadsworth to J. Dennis Haskart, May 10, 2004, NHA.

20. William F. Fox, *Regimental Losses in the American Civil War* (Albany: Brandow, 1898), 139; Jackson, *History of Littleton,* 445; George S. Gove to Julia Parsons, September 17, 1863, UNH.

21. Waite, *New Hampshire in the Rebellion,* 252–296.

22. Child, *Fifth New Hampshire,* 218–219.

23. Livermore, *Days and Events,* 256–257.

24. Bruce Catton, *Mr. Lincoln's Army* (New York: Anchor, 1951), 211; Bruce Catton, *Glory Road* (New York: Anchor, 1952); Donald Richards, "The Fifth New Hampshire Volunteers (Light Infantry)," *Historical New Hampshire* 28, no. 4 (Winter 1973), 241–242.

25. Youngholm, "Edward E. Cross: The Biography of a Civil War Soldier" (bachelor's thesis, Princeton University, 1976); J.P. Wilkins, "'Stand Firm and Fire Low': The Civil War Epic of Colonel Edward E. Cross, USV" (master's thesis, U.S. Army War College, 1993).

26. Pride and Travis, *My Brave Boys; Baltimore Sun,* June 29, 2001; *Civil War News,* August 2001; William Marvel, "Review of *My Brave Boys,*" *Historical New Hampshire* (Spring/Summer 2002), 61–62; Cross, *Stand Firm; University of New Hampshire Magazine,* Fall 2003.

27. Pride and Travis, *My Brave Boys,* xi–xv; MacKinlay Kantor, *Gettysburg* (New York: Random House, 1952), 40–43.

28. Helen Cross Denison, Probate File, CCCH. The granite monument to Cross is located on Main Street in Lancaster, New Hampshire, and the colonel is buried in the Wilder Cemetery.

Bibliography

Manuscripts and Unpublished Materials

American Antiquarian Society, Worcester, Massachusetts
- Ballou, Charles O., Letters.

Antietam National Battlefield, Sharpsburg, Maryland
- Caldwell's Brigade Papers.
- Carman, Ezra, Papers.
- Chase, Benjamin F., Letters.
- Eighty-First Pennsylvania Papers.
- Fifth New Hampshire Papers.
- Fourth North Carolina Papers.
- G.B. Anderson's Brigade Papers.
- Hale, Charles, Memoirs.
- Richardson's Division Papers.
- Sixty-First New York Papers.

Arizona Historical Society, Tucson
- Altshuler, Constance Wynn, Papers.
- Cross, Edward E., Research File.
- Hayden Research Files.
- Mowry, Sylvester, Research File.

Bowdoin College Archives, Brunswick, Maine
- Howard, Oliver O., Papers.

Colby-Sawyer College Special Collections, New London, New Hampshire
- Mather, Cleveland, Papers.

Coos County Courthouse, Lancaster, New Hampshire
- County Vital Records.
- Land Deeds and Records.
- Probate Records.

Coos County Historical Society, Berlin, New Hampshire
- Coos County Enlistment Papers.

Dartmouth College, Rauner Special Collections Library, Hanover, New Hampshire
- McL. Barton, Ira, Papers.
- Mather, Cleveland, Civil War Collection.

Fredericksburg and Spotsylvania National Military Park, Fredericksburg, Virginia
- Burial Records, Fredericksburg National Cemetery.
- Duren, J.A., Letter.
- Irish Brigade Collection.
- Moore, Alexander, Papers.
- Second Corps Papers.
- Sigman, Martin, Diary.

Georgetown University, Washington, DC
- Shea, John Gilmary, Papers.

Gettysburg National Military Park, Gettysburg, Pennsylvania
- Anderson's Brigade File.
- Brooke's Brigade File.
- Caldwell's Division File.
- Cross' Brigade File.
- Eighty-First Pennsylvania Regimental File.
- First Texas Regimental File.
- Fifth New Hampshire Regimental File.
- Fifty-Ninth Georgia Regimental File.
- Kelly's Brigade File.
- New Hampshire State Units, Papers.
- Ninth Georgia Regimental File.
- One Hundredth and Forty-Eighth Pennsylvania Regimental File.
- Robertson's Brigade File.

- Sixty-First New York Regimental File.
- Twentieth Indiana Regimental File.
- Zook's Brigade File.

Lancaster Historical Society, Lancaster, New Hampshire
- Bucknam, John, Diary and Letters.
- Cross, Edward E., Papers.
- Cross Family Papers.
- Kent Family Papers.

Lancaster Town Hall, Lancaster, New Hampshire
- Birth, Marriage, and Death Records.
- Burial Records.
- Militia Records.
- Probate Records.
- Tax Books.
- Town Council Records.

Library of Congress, Washington, DC
- Carman, Ezra, Papers.
- Irwin, Bernard J.D., Papers.
- Lincoln, Abraham, Papers.

National Archives, Washington, DC
- Cook, William W., Service File.
- Cross, Edward E., Adjutant General, Pension, and Service Files.
- Cross, Frank, Service File.
- Cross, Nelson, Service File.
- Cross, Richard, Court-Martial, Service, and Pension Files.
- Fifth New Hampshire Regimental Books and Papers.
- Hale, Charles, Service and Pension Files.
- Hapgood, Charles, Service and Pension Files.
- Langley, Samuel, Service File.
- Livermore, Thomas, Service File.
- Moore, William A., Service File.
- Perry, James, Court-Martial Record.
- Records Group 94, Records of the Adjutant General, Army Papers.
- Records Group 153, Civil War Claims, Department of Washington.
- Records Group 353, Department of New Mexico.
- Second Corps Brigade and Division Records.
- Seventeenth New Hampshire Regimental Papers.
- Sturtevant, Edward E., Service File.
- U.S. Census Records.

New Hampshire Historical Society, Concord
- Cross, Edward E., Letters.
- Davis, Jared M., Letter.
- Hale, John Parker, Papers.
- Kent, Henry O., Papers.
- Kent, Richard P., Papers.
- Larkin, James, Letters.
- Livermore, Elizabeth A., Diary.
- Moore, William A., Letters.
- Pierce, Franklin, Papers.
- Ramsey, Rodney H., Letters.
- Rollins, Edward, Papers.
- Rix, James M., Papers.
- Weeks, John Wingate, Papers.

New Hampshire State Archives, Concord
- Adjutant General Papers.
- *Ayling's Register*, Manuscript Notes.
- Executive Council Minutes.
- Executive Department, Letters Received.
- Fifth Regiment Papers.
- Seventeenth Regiment Papers.
- Sturtevant, Edward E., Letters.

New Hampshire State House, Concord
- Cross, Edward E., Painting and Sword.
- New Hampshire Battle Flags.

New Hampshire State Library, Concord
- Assorted Civil War Papers.
- Cross, Edward E., Artifacts.

Norwich University, Special Collections, Northfield, Vermont
- Balloch, George W., Papers.
- Kent, Henry O., Papers.

Richmond National Battlefield, Richmond, Virginia
- Shannon, George E., Letters.

Tubac Historical Society, Tubac, Arizona
- Cross, Edward E., Research File.
- Cross-Mowry Duel Research File.
- Mowry, Sylvester, Research File.
- *Weekly Arizonian* Research File.

United States Army Military History Institute, Carlisle, Pennsylvania
- Cummings, Albert G., Letters.
- Fifth New Hampshire Volunteers Papers.
- Hale, Charles, Remembrances.
- Moody, Charles T., Letters.
- Peabody, Miles, Letters.

University of New Hampshire Special Collections, Durham
- Cross, Edward E., Papers.
- Gove, George, Papers.
- Foster-Spaulding Family Papers.

Primary Sources

Allen, George H. *Forty-Six Months in the Fourth R.I. Volunteers.* Providence: J.A. and R.A. Reid, 1887.

Barlow, Francis. *"Fear Was Not in Him": The Civil War Letters of Major General Francis C. Barlow, U.S.A.* Edited by Christian G. Samito. New York: Fordham University Press, 2004.

Bartlett, A.W. *History of the Twelfth Regiment New Hampshire Volunteers.* Concord: Ira C. Evans, 1897.

Basler, Roy P., ed. *The Collected Works of Abraham Lincoln.* Vol. 4. New Brunswick: Rutgers University Press, 1953.

Battles and Leaders of the Civil War. 4 Vols. New York: Century, 1888.

Billings, John D. *Hardtack and Coffee: The Unwritten Story of Army Life.* Lincoln: Nebraska University Press, 1993.

Bliss, Zenas R. *The Reminiscences of Zenas R. Bliss, 1854–1876.* Edited by Thomas T. Smith, Jerry D. Thompson, Robert Wooster, and Ben E. Pingenot. Austin: Texas State Historical Association, 2007.

Bonsall, Spencer. *Well Satisfied with My Position: The Civil War Journal of Spencer Bonsall.* Edited by Michael A. Flannery and Katherine H. Oomens. Carbondale: Southern Illinois University Press, 2007.

Browne, J. Ross. *Adventures in the Apache Country: A Tour Through Arizona and Sonora, 1864.* New York: Harper, 1869.

Busey, John W. *These Honored Dead: The Union Casualties at Gettysburg.* Hightstown, NJ: Longstreet, 1996.

Ceremonies at the Dedication of the Monument Erected by the City of Manchester, N.H., September 11, 1879. Manchester: Mirror, 1880.

Child, William D. *A History of the Fifth Regiment New Hampshire Volunteers in the American Civil War, 1861–1865.* Bristol, NH: R.W. Musgrove, 1893.

_____. *Letters from a Civil War Surgeon.* Edited by Merrill C. Sawyer. Solon, ME: Polar Bear, 2001.

Coffin, Charles. *Following the Flag.* Boston: Dana Estes, 1886.

Crafts, James M., and William F. Crafts. *The Crafts Family.* Northampton, MA: Gazette, 1893.

Cross, Edward E. *Stand Firm and Fire Low: The Civil War Writings of Colonel Edward E. Cross.* Edited by Walter Holden, William E. Ross, and Elizabeth Slomba. Hanover, NH: University Press of New England, 2003.

Donaldson, Francis A. *Inside the Army of the Potomac: The Civil War Experiences of Captain Francis Adams Donaldson.* Edited by J. Gregory Acken. Mechanicsburg: Stackpole, 1998.

Dyer, J. Franklin. *The Journal of a Civil War Surgeon.* Edited by Michael B. Chesson. Lincoln: University of Nebraska Press, 2003.

Ellis, Thomas T. *Leaves from the Diary of an Army Surgeon.* New York: John Bradburn, 1863.

Ewell, Richard S. *The Making of a Soldier: Letters of General R.S. Ewell.* Edited by Percy Gatling Hamlin. Richmond: Whittet & Shepperson, 1935.

Favill, Josiah M. *Diary of a Young Army Officer.* Chicago: R.R. Donnelly, 1909.

Fogg, George G. *Reports of Cases Argued and Determined in the Supreme Judicial Court of New Hampshire.* Vol. 32. Concord: Edson C. Eastman, 1872.

Fox, William F. *Regimental Losses in the American Civil War.* Albany: Brandow, 1898.

Frederick, Gilbert. *The Story of a Regiment: Being a Record of the Military Service of the Fifty-Seventh New York State Infantry.* Chicago: Fifty-Seventh Veterans Association, 1895.

Fuller, Charles A. *Personal Recollections of the War of 1861.* Sherburne, NY: News Job Printing, 1906.

Hancock, Almira. *Reminiscences of Winfield Scott Hancock.* New York: Charles L. Webster, 1887.

Haynes, Martin A. *A History of Second Regiment New Hampshire Volunteer Infantry in the War of the Rebellion.* Lakeport: Republican Press Association, 1896.

Hillyer, George. *My Gettysburg Battle Experiences.* Edited by Gregory Coco. Gettysburg: Thomas, 2005.

History of the 118th Pennsylvania Volunteers: Corn Exchange Regiment. Philadelphia: J.L. Smith, 1905.

Howard, Oliver O. *Autobiography of Oliver Otis Howard.* Vol. 1. New York: Trow, 1907.

Hyde, Bill, ed. *The Union Generals Speak: The Meade Hearings on the Battle of Gettysburg.* Baton Rouge: Louisiana State University Press, 2003.

Journal of the Honorable Senate of the State of New Hampshire. Concord: Carroll and Baker, 1846.

Journal of the Honorable Senate of the State of New Hampshire. Concord: Butterfield and Hill, 1849.

Kautz, August V. *The 1865 Customs of Service for Officers of the Army.* Philadelphia: J.B. Lippincott, 1865.

Kent, Charles N. *History of the Seventeenth Regiment, New Hampshire Volunteer Infantry.* Concord: Rumford, 1898.

Ladd, David L., and Audrey J. Ladd, eds. *Gettysburg in Their Own Words: The Batchelder Papers.* 3 Vols. Dayton: Morningside, 1995.

Laws of New Hampshire. Vol. 2. *1829–1835.* Concord: Evans, 1922.

Livermore, Thomas. *Days and Events, 1860–1866.* Boston: Houghton Mifflin, 1920.

Longstreet, James. *From Manassas to Appomattox.* Philadelphia: J.B. Lippincott, 1896.

Massachusetts Soldiers and Sailors of the Revolutionary War. Vol. 5 Boston: Wright & Potter, 1899.

Mathless, Paul, ed. *Fredericksburg.* Alexandria: Time Life, 1997.

_____. *The Peninsula.* Alexandria: Time Life, 1997.

_____. *The Seven Days.* Alexandria: Time Life, 1998.

McCarter, William. *My Life in the Irish Brigade: The Civil War Memoirs of Private William McCarter, 116th Pennsylvania Infantry.* Edited by Kevin E. O'Brien. Campbell, CA: Savas, 1996.

McClellan, George B. *The Civil War Papers of George B. McClellan: Selected Correspondence, 1860–1865.* Edited by Stephen W. Sears. New York: Ticknor and Fields, 1989.

_____. *Report on the Organization and Campaigns of the Army of the Potomac.* New York: Sheldon, 1864.

The Medical and Surgical History of the War of the Rebellion. 12 Vols. Washington: Government Printing Office, 1883.

Moore, Frank, ed. *The Rebellion Record: A Diary of American Events.* 10 Vols. New York: G.P. Putnam, 1862–1869.

Muffly, J.W. *The Story of Our Regiment: A History of the 148th Pennsylvania Volunteers.* Des Moines: Kenyon, 1904.

Neill, Edward D. *Incidents of the Battles of Fair Oaks and Malvern Hill.* New York: D.D. Merrill, 1893.

New York Monuments Commission. *Final Report on the Battlefield of Gettysburg.* Vol. 2. Albany: J.B. Lyon, 1902.

Osborne, William H. *The History of the Twenty-Ninth Regiment of Massachusetts Volunteer Infantry.* Boston: Albert J. Wright, 1877.

Proceedings of the Editors, Publishers, and Printers' Association of the State of New Hampshire. Manchester: C.F. Livingston, 1872.

Report of the Eighth Annual Reunion of the 64th N.Y. Regimental Association. Randolph, NY: Enterprise, 1896.

Report of the Ninth Annual Reunion of the 64th N.Y. Regimental Association. Randolph, NY: Enterprise, 1897.

Report of the Proceedings of the Society of the Army of the Tennessee at the Thirty-Fourth Meeting, Held at Washington, D.C., October 15–16, 1903. Cincinnati: F.W. Freeman, 1906.

Richardson, Albert D. *Beyond the Mississippi.* Hartford: American, 1869.

_____. *The Secret Service, the Field, the Dungeon, and the Escape.* Hartford: American, 1866.

Rowell, George P. *Forty Years an Advertising Agent, 1865–1905.* New York: Printer's Ink, 1905.

Silber, Nina, and Mary Beth Sievens, eds. *Yankee Correspondence: Civil War Letters Between New England Soldiers and the Home Front.* Charlottesville: University of Virginia Press, 1996.

Spencer, William H. "How I Felt in Battle and in Prison." *War Papers Read Before the Maine Commandery of the Military Order of the Loyal Legion of the United States.* Vol. 2. Portland: Lefavnour-Tower, 1902.

Third Annual Report of the State Historian of the State of New York, 1897. Albany: Wynkoop, Hallenbeck, and Crawford, 1897.

Turner, Thompson M. *Latest from Arizona!: The Hesperian Letters, 1859–1861.* Edited by Constance Wynn Altshuler. Tucson: Arizona Pioneers' Historical Society, 1969.

Walker, Francis A. *History of the Second Army Corps in the Army of the Potomac.* New York: Charles Scribner's Sons, 1887.

War of the Rebellion: A Compilation of the Official Records of the Union and Confederate Armies. 128 Vols. Washington, DC: Government Printing Office, 1880–1901.

Woodhead, Henry, ed. *Antietam.* Alexandria: Time Life, 1996.

_____. *Chancellorsville.* Alexandria: Time Life, 1996.

Secondary Sources

Addelman, Gary E., and Timothy H. Smith. *Devil's Den: A History and Guide.* Gettysburg: Thomas, 1997.

Anbinder, Tyler. *Nativism and Slavery: The Northern Know Nothings and the Politics of the 1850s.* New York: Oxford University Press, 1992.

Armstrong, Marion V. *Unfurl Those Colors!: McClellan, Sumner, and the Second Army Corps in the Antietam Campaign.* Tuscaloosa: University of Alabama Press, 2008.

Behling, Laura L. *Hospital Transports: A Memoir of the Embarkation of the Sick and Wounded from the Peninsula of Virginia in the Summer of 1862.* Albany: State University of New York Press, 2005.

Bilby, Joseph G., and Stephan D. O'Neil, eds. *"My Sons Were Faithful and They Fought": The Irish Brigade at Antietam.* Hightstown, NJ: Longstreet, 1997.

Brown, Roger Hamilton. *The Struggle for the Indian Stream Republic.* Cleveland: Western Reserve Historical Society, 1955.

Brownell, Elizabeth R. *They Lived in Tubac.* Tucson: Westernlore, 1986.

Carman, Ezra A. *The Maryland Campaign of September 1862.* Vol. 1. *South Mountain.* Edited by Thomas G. Clemens. El Dorado Hills, CA: Savas Beatie, 2010.

Catton, Bruce. *Glory Road.* New York: Anchor, 1952.

_____. *Mr. Lincoln's Army.* New York: Anchor, 1951.

Chace, Persis. *The Lancaster Sketch Book.* Brattleboro, VT: Frank E. Housh, 1887.

Chaplin, W.J., ed. *The Michigan Freemason.* Kalamazoo: Chaplin & Ihling, 1872.

Clarke, Maurice D. *Manchester: A Brief Record of Its Past and a Picture of Its Present.* Manchester: John B. Clarke, 1875.

Cole, Donald B. *Jacksonian Democracy in New Hampshire, 1800–1851.* Cambridge: Harvard University Press, 1970.

Conn, Granville P. *History of the New Hampshire Surgeons in the War of Rebellion.* Concord: Ira C. Evans, 1906.

Crawford, Lucy. *Lucy Crawford's History of the White Mountains.* Hanover: Dartmouth, 1966.

Dell, Christopher. *Lincoln and the War Democrats: The Grand Erosion of Conservative Tradition.* Rutherford: Farleigh Dickinson University Press, 1975.

Echoes of Glory: Arms and Equipment of the Union. Edited by Henry A. Woodhead. Alexandria: Time Life, 1995.

Ellis, William A. *Norwich University, 1819–1911: Her History, Her Graduates, Her Roll of Honor.* Vol. 2. Montpelier: Capital City, 1911.

Flood, Theodore L. *The Chautauquan.* Meadville, PA: T.L. Flood, 1895.

Fogg, Alonzo J. *The Statistics and Gazetteer of New Hampshire.* Concord: D.L. Guernsey, 1874.

Forney, John W. *Life and Military Career of Winfield Scott Hancock.* Philadelphia: Hubbard, 1886.

Gallagher, Gary W., ed. *Chancellorsville: The Battle and Its Aftermath.* Chapel Hill: University Press of North Carolina, 1996.

_____. *The Fredericksburg Campaign: Decision on the Rappahannock.* Chapel Hill: University of North Carolina Press, 1997.

_____. *The Second Day at Gettysburg.* Kent, OH: Kent State University Press, 1993.

Gambone, A.M. *Hancock at Gettysburg and Beyond.* Baltimore: Butternut and Blue, 1997.

_____. *If Tomorrow Night Finds Me Dead: The Life of Samuel K. Zook, Another Forgotten Union Hero.* Baltimore: Butternut and Blue, 1996.

The Grafton and Coos Counties Bar Association: Rolls of Membership, Officers, Proceedings, and Miscellaneous Papers. Vol. 3. Littleton: The Association, 1899.

Griffith, Paddy. *Battle Tactics of the Civil War.* New Haven: Yale University Press, 1989.

Harsh, Joseph L. *Taken at the Flood: Robert E. Lee and Confederate Strategy in the Maryland Campaign of 1862.* Kent, OH: Kent State University Press, 1999.

Heald, Bruce D. *New Hampshire in the Civil War*. Charleston, SC: Arcadia, 2001.

Heffernan, Nancy Coffey, and Ann Page Stecker. *New Hampshire: Crosscurrents in Its Development*. Hanover: University Press of New England, 2004.

Heidemann, Derek. "The Transformation of the Massachusetts Militia, 1785–1840." Honors Thesis, Clark University, 2009.

Hess, Earl J. *The Union Soldier in Battle: Enduring the Ordeal of Combat*. Lawrence: University Press of Kansas, 1997.

Humphreys, Andrew A. *From Gettysburg to the Rapidan: The Army of the Potomac, July 1863 to April 1864*. New York: Charles Scribner's Sons, 1883.

Jackson, James R. *History of Littleton, New Hampshire*. 3 Vols. Cambridge: Harvard University Press, 1905.

Johnson, Curt, and Richard C. Anderson, Jr. *Artillery Hell: The Employment of Artillery at Antietam*. College Station: Texas A & M University, 1995.

Jordan, David M. *Winfield Scott Hancock: A Soldier's Life*. Bloomington: Indiana University Press, 1988.

Jorgenson, Jay. *Gettysburg's Bloody Wheatfield*. Shippensburg: White Mane, 2002.

_____. *The Wheatfield at Gettysburg: A Walking Tour*. Gettysburg: Thomas, 2002.

Kantor, MacKinlay. *Gettysburg*. New York: Random House, 1952.

Lossing, Benson. *Pictorial History of the Civil War in the United States of America*. Hartford: Thomas Belknap, 1877.

Marvel, William. *Burnside*. Chapel Hill: The University of North Carolina Press, 1991.

_____. *Finishing Lincoln's War*. Boston: Houghton Mifflin, 2011.

_____. *The First New Hampshire Battery, 1861–1865*. South Conway, NH: Lost Cemetery, 1985.

_____. *The Great Task Remaining: The Third Year of Lincoln's War*. Boston: Houghton Mifflin, 2010.

_____. *Lincoln's Darkest Year: The War in 1862*. Boston: Houghton Mifflin, 2008.

_____. *Mr. Lincoln Goes to War*. Boston: Houghton Mifflin, 2007.

_____. *New Hampshire's Hall of Flags: Preserving a Legacy*. Concord: State of NH, 1993.

_____. *Race of the Soil: The Ninth New Hampshire in the Civil War*. Wilmington, NC: Broadfoot, 1988.

Mason, Jack C. *Until Antietam: The Life and Letters of Major General Israel B. Richardson, U.S. Army*. Carbondale: Southern Illinois University Press, 2009.

Mather, Cleveland. *New Hampshire Fights the Civil War*. New London, NH: n.p., 1969.

Maust, Roland. *Grappling With Death: The Union Second Corps Hospital at Gettysburg*. Dayton: Morningside, 2002.

New England: A Collection from Harper's Magazine. New York: Gallery, 1990.

Noon, Jack. *Muster Days at Musterfield Farm: New Hampshire's Muster Day Tradition, 1787–1850*. Portsmouth, NH: Peter E. Randall, 2000.

O'Reilly, Francis A. *The Fredericksburg Campaign: Winter War on the Rappahannock*. Baton Rouge: Louisiana State University Press, 2003.

Page, Elwin L., and Mike Pride. *Abraham Lincoln in New Hampshire*. Concord: Monitor, 2009.

Palfrey, Francis W. *The Antietam and Fredericksburg*. New York: Charles Scribner's Sons, 1906.

Pfanz, Donald C. *Richard S. Ewell: A Soldier's Life*. Chapel Hill: University of North Carolina Press, 1998.

Pfanz, Harry W. *Gettysburg: The Second Day*. Chapel Hill: University of North Carolina Press, 1987.

Pickett, LaSalle Corbell. *Pickett and His Men*. Philadelphia: J.B. Lippincott, 1913.

Powers, Grant. *Historical Sketches of the Discovery, Settlement, and Progress of Events in the Coos County and Vicinity*. Haverhill, NH: J.F.C. Hayes, 1847.

Pride, Mike, and Mark Travis. *My Brave Boys: To War with Colonel Cross and the Fighting Fifth*. Hanover, NH: University Press of New England, 2001.

Quiesenberry, Anderson C. *Lopez's Expeditions to Cuba, 1850 and 1851*. Louisville: John P. Morton, 1906.

Renda, Lex. *Running on the Record: Civil War Era Politics in New Hampshire*. Charlottesville: University Press of Virginia, 1997.

Report of the Adjutant General of the State of New Hampshire. 2 Vols. Manchester: John B. Clarke, 1866.

Schmitt, Jo Ann. *Fighting Editors: The Story of Editors Who Faced Six-Shooters with Pens and Won*. San Antonio: Naylor, 1958.

Sears, Stephen W. *Chancellorsville*. Boston: Houghton Mifflin, 1996.
_____. *Controversies and Commanders: Dispatches from the Army of the Potomac*. Boston: Houghton Mifflin, 1999.
_____. *George B. McClellan: The Young Napoleon*. New York: Ticknor and Fields, 1988.
_____. *To the Gates of Richmond: The Peninsula Campaign*. New York: Ticknor and Fields, 1992.
Seitz, Don Carlos. *Artemus Ward: A Biography and Bibliography*. London: Harper, 1912.
Sewell, Richard H. *John P. Hale and the Politics of Abolition*. Cambridge: Harvard University Press, 1965.
Shaffer, Duane E. *Men of Granite: New Hampshire's Soldiers in the Civil War*. Columbia: University of South Carolina Press, 2008.
Somers, A.N. *History of Lancaster, New Hampshire*. Concord: Rumford, 1899.
Stearns, Ezra. *Genealogical and Family History of the State of New Hampshire*. Vol. 1. New York: Lewis, 1908.
Tucker, Glenn. *High Tide at Gettysburg: The Campaign in Pennsylvania*. Gettysburg: Stan Clark, 1995.
Wagoner, Jay J. *Early Arizona: Prehistory to Civil War*. Tucson: University of Arizona Press, 1975.
Waite, Otis F.R. *New Hampshire in the Great Rebellion*. Claremont: Tracey, Chase, 1870.
Wallner, Peter A. *Franklin Pierce: Martyr for the Union*. Concord: Plaidswede, 2005.
_____. *Franklin Pierce: New Hampshire's Favorite Son*. Concord: Plaidswede, 2004.
Weeks, Stuart. *The Lord of Cat Bow*. Brookline, NH: Hobblebush, 2003.
Wilkins, J.P. "'Stand Firm and Fire Low': The Civil War Epic of Colonel Edward E. Cross, USV." Master's thesis, U.S. Army War College, 1993.
Yerrington, J.M.W. *The Centennial Celebration of the Settlement of the Town of Lancaster, N.H.* Lancaster: E. Savage, 1864.
Youngholm, Janet R. "Edward E. Cross: The Biography of a Civil War Soldier." Batchelor's thesis, Princeton University, 1976.

Primary Articles

Cram, Thomas J. "Railroads and Mines in Arizona: The Cram Memoir of 1858." Edited by Gerald E. Thompson. *Arizona and the West* 10, no. 4 (Winter 1968), 363–376.
Livermore, Thomas L. "The Northern Volunteers." *Granite Monthly* 10 (1887), 239–266.
Mowry, Sylvester. "Arizona and Sonora." *Journal of the American Geographical and Statistical Society* 1, no. 3 (March 1859), 66–75.
Way, Phocion R. "Overland via 'Jackass Mail' in 1858: The Diary of Phocion R. Way, Part I." Edited by William A. Duffen. *Arizona and the West* 2, no. 1 (Spring 1960), 35–53.
_____. "Overland via 'Jackass Mail' in 1858: The Diary of Phocion R. Way, Part II." Edited by William A. Duffen. *Arizona and the West* 2, no. 2 (Summer 1960), 147–164.
_____. "Overland via 'Jackass Mail' in 1858: The Diary of Phocion R. Way, Part III." Edited by William A. Duffen. *Arizona and the West* 2, no. 3 (Autumn 1960), 279–292.
_____. "Overland via 'Jackass Mail' in 1858: The Diary of Phocion R. Way, Part IV." Edited by William A. Duffen. *Arizona and the West* 2, no. 4 (Winter 1960), 353–370.
Whetten, Harriet Douglas. "A Volunteer Nurse in the Civil War: The Letters of Harriet Douglas Whetten." Edited by Paul H. Hass. *Wisconsin Magazine of History* 48, no. 2 (Winter 1964–1965), 131–151.

Secondary Articles

Altshuler, Constance Wynn. "The Case of Sylvester Mowry: The Mowry Mine." *Arizona and the West* 15, no. 2 (Summer 1973), 149–174.
_____. "The Life and Death of the *Weekly Arizonian*." *Arizona and the West* 18, no. 2 (Summer 1976), 265–276.
Hatch, Mary R.P. "Lancaster, New Hampshire." *Granite Monthly* 51 (1919).
Holden, Walter. "The Bridge That Saved the Army." *Historical New Hampshire* 35 (Winter 1980), 393–416.
Hufford, Kenneth. "Journalism in Pre-Territorial Arizona." *Smoke Signal* 14 (Fall 1966), 77–96.
_____. "P.W. Dooner: Pioneer Editor of Tus-

con." *Arizona and the West* 10, no. 1 (Spring 1968), 25–42.

Jorgensen, Jay. "Anderson Attacks the Wheatfield." *Gettysburg* 14 (January 1996), 64–76.

Joslyn, Mauriel P. "'For Ninety Nine Years or the War': The Story of the 3rd Arkansas at Gettysburg." *Gettysburg* 14 (January 1996), 52–63.

Mook, H. Telfer. "Training Day in New England." *New England Quarterly* 11, no. 4 (December 1938), 675–697.

North, Dianne. "'A Real Class of People': A Biographical Analysis of the Sonora Exploring and Mining Company, 1856–1863." *Arizona and the West* 26, no. 3 (Autumn 1984), 261–274.

Park, Joseph F. "The Apaches in Mexican-American Relations, 1848–1861: A Footnote to the Gasden Treaty." *Arizona and the West* 3, no. 2 (Summer 1961), 129–146.

Richards, Donald H. "The Fifth New Hampshire Volunteers (Light Infantry)" *Historical New Hampshire* 28, no. 4 (Winter 1973), 241–261.

Sacks, B. "The Creation of the Territory of Arizona." *Arizona and the West* 5, no. 1 (Spring 1963), 29–62.

_____. "The Creation of the Territory of Arizona." *Arizona and the West* 5, no. 2 (Summer 1963), 109–148.

_____. "Sylvester Mowry: Artilleryman, Libertine, Entrepreneur." *American West* 1, no. 3 (Summer 1964), 14–24.

Tatham, David. "David Claypoole Johnston's 'Militia Muster.'" *American Art Journal* 19, no. 2 (Spring, 1987), 4–15.

Weitz, Mark A. "Drill, Training, and the Combat Performance of the Civil War Soldier: Dispelling the Myth of the Poor Soldier, Great Fighter." *Journal of Military History* 62, no. 2 (April 1998), 263–289.

Wyllys, Rufus Kay. "Henry A. Crabb: A Tragedy on the Sonora Frontier." *Pacific Historical Review* 9, no. 2 (June 1940), 183–194.

Newspapers and Periodicals

Amherst (NH) Charge Bayonets!
Amherst (NH) Farmer's Cabinet
(Prescott) Arizona Enterprise
Baltimore Sun
Boston Herald
Charleston (SC) Mercury
Cincinnati Dollar Weekly Times
Cincinnati Times
Claremont (NH) National Eagle
Claremont (NH) Northern Advocate
Cleveland Plain Dealer
Concord New Hampshire Patriot
Concord (NH) Monitor
Concord (NH) Statesman
Denver Rocky Mountain News
Dover (NH) Gazette
Fayetteville (NC) Observer
Gettysburg Times
Harper's Weekly
Keene (NH) Sentinel
Lancaster (NH) Coos Democrat
Lancaster (NH) Coos Republican
Lancaster (NH) Sketch Book
Lebanon (NH) Granite State Free Press
Littleton (NH) People's Journal
Lyndonville (VT) Caledonia Record
(New York) Frank Leslie's Illustrated
New York Herald
New York Irish-American
New York Sunday Mercury
New York Times
Newark (NJ) Advocate
News and Observer (Raleigh, NC)
Raymond (MS) Hinds County Gazette
Salt Lake City Deseret News
Salt Lake Semi-Weekly Tribune
San Antonio Register
Sandusky Register
St. Louis Missouri Republican
Tubac (AZ) Weekly Arizonian
Tucson Arizona Daily Star
Washington (DC) Constitution
Washington (DC) National Tribune
Washington (DC) States
Wooster (OH) Republican

Index

Page numbers in ***bold italics*** indicate illustrations.

Adams, Francis 96–97, 123
Alamo, Battle of 50
Anderson's Brigade 154–160
Antietam, Battle of 100–115

Ballou, Charles O. 98, 114, 120, 123, 133
Barlow, Francis C. 113
Bass, M.J. 155
Bean, J.W. 91
Bedel, John 73
Berry, Nathaniel 71–73, ***73***, 78, 84, 86, 100, 120, 129, 131, 139
Bliss, Zenas R. 138
Brooke, John Rutter 110, 157
Brown, James B. 84
Browne, Charles 19–22, ***21***, 59, 64–65
Buchanan, James 44, 46
Bucknam, John W. 76, ***77***, 84, 133, 158–161
Burnside, Ambrose E. 119–122

Caldwell, John C. 100–109, ***102***, 111–113, 117, 126, 136, 145, 154–160
Camp California 79–83
Camp Jackson 75–78
Catton, Bruce 176
Chancellorsville, Battle of 136–147
Chase, Dexter 124
Chase, Salmon P. 42
Child, William 99, 108, 115, ***138***, 141, 143, 145, 154, 158–161, 173, 175
Cincinnati, OH 25–47
Cincinnati Times 25–26, 31, 35, 42–43, 49, 54
Clarke, Daniel 128
Cleveland, Mather 167
Coffin, Charles 116
Colby, Anthony 111
Conner, Edward J. 76
Cook, William W. 76, 84–86, 98
Coos Bank 13–14, 23, 34, 67

Coos County, NH 9–20
Coos County Democrat 17–21, 27, 39
Corser, Norman 90
Couch, Darius 136, 142, 145
Crafts, Welcome 133, 162
Craig, Joseph 161
Cross, Abigail 12–13, 24, 67, 162, 166–168
Cross, Daniel 123
Cross, Ephraim 12–16, 22–23, 34, 46, 67, 124, 168
Cross, Frank 12, 26, 67, 82, 97, 101, 171
Cross, Helen 12, 67, 180
Cross, Nelson 12, 25, 101, 158, 171
Cross, Persis 12, 166
Cross, Richard 12, 15, 19, 36, 51, 66, 75, 81, 91, 101, 108, 120, ***121***, 132–133, 136, 143, 158–161, 170–171
Crowley, Rodney 158–159
Cuban Filibuster 24

David, James B. 84–86
Davis, John M. 162
Denison, Henry 19
Dolbear, Samuel 161
Donaldson, John 62–64
Duren, John 120–121, 124

Edwards, Thomas M. 83
Eighty-First Pennsylvania 78, 109–110, 151, 154–158
Ellis, Thomas 97
Everett, Persis 11–12
Everett, Richard 9–12, ***10***
Everett, Richard (alias) 30–32
Ewell, Richard 54–55, 59, 66, 68, 87

Fair Oaks, Battle of 91–97
Farnsworth, John F. 131
Fifth New Hampshire Vols. 71, 74–175, ***179***

215

Index

Fillmore, Millard 36, 42, 44
Fitch, Everett S. 171
Foney, John W. 130
Fourth Rhode Island 78
Fredericksburg, Battle of 116–126
Frémont, John C. 44

Gay, George 110
Gettysburg, Battle of 148–161
Gilman, John T. 11
Gilmore, Joseph 130
Gove, George 82, 96, 104, 109, 122, 128, 137, 144, 155, *156*, 161, 174
Grapevine Bridge 90–93, *91*

Hale, Charles 94, 107–109, 112, 128, 134, 149–160, *150*, 162, 166
Hale, John P. 40, 44, *45*, 58, 68–69, 80, 85–86, 164
Halstead, Murat 120
Hancock, Winfield Scott 110–111, 121, 126, 128, *129*, 142, 144, 151–160
Hapgood, Charles 75, 114, 132, 139, *140*, 144, 158, 162, 166
Hazard, John 95
Heintzelman, Samuel P. 48
Heywood, Frank 79
Hill, Daniel H. 104, 106–109
Hillyer, George 155–156
Holden, Walter 178, 180
Hooker, Joseph 136, 139–140, 148
Howard, Oliver O. 78–82, 87, 93, 95, 97
Hurd, Sumner 144

Jackson, John H. 73
Johnson, Elijah W. 76, 84
Juarez, Benito 71

Kansas-Nebraska Act 35, 44
Kantor, Mackinlay 179
Kent, Faith 179
Kent, Henry O. 15, 22, 24, 26, 29, *30*, 32, 39–42, 47, 49, 57, 65, 70–71, 76, 80, 88, 95, 98, 111, 113, 129, 152, 163–166, 171–172, *177*, 180
Kent, Richard P. 17, 162
Know-Nothing Party 28–31, 33, 35–46

Lancaster, NH 10–20, *16*, 98–99, 162–163
Langley, Samuel 76, *83*, 94, 118
Larkin, James 76, 93, 95, 117–119, 124, 132, 135, *143*, 172
Lincoln, Abraham 134
Livermore, Thomas L. 76–78, *103*, 104–107, 109, 121, 123, 142–145, 150, 173, 175
Long, Charles 73, 101, 114, 132
Longstreet, James 106, 111, 119

Lossing, Benson 166
Lynch, John 115

Marston, Gilman 127–129
Masonry 13, 39, 67, 110, 163
McClellan, George B. 79, 84, 88, 100, 102, 104, 108, 116
McKeen, H. Boyd 109–110, 138, 151, *153*, 158, 160
McL. Barton, Ira 76, 84, 114, 146, 162
Meade, George G. 152
Meagher, Thomas F. 97, 104, 112, 121, 144
Mercer, George D. 62–64
Messer, Lucy P. 12
Mexican War 16, 37–38
Mexico 70–71
Moody, Charles T. 161
Moore, Adams 124
Moore, Alexander 140
Moore, William Adams 76, 94, *124*
Moultrie, Francis 41
Mt. Washington, NH 36–37, 98
Mowry, Sylvester 59–67, *63*
Mowry-Cross duel 61–65
Murray, John 76, 101, 118, 124

Nettleton, George 110
New Hampshire Militia 11–18, 24, 35, 71
New Hampshire Veterans Association 169–170
Ninth U.S. 16, 38
Norwich University 26, 32, 39, 76
Nugent, Robert 121

One Hundred and Forty-Eighth Pennsylvania 148–149, 151, 154–158, 160
Osmer, Nathan 161

Peabody, Miles 81–82, 134
Peninsula Campaign 88–99
Perry, James 110, 117, *118*, 122, 124
Pierce, Franklin 28, 35, 129, 133, 137, 165–166
Pope, John 100
Potter, Joseph H. 72
Pride, Mike 178
Putnam, Haldimand 73

Quebec 23, 36

Ramsey, Rodney H. 124, 161
Rappahannock, Battle of 87–88
Regular Army 66–68
Republican Party 40–41, 130
Rice, Thomas 146
Richardson, Israel B. 90, 93–94, 100, 104–107

Rix, James Madison 18–20, **18**, 36, 46
Rollins, Edward H. 131

Sanborn, Augustus 134, **135**
Scott, Winfield 25, 29
Sears, Lee 82
Second Corps 80, 87, 105, 135–136, 142
Second New Hampshire 136
Seven Days Battles 98–10
Seventeenth New Hampshire 133
Shannon, George E. 95
Sickles, Daniel 151–152
Sixty-First New York 78, 87, 93, 113, 151, 154–158
Sixty-Fourth New York 78, 91, 93
Sixty-Ninth New York 91, 96, 97, 104, 121, 155
Smith, Jeremiah 12
Spencer, William 95
Stark, John 15, 71, 163
Stevens, Josiah 118
Sturtevant, Edward E. 76, 85, 90, 93, **96**, 98, 102, 118, 122
Sumner, Edwin Bull 80, 86, 91, 104–107, 120, 136–137

Tactics 79
Tenney, Allen 85–86 88

Texas, journey across 48–55
Thomas, Lorenzo 83
Trask, Charles 139
Travis, Mark 178
Tubac, AZ 48–65, **56**
Twelfth New Hampshire 141, 147
Twentieth Indiana 156
Twenty-Ninth Massachusetts 106

Verry, Orastus J. 82–84, 172

Waite, Otis 175–176
Walker, Francis 107
Weekly Arizonian 55–62
Welch, Richard 84–86
Whetten, Harriet 97
Whipple, Thomas J. 73
White Mountain Aegis 17
Wilder, Jonas 10
Wilder, Susan M. 12
Wilkins, J.P. 178
Wrightson, William 48–49

Young Volunteers 181–191
Youngholm, Janet R. 177

Zook, Samuel 155–158

www.ingramcontent.com/pod-product-compliance
Lightning Source LLC
Chambersburg PA
CBHW032052300426
44116CB00007B/709